1

'Becoming Bavarian'

Copyright © 2021 by Tim Howe

ISBN Nr. 9798648591158

'Learning another language is like becoming
another person.'

Haruki Murakami, novelist.

Becoming Bavarian

in six short steps

Tim Howe

Tim Howe

Ever since over 900 young Germans answered his call for a *Brieffreundin*, Tim Howe's been hooked on *alles Deutsch*. His first job was in a Kent comprehensive school, teaching the tongue to not always motivated British school kids.

He moved to Germany in 1998 to take up a post as staff translator with a truck manufacturer in Munich. Since leaving this secure job, Tim divides his time between less secure jobs as free-lance Business English Teacher, Translator and Writer. *'Becoming Bavarian'* is Tim's first stab at non-fiction.

Tim and his family live in the Hallertau, home to the largest intact hop-growing area in the world.

knowhoweforenglish.blogspot.de
https://twitter.com/TimKnowhowe

Author's note

While there's no shortage of guidebooks on touring Germany, there seems to be a scarcity of titles describing what it's like to actually live here. As far as I know, I'm the very first Brit to write about life in The Hallertau, Lower Bavaria.

And yet Germany is the third most popular destination for Brits seeking to 'transplant'. Around 240,000 native-English speakers currently live in Germany, and Brexit boosted the number of Brits becoming *Deutsch* almost threefold.

So here goes with a bid to plug a gaping market gap.

Or, at the very least, to put The Hallertau on the map.

The overall timeline of *'Becoming Bavarian'* has been slightly altered in places to improve the narrative pace. Conversations throughout the book have been recalled to the best of my ability, but are not verbatim. Some identities have been changed for all the usual reasons.

Contents

Preface

As a British expat 'guest worker' living smack bang in the middle of Europe, I probably should have shown greater enthusiasm about either loving or leaving the EU. But I'd scarcely followed the referendum debate. Like so many of my 100,000 compatriots in Germany, I'd been taking it for granted that the sensible British electorate would vote YES to Europe.

Yes, it's all sorted. After all the excitement dies down, we'll simply return to doing what we've always done rather well. Such as successfully negotiating special privileges – fondly known in Germany as 'extrawurst', or an extra helping of sausages. That's the gist of a facebook commentary I post on the eve of the Brexit ballot. I feel endorsed when Jenny in Bath replies 'You got it sussed Tim.'

Our lips on God's ear.

Sadly, whatever God's ear was glued to, it wasn't the Brexit vote.

That was it, then. Being British in Bavaria had been good fun. But now it was time.

Time to become one of them.

A knee-slapping, *Bierstein*-sloshing Bavarian.

Step One:

Watch out what you wish for...

*22% of Germans wish for nothing more
than more money.*

4% wish for nothing at all.

Bravo

When an *Engländer* falls in love with *Deutschland,* it typically has something to do with either *Bier, Autos* or *Frauen.*

Or all three. Great beer, great cars, great girls.

But not me. On an 'A-Level Studies Trip' to Cologne, while school mates 'researched' German pub culture and flirted with *Fräulein,* I had my head buried in a magazine called *Bravo.* While its pop music content bore striking similarity to *Smash Hits* in Britain, *Bravo* was blazing a trail in a totally different direction – relationship and sex counselling.

As well as educating young minds about the birds and the bees, the sex advice feature known as 'Dr. Sommer' was also quite graphical. It depicted kids going about ostensibly normal activities. Such as unpacking their schoolbag or grabbing a Coca Cola from the fridge.

Trouble was, these pictures were not in the least bit normal. The youngsters in Dr. Sommer's pull-out centre-spreads were totally in the buff. Germans, I discovered on that life-changing school trip, don't regard this as porn at all. They call it *sexuelle Aufklärung.*

Forty years on and *Bravo* remains in a league of its own. Spiegel International describes the youth magazine's open-minded approach to nudity as 'The kind of thing that would land publishers in jail were it to hit newsstands on the other side of the Atlantic.'

It's also the kind of thing which can get you fired from a British state school. As I discovered just days after successfully completing my probationary period as a *Deutschlehrer*.

Entering the headmaster's office, I immediately recognised the pictures and posters. Ripped out at random, the pages were demonstratively strewn around his study. Some had been torn into a thousand shreds. They littered his desk like a blanket of confetti. Lying at his feet was a fully intact double spread. It graphically depicted a naked body.

In my defence, I contended that *Bravo* is the largest youth magazine in central and western Europe. A supreme example of typical 'realia' – authentic material which students needed exposing to in modern foreign language lessons. The very type our postgraduate tutors had so heartily encouraged us to exploit.

Reporting to the Chairman of the Governors, the headmaster conceded that it was indeed *authentic* teaching material. I just shouldn't have been *teaching* with it.

Angered at my sheer stupidity, I raced home and ransacked my room, binning every single *Bravo* I could lay my hands on. Until I came across *that* one. Snatching it off the shelf, I sniggered at the sight of Bucks Fizz festooning the front cover, their bleach-permed manes sprawling in all directions. But it wasn't Britain's jubilant Eurovision winners, best remembered for skirt-rip striptease, that caught my eye. Inside, halfway down the pen-pal page was an advert:

Engländer (18) sucht nette deutsche Brieffreunde/innen.

It had been a rain-sodden Saturday afternoon in spring 1982. On a whim, I'd pulled out a postcard and scribbled on the back something about an Englishman seeking German penfriends. I distinctly remember holding the card to my lips and planting a good-luck kiss on the stamp, before posting it off to *Bravo*. Equally clearly, I recall the day a fortnight or so later when the postman rang the bell. He was lugging a sack full of assorted letters and packages, and they were all for me. The senders were mostly German, Austrian and Swiss, aged 15 to 17. And they were *all* female.

Within weeks, roughly a thousand more letters had descended on our doormat. For a brief period, I even possessed my own sorting shelf at Her Majesty's Royal Mail.

Many replies enclosed photographs which I taped to my bedstead. I soon ran out of bedstead and coated the bedposts too. Judging by their photos, these *deutsche* girls were *gut*.

I did my level best to answer as many as I could, rattling off responses on an almost industrial scale. There was just one *kleines Problem*. Spending almost every spare moment of my final school year immersed in mounds of mail from abroad was isolating me from friends in and outside school. And scribbling away in *Denglish* – a mad mixture of English and German – was unlikely to land me best examination results either. I eventually scraped through with a batch of 'C' grades.

Deutsch was, and remains a tough option. Only around 5% of British pupils currently learn the subject. Most ditch it by the age of 16. The trend is downward.

All the while, my love-in with Germany was escalating. Letters sealed and stamped, I'd crawl into bed, collapsing alongside my portable radio. My sleep-inducer was *Berichte von heute*, North German Radio's roundup of the day's news. In those days, just how much you could follow on short-wave, even on local BBC Radio, largely depended on the strength of signal. Still, I also managed to pick up crackly Radio Luxemburg, catching bits and pieces of their breakfast show, *Der Fröhliche Wecker*, which played a hodgepodge of *Deutsche Schlager* and Euro pop. Sung in passable yet utterly puerile English, the latter never troubled the charts in Britain. Give or take the odd freak exception like 'Da Da Da', by Trio. This *Deutsche Welle* group even made it onto Top of the Pops. The lyrics of their hit make for surprisingly interesting linguistic analysis:

'Da, da, da. Ah ha, ah ha, ah ha.'

A sure shoo-in for Eurovision. Pity they passed that one up. As for understanding the rest of the chorus line, beginner-level German probably suffices:

'Ich liebe Dich nicht
Du liebst mich nicht
... Ah ha!'

To any Germans who might feel the need to say sorry for giving us 'Da Da Da' – don't worry. You don't have to. We were worse still.

The thing is, 'Da Da Da' *only* made Number Two in the UK. The very week I left school it was pipped to the post by Captain Sensible's 'Happy Talk'. It's quite possible that whoever subsequently toppled Sensible was singing something along the lines of 'Bla Bla Bla'.

Not that I'd have noticed. I was far too occupied applying for universities and going for interviews. In hindsight, I should have done something such as trainee journalism or a B.A. in Media Studies. Instead I chose to study 'Language and Linguistics' at a university in South East England. Alas, despite the all-alluring blurb splattered around the college prospectus ('cutting-edge, interdisciplinary approach to study of language', 'state-of-art research'), the Linguistics part of the course turned out to be a huge disappointment. The college location, on the other hand, couldn't have been better. Just down the road was the port of Harwich; a quick and affordable escape route to Continental Europe. From the Hook of Holland, it was just an eleven-hour train ride down to Bavaria, my favourite part of Germany. It was a few more years before no-frills airlines revolutionised the way we travelled abroad. For the time being it was the Stena Line ferry for me.

Had you asked, in those halcyon pre-Brexit days, if I'd rather be Bavarian than British, the answer would have been a resounding *'jawooooi!'* I'd already picked up basic Bavarian dialect and had a crush on everything German. As far as I was concerned, Germany could do no wrong.

Despite 'Da Da Da'.

Mad about Munich

The form instructs students of 'Modern Foreign Languages' to list, in order of preference, three places where they wish to spend their study year abroad. If unable to grant first choice, the German Academic Exchange Service guarantees to fulfil one of the other two requests. Nowhere does it say you have to apply for three *different* places.

Mad about Munich, and determined to go nowhere else, I make the city my first, second and third choice. Confident I've clinched it, I rush out and buy a brand-new ski jacket and some long johns to see me through the harsh Bavarian winter.

Staff processing applications back in early 1984 don't fall for the ploy. They pack me off to Schleswig-Holstein. That's about as far away as you can travel from Munich without leaving Germany. It's like a Brit requesting Bath and being banished to Barrow-on-Furness.

Over 500 miles (800 km) away from Munich, Germany's most northern state isn't quite the punishment I'd feared. Just an hour's drive from the Baltic, the small town of Neumünster is gateway to windswept sandy beaches to the east, bleak but beautiful coastal mudflats to the west and heathlands to the north. Still, I vow there and then that if I ever spend any longer length of time in Germany it had better be Bavaria. A good 16 years pass before I secure my first job in Munich. In between, I again apply to the Deutscher Akademischer Austausch Dienst – DAAD for short. My heart's still yearning for Bavaria. But I'm in for another disappointment. All the popular places – even less desirables such as Buxtehude and Wolfenbüttel – have already been allocated. Munich's not even mooted. All that DAAD can offer are several towns in remote Mecklenburg-West Pomerania. That's as far as you can travel due northeast of Bavaria without having to exchange your euros for zloty. Being ousted to the country's furthest outpost once again feels like punishment for something I've not done.

But it could have been far worse. Tom, whom I meet on the plane going over, was given no choice whatsoever. He'd been ordered right up to the *Deutsch-Polski* border, to a town called Pasewalk. Tom's clearly drawn the short straw, or *Arschkarte* as the Germans call it. Pasewalk regularly ranks in online surveys as one of the most depressing places in the whole of Germany. Even neighbouring Poles, who'd flocked over after the Iron Curtain fell, have long since thrown in the towel and gone home.

I'd picked out a town called Neustrelitz. Compared to Pasewalk, this place actually has a lot going for it. It provides all the essentials you'd expect from a nice little German town, including Aldi, Lidl and drive-in McDonalds.

Tom and I are part of a cohort of young Brits recruited by Manchester University. Which, in turn, have been recruited by Mecklenburg's *Kultusministerium*. The state ministry is crying out for native-English speakers to help retrain their soon-to-be-redundant teachers of Russian. We instruct *The Russkis*, as we playfully call them, just once a week. In order to top up our teaching hours we're dispatched to local schools for the remaining time. Unlike their teachers, the pupils – Russian had always been *bête noire* in East German schools – are delighted with the deal.

Thanks to a joint agreement between Britain and Germany, English teachers can work tax free for up to two years. And with just 14 teaching hours a week, I have plenty spare time. Much of which I spend trying to impress staff at the local newspaper, the *Nordkurier*. After a month or more peering over shoulders and penning the odd by-line, they finally give me a reporting assignment – a pop concert in nearby Neubrandenburg. It's an up-and-coming American boy band, and the *Chefredakteur* has reserved the full features page for my 1000-word report and pictures.

The Backstreet Boys are indeed hot stuff in Eastern Germany. The venue, a disused warehouse, is packed to the rafters. Crowds of ticketless teenagers are even trying to worm their way in through the toilet block. Acoustically, the show's nothing short of eardrum-shattering. Even Led Zepp would have pulled the plug. Any less loud, however, and sounds from the stage would have been drowned by the screaming and sobbing of the thousand-strong, all-girl audience.

Relieved when it's finally all over, I catch a lift back home and set about writing up my report in peace. I duly submit some great pictures of fainting fans and something vaguely akin to a boy band cavorting around amidst the general confusion. But that's also the problem. The love-struck audience are so delirious that I can barely hear or see anything of the performance. I struggle to scrape together even half a report. The resulting review graphically describes gaggles of fanatic females being carted off by overwhelmed ambulance attendants but falls short on just about all other fronts.

Eclipsed by a jumbo-size photo of hysterical teenyboppers, my apology for a report appears the following Monday. Heading the *Feuilleton* arts pages of Mecklenburg's best-selling newspaper, the article is both blessing and bane. While I'm prancing around, proudly waving it to colleagues, the *Chefredakteur* is having to justify to the Executive Board why he didn't send a more senior reporter to the event. From then on, I'm commissioned to do only school jumble sales and flea markets.

Although I soon tire of reporting on *Trödelmärkte*, life in 'Meck-Pomm' isn't too bad. When my teaching contract expires, I resist the lure of creature comforts back home in England. Instead, I carry on renting my drab but dirt cheap *Altbauwohnung* and somehow eke out a living from freelancing for the local *Strelitzer Zeitung* and tutoring a group of anglophile dentists. I'm grateful for this modest income, given my third 'job' doesn't pay a single cent. I'm hosting *'Hits 'n' Tips'* on the local citizens' channel *'NB-Radiotreff 88,0'*. The show's format is dead simple – chart hits interspersed with shout-outs for events around and about town. To attract listeners, I prowl around with a 'roving mike'. Lurking under bus shelters and leaping out from behind bottle banks, I encourage passersby to speak out on current topics. 'Current' could be just about anything – from Angelo Kelly's *Note Sechs* in maths (pure make-believe on my part – I doubt whether the Irish *Wunderkind* ever gained such a dismal grade) to how to deal with disturbances of the peace in public places. It's 1996, and already the mobile phone is a veritable street-rage phenomenon, fuelling heated debates in the media.

'*Hits 'n' Tips*' goes out live from a pre-fab tower block in Neubrandenburg every Tuesday afternoon at 2 o'clock. Spinning sounds by forgettable acts such as DJ Bobo and Caught in the Act, I speak in the sort of throaty, cut-glass accent that possibly even the Queen would be hard pushed to outperform. Listening to these recordings over twenty years later – I've kept all the tapes – I'm not sure whether to cringe or just laugh out loud.

Unfortunately, the fun has a flipside. For every piece of music played I have to shell out *GEMA-Gebühr*, a fee to the Performing Right Society. And, in stark contrast to my fellow presenters who sensibly play little and talk lots, I mostly do just voice-overs. Spinning discs back to back, I very soon exhaust my private music collection. My unemployment benefit clearly doesn't stretch to splashing out on brand new CDs every week. Luckily, I manage to persuade the owner of my local *Musikladen* to lend me the latest hits in return for regular name checks.

He continues to do so even when I return his copy of Phil Collins' 'Dance into the light' with a beastly scratch strewn across tracks three and four. Sorry Stephan.

Building up a fan following at the radio station earns me the accolade *'Neubrandenburg's bekannteste britische Stimme'*. Not that I need work too hard for this coveted title – I'm the *most famous* British voice in town simply because I'm the *only* British voice in town. This is merely four years after reunification. Most expat Brits are probably still living the boho lifestyle some 100 km down the road in hip-and-happening Berlin. Lolling around barefooted, they're no doubt consuming vast quantities of absinthe, patiently treading water till conditions in the former *Ostblock* land shape up sufficiently to entice them further east.

But what of Bavaria? Being rebuffed for listing Munich as all three choices had certainly taught me a lesson or two. Would I have ended up closer to my goal if I'd listed other cities – Frankfurt and Brunswick maybe – as wishes number two and three? Chances are the exchange service staff would have still packed me off to some God-forsaken place.

Such as Pasewalk.

Wake up with Verona

I land my next job some 220 miles closer to the Bavarian capital. Couchsurfing at a student friend's place in Bonn, someone mentions that just down the road Deutsche Telekom are seeking a recently qualified linguist for their *Sprachendienst*. Offered the position on the spot, I'm delighted when they immediately put me to work on translating press releases.

First day or two I'm on a high. Particularly when a text advertising a wake-up call service from former Miss Germany Verona Feldbusch lands on my desk. The piece is packed with innuendos which I translate under the saucy headliner 'Get a Buzz – Wake up with Verona!' Handing my polished text to the department secretary, I glibly announce in German:

'Hee-hee, what a titillating way to start the day!'

Warning to novices – be careful what you say to the boss's *Sekretärin* just two days into a new job. Because at the workplace in Germany all lines of communication pass via this one person. It's almost like she *is* The Boss.

The throw-away remark, uttered like some lustful *Carry On* star, immediately gets back to my superior. The following morning I'm removed from press translation and relegated to manning the clippings cubicle. This, I discover, is the least popular workplace in the whole department – one normally assigned to school pupils on job experience week. My instructions are to 'fillet' the daily *Fachpresse*, or specialist press, cut out everything connected with telecommunications and stick it into a scrapbook. The practice was obsolete even by nineties' standards. I'd heard from former novices that new full-time entrants were also occasionally put to work on this peripheral task. But for just a day or two, before being moved on to more key, translation-based tasks. Apart from being released to translate the odd text whenever a colleague goes sick, I'm stuck in Clippings a whole month.

I should have taken the hint. Especially when the co-worker charged with keeping an eye on my efforts hands me copies of the *Stellenangebote* – situations vacant – from the *Süddeutsche Zeitung* and suggests I apply to one or two.

The following day, sitting in the boss's office, I receive my first and, most likely, very last performance review:

'So, let's just get this straight.'

Frau Gürtelmann, removes her spectacles and fixes me slap bang in the eyes with a studied, concentrated gaze.

'In your application you say you are PC literate. But it turns out you can't touch-type, you can't tell the difference between pdf and PowerPoint and Frau Bichlbecher had to show you how to send an email.'

True. I'd needed to ask her secretary how to dispatch an email.

'All you're able to do, is open, save and exit Word.'

Also true.

Looking for confirmation she cocks her head promptingly.

'Right so?'

Frau Gürtelmann is smiling with all the serenity of a psychiatrist. Her scathing appraisal of my practically non-existent PC skills is, alas, spot-on. Humiliated and unable to return her gaze, I lower my eyes, bringing them to rest on a stain on the lacquered wood floorboards. Then, as if attempting to redeem myself, I look up. Our eyes meet briefly as I whimper:

'Yes, but I also copy and paste.'

On reflection, maybe I'd taken 'PC literate', buzzword of the day, a bit too literally. Yet my ignorance of all things IT was not totally *mea culpa*. I'm one of the so-called 'lost generation'. The very year after I left school, Information Technology was introduced to the British National Curriculum. But the idea of scrambling to 'catch up' on this essential life-skills subject was never mooted. Not even when, much later, I take my Diploma of Translating is there any talk of computer literacy being *de rigueur* for those wishing to enter this IT-driven profession. As a mature student, I'm easily ten years older than most fellow peers – every single one of them PC proficient.

Following the dressing down in Frau Gürtelmann's office, I knuckle down and sharpen up my IT skills. For starters, I salvage an old typewriter and teach myself touch-typing.

Shortly after, when I start reapplying for jobs, I'm able to say hand on heart that I'm PC literate. The translation department of a major truck manufacturer just outside Munich is sufficiently impressed to offer me a full-time post.

Home to Hops

'Listen to this,' says Bea, as we relax over a leisurely breakfast one wintery weekend. Clicking open a website advertising plots of land for sale, she reads out the description:

'140 m² potential building plot with planning permission in open countryside. Adjacent to hop fields, stream trickling along perimeter of back garden.'

One finger pointing at the screen, another dusting croissant flakes off her front, she's visibly excited: 'Sounds idyllic, huh?'

I'm wooed too. But more by the attractive price tag.

It's five years since showdown at the telecommunications giant. And the pretty Pole from Internal Sales with whom I'd loped off into a leafy lane at lunchtime is now my wife. When I received the job offer in Munich we decided to head south together. Soon after, Bea also found employment in the Bavarian capital. We rented a flat in Groß Inzemoos, a nondescript dormitory *Dorf* close to Dachau. The place is just half an hour by *S-Bahn*, the very efficient suburban train, from central Munich.

After years spent languishing in the far north and remote east of the country, I'd ended up only 15 miles from the city of my dreams. And now I was living that dream. Or so I thought.

There was just one small problem. Like 57% of Germans, we were also living in rented accommodation. It worked well, at first. Until dear *Oma*, our late landlady, suddenly hiked the monthly rent up by an extra hundred euros. And then presented us with an itemised bill. She'd outsourced all the odd jobs which we'd automatically done ourselves: lawn mowing, cleaning windows and that quintessential, almost sacrosanct chore carried out each week by every law-abiding German household – *Treppenhausreinigung und Gehsteigputzen.* That's the sweeping clean and mopping of communal stretch of stairs and/or pavement directly outside your front door (neglecting to do so can cost you dearly). All at once, renting no longer seemed an attractive option. We started looking around at other options. One idea was to buy some land and build our own property.

We find our *Schnäppchen* almost immediately.

There's a good reason why this plot of land is such a *Schnäppchen*, or bargain. The picture-perfect plot advertised online is smack bang in the middle of nowhere. We'd never heard of the 'Hallertau' before. And neither, apparently, have very many Germans. Even though the area is listed as the largest continuous hop-growing area in the world. Stretching over almost 19,000 hectares and home to some 20 different types of *Hopfen*, this little-known region has been growing hops since the eighth century. Producing around 86% of Germany's harvest, and over a third of global output, the Hallertau exports to around 170 countries. The region's pungently aromatic cones are particularly popular in Thailand, where Bavarian buds are used to brew 'Singha beer'.

One reason why the Hallertau is such a *Geheimtipp*, or hidden gem, is because it's more commonly known by two other names: 'Hoiertau' and 'Holledau'. But since only local people use these names, neither one makes it onto the map. And guidebooks aren't much help here either. Search for 'Hallertau' on Lonely Planet, for example, and you'll certainly find it. But as one of the Top Ten Country Pubs in *New Zealand*. Located in West Auckland's main wine-producing area, the 'Hallertau' is family friendly and apparently their gourmet food really cuts the mustard. Look up *The* Hallertau, however, and you'll draw a complete blank. To its credit, the Lonely Planet Guide to Lower Bavaria does include major towns such as Landshut and Passau. The 242-km^2 Bavarian Forest, a region of low mountains, rivers and pastures, also features prominently. Yet anyone looking for even a cursory mention of the Hallertau in Germany is in for a disappointment.

Isn't the only reason for not listing a region in Lonely Planet because it's not worth going there? Seems like they're being rather harsh on the 'Hoiertau'.

Had the guide included the Hallertau, it might have acknowledged that this region is unique in more ways than one. It boasts a twelfth-century trade route, for instance. Back in 1955, the Bavarian Tourist Board had a brain wave. Concerned that the historical road was being abused by juggernauts as a short cut between A9 and A93, they decided to rechristen it. Overnight, signs sprung up along the way informing travellers that they were now riding 'The German Hops Route'. It certainly sounded nicer than Federal Highway B301. The renamed 49-km road connects Abensberg with Freising, one of the oldest settlements in Bavaria. Our delightful little village lies smack back in the middle.

Set just beyond hearing distance of the traffic-heavy 'German Hops Route', our plot of land turns out to be every bit idyllic as pitched to us online. Within six months of purchasing the parcel, our prefabricated house, framed by hop fields and babbling brook, is ready to celebrate *Richtfest*, a very German tradition of giving thanks to the builders and all involved in the construction work. Our construction supervisor, Herr Himmelreich, reads out a *Richtsspruch* which marks the completion of building and declares the house 'open'. But before we can clump our beer mugs together and roar '*Prost*', Herr Himmelreich has one final duty to perform. With hands clasped prayerfully and head tilted heavenward, he calls upon God to protect and bless our new home.

Painted ocean green, the house is all wooden and wide gables, save for floor-to-ceiling windows spanning two sides. Given almost every other house in our neighbourhood comes white washed with teeny-weeny windows, ours sticks out like a sore thumb. We love it to bits. I hope God likes it a bit too.

These past five years I'd been working a comfortable 35-hour week office job. I'd enjoyed 30 days annual paid holiday coupled with a generous company-funded social security programme. But, shortly after moving to the Hallertau, I do the very thing that no sane and sensible German employee would ever dream of doing. No matter how much things suck.

I quit.

Job satisfaction had always meant far more to me than job security. Yet I'd spent those last five years cowered over a PC eight hours straight, punctuated only by lunch *al desko* and a brisk stroll around the truck yard. This was definitely *not* my idea of dream job Germany.

Although the work bored me to tears, this wasn't actually the straw that broke the duck's back. Germans have a lovely expression for announcing approaching trouble: *'da ist dicke Luft'*. The air is thick, literally. In my case it wasn't just thick, it was positively stale. And I wanted it fresh. A disagreement on ambient room temperature had meant spending half the previous year at the truck company on near non-speakers with my new office mate.

It's a shame, because when Annika joined our team the previous spring, we'd hit it off surprisingly well. Probably because we happened to shop at the same discounter. We took turns to leave work early on Mondays and Thursdays and pick up special offers for each other at Aldi. For extra-special offers, such as cut-price computers and bargain automatic coffee machines, we even stood in line for one another, patiently waiting for the store to open at eight.

But, with winter on its way, trouble was in the offing. I like the office cool; Annika likes it warm. Interestingly, 61% of German employees describe themselves as *Frischluftfanatiker*, or fresh air fanatics. They prefer to work with the window open – even in the grips of winter. Annika, evidently, does not belong to this demographic.

Me: 'Fresh air, fresh minds.'

She: 'Nah, warm air, warm thoughts.'

There's no way we'll ever see eye to eye here. Fresh air is to me like fresh-brew coffee is to Annika. And she drinks it by the bucket. Our failure to compromise on ambient room temperature comes to a head when I arrive one morning in early November and, as per usual, promptly set about opening the window.

'Look,' she sighs demonstratively, 'if you want it freezing cold you know where you can go.'

'What do you mean?'

It's clear where this is leading.

Putting her coffee down for a split second, she points at the offending window.

'Get the IT department to move your PC outside!'

Most likely she's just teasing, but the sudden sharp tone puts me firmly in my place. And so the window stays shut. Not until the following spring, as temperatures tentatively creep up to 15 C, do I dare ease the window open.

'You don't mind, do you?' I enquire sheepishly.

We're finally on speakers again.

I hang on in a further fortnight and then hand in my notice.

Leaving the truck giant turns out to be a good move. A year or two afterwards, the whole translation department is disbanded; the work farmed out to translation agencies. Many of my colleagues are offered, and gleefully accept, early retirement. They'd be foolish not to. Gold-plated pension schemes in Germany range from 45 to 70 % of former salary.

All the while, remarkable changes are unfolding in Germany. This is the year the country hosts the World Cup. It's also the year the world falls in love with Germany. And, perhaps even more surprising, Germany falls in love with itself. For one long stifling hot summer, the nation is swept away on a wave of patriotic hysteria. Suddenly everyone's painting black, red and gold all over their faces and flying flags almost anywhere they can stick them – something unheard of since darker days in the country's history.

I remember 2006 with equal affection. But not on account of the 'football fairy tale', as everyone was calling it.

2006 is the year I make the three-hour round-trip to the International Press store at Munich central railway station to pick up *The Weekly Telegraph*. It carries my very first report on expat life in Germany. Over the following decade the newspaper prints several dozen. They span scintillating subjects from law and order, waste disposal and recycling, to why Germans find my surname such a pain to pronounce. Looking back, I must have been a hopeless negotiator. The full-page features, which take hours on end to pen, fail to make any great impact on my bank balance.

Luckily, I manage to negotiate a slightly better rate for my translations, and soon start picking up regular work, translating press releases and tourist brochures.

I'm even offered some lucrative interpreting assignments at a cosmetics fair in Munich.

No longer sat bent over a screen in the office all day, working from home – finally free to open and close the window as I wish – immediately hits the right spot.

From now on, surely, it's going to be roses all the way.

Testing Times

When everyone else leaves the house at 7 a.m., peace and quiet reign supreme. Homeworkers can enjoy their second or third coffee of the morning totally undisturbed. Possibly even crawl back into bed, finish off reading a novel, or do press-ups on the living room floor while tuned into the 'Today' programme on BBC Radio 4. But then, slowly and surely, this glorious solitude starts to lose its shine. The rest of the day stretches out ahead like an endless carpet, trailing off to some distant speck on the horizon. All that's left for company is the Internet.

Gone is the novelty of homeworking. Bereft of regular office routine or structure, fritting away time becomes the new *modus operandi*. In between sporadic bursts of work, increasingly prolonged periods are spent engrossed in activities that boost morale yet fail to boost income. Activities such as vanity googling and monitoring fan numbers on facebook. While devouring bar after bar of party-pack *Snickers*. The office carpet is strewn with confectionary wrappers. Sitting at the PC in nothing but underwear, it's almost too much effort to bend down and put them in the bin.

This is my own lifestyle right now.

Yep, keeping tabs on my facebook fanship, doing the

odd translation and stuffing myself with peanut choc bars. Not such a bad life, actually. Until one or two things gradually become clear: I miss more regular face-to-face contact with other people. And I can't live from translating and interpreting alone.

It's also clear that my insatiable appetite for *Snickers* has to stop.

'*Tja*,' as Germans typically say.

While Brits tend to dash off and put the kettle on, '*Tja*' is the quintessential German knee-jerk reaction to first signs of trouble. And while Brits quietly enjoy a nice 'cuppa', wondering what to do next, Germans are already back on the job, working flat out to fix it.

There's no quick fix here though. Bottom line is I need a part-time job to fall back on, whenever I'm not inundated with translations. Which seems to be increasingly often.

As for social contact, sharing an office with someone maybe wasn't so awful after all. Despite frequent feuds over fresh air.

But no. I'm not returning to another full-time office job. And I'm in no hurry to return to the classroom either. Least of all in England. Memories of that showdown in the headmaster's study, pages from *Bravo* ripped out and strewn over the floor, still haunt me. I flinch whenever I see the magazine displayed on news stall racks. Besides, hadn't I left my job in England because I'd grown tired of teaching largely disinterested juveniles? That's the official version of events, at least.

One sticky hot summer's day in 2008, however, I'm listening to 'Guten Morgen Bayern' on local radio

Antenne Bayern. Attracting around 1.2 million listeners daily, 'Good Morning Bavaria' purports to be Germany's most successful breakfast show. They're interviewing an officer from the *Kultusministerium*. He's saying that Bavarian schools are hiring what they call *Quereinsteiger*, or lateral entrants. Back in the noughties, the *Kultusministerium* grossly miscalculated not only pupil numbers but also the amount of *Lehrer* required. In a bid to boost numbers, rules are finally being relaxed. Some schools have started recruiting *Ausländer* – teachers qualified from federal German states *outside* Bavaria. Others, bolder still, are even hiring from other EU lands.

Attempting to swipe a tea towel at a wasp crawling over my *Marmeladensemmel*, I'm really only half listening. But my ears prick up when I hear these jobs also pay employee social security contributions. As a freelancer, forking out for this myself has started to become costly. Pushing the *Bravo* fiasco to the back of my mind, I begin to wonder whether going back to the classroom might not be such a bad move after all.

Upshot – I shoot off a speculative application to the Ministry of Culture. After submitting certified copies of all my qualifications – some of which, curiously, require witnessing and countersigning by the manager of my local *Sparkasse* bank – I'm informed that my Postgraduate Certificate of Education is equivalent to just part of the *Staatsexamen*. Without this state exam they'll accept me only as an *Aushilfslehrer,* or a casual teacher. This country, and the *Freistaat* of Bavaria in particular, has some of the most rigid teaching qualification requirements in the world.

To secure a permanent post, I'll need to undergo a series of *Nachqualifizierungsexamen* – additional public exams testing my knowledge of English language, linguistics and literature. Thanks to my 'native speaker status' I'm excused the language proficiency test. I dutifully start preparing to take the written tests. One morning I have my head stuck particularly deep in a book on Olde English. I vividly recall the topic – the five cases and three grammatical genders in the language of Anglo-Saxons. I'm trying to work out why personal pronouns have dual forms when the phone rings. It's the *Direktor* of a nearby *Gymnasium.* One of the grammar school's regular English teachers has been signed off with a long-term illness; would I like to cover for him? I hesitate. It takes a while to sink in that this is an actual job offer. Putting the phone down a moment or two later, I shove my revision notes to the side. The *Staatsexamen* will have to go on hold until next year.

While happy to forget about Olde English dual verb forms, for a while at least, there's also a downside. Without the formal state qualification, I'm merely what they call an *Ersatzlehrer.* Germans use the word *Ersatz* to describe replacement, make-do and non-original items, such as teeth, tyres and coffee. Further ominously, it's used to talk about emergency bus services. My suspicions are borne out when I bank my first paycheck. I'm earning only half as much as my tenured colleagues.

Still, life in the classroom gets off to a good enough start. Pupils appreciate the wide opportunity to speak in these classes – some say that having the lesson totally in English feels just like being in England.

Things are looking good too when, a little later, we officially become a *Seminarschule*. The school welcomes a dozen young trainees to its ranks. All have just completed their *Erstes Staatsexamen* in either German, English, French or History. They're predominantly female and rather attractive. Some of my male colleagues start turning up for classes every morning with a spring in their step.

Welcome distraction notwithstanding, it soon becomes clear that this is going to be no easy ride. These are, quite literally, testing times.

Each class is required to take three to four formal tests a year, plus a steady flow of *Stegreifaufgobn* (short, unannounced tests). This, and the constant need to be collecting oral grades, seems to be the biggest bugbear of most teachers in the German school system.

I spend each weekend marking and making assessment tests. All that, however, goes on hold in early December, as we set about welcoming a new addition to the family. We're expecting a boy. His name's to be Daniel. Then, just days before the birth, the gynaecologist springs a surprise. How would we feel about Daniela? Not so sure. We spend a whole weekend throwing random girl names at each other:

'What about Anja?'

'Wasn't that the name of your last girlfriend? No way!'

'OK, how about Sophia?'

'Naah! Girl with that name bullied me at school.'

And so we carry on. In the end we settle on a name of Germanic origin: *Mathildis*, or Matilda, meaning 'strength in battle'. On the happy day, the school gives me time off. I'm the proudest dad in the world.

From then on, it's life in turbocharge. Every single second not spent at school or nursing the new arrival is devoted to preparing lessons and marking the never-ending tests.

One test turns out to be particularly troublesome. Rules stipulate that each *Klassenarbeit* in the upper school last *exactly* sixty minutes. We begin at 11:02. Officially I should finish at *exactly* 12:02. On this occasion, however, hearing nearby church bells chime at the stroke of midday, I instinctively call time at twelve o'clock precisely. I spot the *Schnitzer*, a clumsy blunder, just as I'm handed the final script. Fortunately, everyone seems to have finished anyway and nobody points out the discrepancy.

The following Tuesday when I return the paper, a handful of pupils who have received *Note* 3, and one with *Note* 4, protest. The test, they say, had been cut short by 120 seconds. Time in which they could easily have written an extra word or two and boosted their grade. Word of the misfortune spreads through school like a volley of emojis ricocheting across a social media platform. Called into the office of the *Studiendirektor*, I suggest resolving the issue simply by reassessing the three or four controversial test papers 'appropriately'. I'm basically offering to jack up each candidate one full grade. But the *Studiendirektor* is having no such thing. He instructs me to declare the whole thing *null und nichtig*. The pupils must do it all again.

I spend the best part of that week devising a

completely new test. Pupils have a full further week to revise before sitting the new paper. But this time I'm taking no chances. *Stoppuhr* in hand, I time the whole thing right down to the very last second, ensuring that it lasts *exactly* sixty minutes.

Halfway through marking the retake, however, it becomes clear that I have a brand-new problem. Even though I'd taken great care not to make the revised test any harder than the original, some four or five pupils now have lower grades. Our next class isn't till the following Tuesday. Monday evening feels like the calm before the storm as I bravely steel myself for the inevitable.

The smartest thing would be to call in sick, of course. I could say I had *Kreislaufstörung* or circulatory collapse. What sounds like some life-threatening illness is actually a quite common complaint which besets only Germans, typically striking on Monday mornings.

I reflect on this a moment. At least it would buy me a day's reprieve to think it over. But to think over what? My resignation speech?

Ho, don't tempt me.

Bottom line: regardless of whether I delay one or two days or go and in and face the music straight away, the outcome will be equally disastrous. Better get it over and done with.

The following day I return the marked papers without commentary. Just as expected, the youngsters demand these results be declared *null und nichtig* and call for the original results to be revalidated. Only those grades should be entered on their *Zeugnis*, they argue.

Any teaching plan I might have had up my sleeve flies straight out of the window.

I dismiss class before the bell rings, once again short-changing them by 120 seconds. This time, interestingly, everyone cheers.

While all this is going on another problem is unfolding. Every teacher is required to perform *Pausenaufsicht* – break duty once a week. Technically, I should really be roped into this just once a fortnight, since I teach here only two and a half days a week. First break duty invariably makes me late for the lesson straight after. I arrive totally flustered, *'duach den Wind'*, as the Bavarians say, after racing from school yard back to staffroom and then on to the next lesson in almost one fell swoop. By the time I finally set foot in the classroom, dump my bag on the desk and announce 'Good morning 9C,' I'm already exhausted.

One such morning, I'm counting down the seconds until the bell rings. That's my cue to sprint back inside and collect together everything I need for the following lesson. All of a sudden, I feel something solid and missile-like nip the nape of my neck. Pain shoots through my left shoulder. I swing round instinctively, just in time to spot two boys high-fiving each other. Before I can catch them, they disappear around the corner. I recognise one of the pupils though, he's in my eight-year French group. I head straight to the main office to report the incident. Both boys are eventually pulled out of class and sent to the *Direktor*.

I never hear if the miscreants are brought to justice or simply let off with a curtain lecture. Still, one good thing comes out of the incident. Shortly afterwards I'm relieved of all *Pausenaufsicht* for the rest of the year.

I arrive at my remaining lessons on time and unflustered.

Wandertag

Once a semester, every mainstream state school in Germany is supposed to up sticks for the day on a so-called *Wandertag*. Each year group is encouraged to collectively undertake an educational activity outside the classroom. It's a great idea. In theory, at least.

By now, after all that hassle with *Notendrama* and *Pausenaufsicht,* a little light relief sounds just the ticket. Perusing the board in the main hall, I see quite a few classes are planning some really interesting excursions: years 6 and 7 are travelling to Bayern Park, an enormous fun arena in the Bavarian Forest. 11th grade is gearing up to go white-water rafting down the River Altmühl, also in one of Bavaria's prettiest national parks. And art students in the upper school are visiting The Old and New Pinakothek galleries in Munich. I go home toying with the various options, trying to decide which excursion I should sign up for.

And then my heart drops. It turns out that since I'm just a temporary teacher I don't get to cherry pick at all. I'm simply assigned to Year 10. My heart sinks further into my pants when I hear what these youngsters have unanimously voted to do. It's as if they've opted for something as non-sporty and un-outdoorsy as possible. They're going ten-pin bowling.

Sensing my scepticism, one colleague helpfully suggests that the prime purpose of class excursions is to raise group dynamics and strengthen the class sense of community. Another colleague wryly points out that it's simply an excuse to get out of the classroom and avoid 8B for a whole day. Whichever way you look at it, the pin-bowling trip is probably doing what it's pedagogically supposed to do. The three or four of us, 'volunteered' to supervise the venture, arrange to meet at 8 o'clock in the carpark opposite the school tennis courts.

On the day of the outing, I get stuck in a six-kilometre traffic jam on the short stretch of autobahn between home and school. I miss the coach. Stranded on a wind-swept parking bay, I deliberate whether I should really bother going at all. I go through the motions of pulling my cell phone out, punching in the school secretary's number and uttering that unutterable word: *Kreislaufstörungen.*

Yes, why not? I have every reason to pass up on the ten-pin bowling. The only time I've ever played this 'sport' was at a stag party in Bluewater, Kent. The largest indoor shopping centre in Britain, and home to a dinosaur adventure park, there are probably better places for gallivanting around half drunk in celebration of your best mate getting hooked.

Although tempted to cop out of bowling, I can't quite bring myself to faking *Kreislaufstörung.* I decide to catch the pupils up in my car. I pull up at the bowling centre just as they've finished sorting themselves out into teams and are sending the first balls sliding down the alley. Some of the boys are showing off their side-spinning skills, getting the ball to spin on its base before hitting all ten targets in one fell swoop. I initially manage to show some enthusiasm:

'Wow! Hey! Cool!'

After seeing the act repeated a few times, however, the novelty begins to wear off. Curiously, I seem to be the only adult supervising the whole thing. Where are all my colleagues? I finally find them comfortably ensconced in the bowling bistro, sipping café lattes and busily devouring a *zweites Frühstück*. That's the extra meal which German employees love to slap in between early breakfast and equally early lunch. They typically down tools and tuck into their second breakfast around 9 o'clock every weekday.

Huddled up on blood-red, fifties-style American sofas, these mostly young colleagues turn out to be a fun bunch, and I'm soon glad I've taken the trouble to turn up. We spend most of the time trading tales about classroom nightmares. Evidently, I'm not the only member of staff relieved to be escaping class 8B for the day.

There's just one *kleines Problem*.

Cosily ensconced amidst a warren of retro diner décor, we're enjoying swapping stories so much that we totally lose track of time. A good two hours later a responsible-looking pupil finally pokes her head around the door:

'Tschuidigung, mia san fertig.'

Our Year Tens are patiently waiting for us on the coach and wondering how much longer we'll be.

Fortunately, upon return to school, the pupils keep as quiet as church mice. Our somewhat brief report on the 'action-packed' excursion duly lands on the *Direktor's* desk and we all agree that if pushed to supply further details we'll simply confirm that the trip was a huge success.

Schönen Feierabend!

'*Endlich Freitag!*' sighs my colleague Barbara, wobbling into the staffroom with a pile of exercise books balanced precariously between her arms. Seconds later Barbara has dumped her books in a corner and is bouncing back through the main door.

'*Schönen Feierabend!*' she calls over her shoulder.

Her mood, it seems, has suddenly swung from stressed to sparkling.

'*Merci, gleichfois!*' everyone around me choruses.

I catch myself automatically echoing this classic Bavarian response to well-wishers. Even though I'm sat with my back to her and don't even bother looking round to reply. But then a puzzling thought – doesn't '*Schönen Feierabend!*' mean 'Have a nice celebration evening!'? Hearing colleagues call out this well-wish feels funny at 11 o'clock in the morning. Particularly when you're just tucking into your *zweites Frühstück*.

Historically, *Feierabend* was very much an evening celebration, as church bells called burghers to sunset praise and worship. These days, however, *Feierabend* is more a byword for the end of the working day and the official act of switching off from work all together. In some companies, a six-thirty start, for example, lets you clock off at 11 a.m. Starting work only slightly later, most teachers are also done by midday. Staying behind at your workplace after hours – perfectly normal in Britain and America – is seen in Germany as an admission of inefficiency. Barbara, quite clearly, wishes nobody to question her personal productivity.

Germans cherish their abundant *Freizeit*. But not all burghers are so thrilled about its ramifications. With weekends starting up to half a day earlier than in most other countries, it's difficult to reach many employees after Friday midday. Germans currently work an average of 37.7 hours a week, compared to just over 42 in the UK. While British employees are only just drifting back to the office from lunch break, their German counterparts are already downing tools and heading home for *Kaffee und Kuchen*. And when Brits finally knock it on the head and pour into the pub at five or six o'clock for after-work drinks, *Bundesburghers* are already in the throes of going out 'proper'.

Just like me on this still blazing hot early evening in June. Having spent all afternoon puttering around the garden, I'm off to a concert. Only problem is I'm not so sure what to wear. I finally plump for *sportlich elegant* – smart casual, with checked-pattern polo shirt, jacket, shorts and sandals. Default summer wear for middle-aged male Germans.

It's soon clear that I'm totally out of synch with local dress code.

Everyone around me is totally glammed up: glittery romper suits and gowns, Lurex pants studded with sequins and earth-goddess hairstyles all round. Equally striking is the unashamedly retro music. Pumping out of the p.a. system is Boney M's 'Hooray! Hooray! It's a Holi-Holi-Day!' Staring disbelievingly at the date on my mobile, I do a double take. This can't possibly be 2009. It feels more like *1979*.

I've come to Flora Mediterranea, a rather swish garden centre which occasionally serves as a venue for pop concerts. Tonight's offering is A4U. What sounds like a sporty hatchback from Audi is actually a tribute to a bunch of Swedish popstars. A4U is one of some dozen Abba sound-and-look-alike bands currently touring Germany. Tribute acts – 'Re-vival Bands' as Germans call them – are big business in this country. They have their own festivals, stars and fans too. Judging by their garish garb, these Abba aficionados are going the whole hog. What bewilders me is not so much the comic costumes but that no one seems at all troubled that the group they've paid through the nose to see isn't actually the real deal.

Personally, I'd have given my last breath to see the originals. I'm not too sure about this particular tribute band though. The Oxford English Dictionary defines the word 'tribute' as 'an act, statement, or gift that is intended to show gratitude, admiration or respect.' Respect? With tickets being snapped up for over fifty euros a piece, tribute bands have clearly worked out that paying respect also pays dividends. Fortunately, I've got in free. Simply by offering to review the event for the *Hallertauer Zeitung*, my local newspaper. German *Regionale Zeitungen* are often so short of staff that when it comes to reporting on local events, they largely rely on freelancers to pack their pages.

As I take my place beside two kohl-eyed middle-aged females, the band is already belting out their first offering: 'Ring Ring, Why Don't You Give Me a Call?' The impersonators are drawing circles with their fingers, presumably dialling imaginary rotary phones. I eavesdrop on my neighbours' conversation. One of them is scrutinising the two 'Abba' males larking around on stage in hilariously tight spandex playsuits. Turning to the other, she says 'Oooh, those boys are so much sexier than Benny and Björn!'

I don't know about clean-shaven Björn, but his bearded sidekick looks like he needs fattening up a bit. The skinny 'Swede' can barely weigh sixty kilos. As for the girls, Fake Frida's hair-do looks more salmon pink than the dark ginger-head from the seventies.

Actually, to give the 'copycats' credit, they at least sound remarkably like the real thing. Especially when it comes to 'Dancing Queen'. Sashaying sexily from one side of the stage to the other, 'Agnetha' calls out in a fake Swedish English accent, '*Wheesper* in your neighbour's ear I'd like to get to *knoooow* you!' It's the ultimate in audience participation – a sure tell-tell sign that they're psyching us all up for 'Knowing me, Knowing you.' I turn to my kohl-eyed neighbour. Too late. She's already whispering sweet nothings in her other neighbour's ear.

Meanwhile A4U are jollying us up for the grand finale. Some of the crowd have already donned the bicorn, Napoleon's famous triangular hat, gearing up for the greatest Eurovision hit of all.

I've enjoyed the show greatly, but it's getting late and I've promised to file my report by tomorrow noon. There are also words I need to look up – what's German for 'copycats'? Leaving now of course means missing the after-show party. And, fortuitously, all those other Boney M hits. Shaking glitter dust out of my hair, I shuffle towards the exit.

Toga and Temptress

Late June, and there seems to be one sole topic of conversation in the upper school – the *Abistreich*. That's the prank which final-year pupils play on the rest of the school. And, when it comes to firing a parting shot at the establishment, German pupils certainly know how to go out with a bang. Word is out that this year's leavers are set to deliver something unparalleled in the school's entire history. Roped into negotiating terms and conditions with pupils, one colleague describes the practical joke as little short of 'epic'.

Going by previous *Abi* jokes, it's unlikely that this year's leavers will have *too* much to top. Last year, outgoing pupils locked the *Direktor* in a cage on the main stage and had staff scuttle around searching for the matching key. Seven identical-looking specimens were stowed around the hall, and only one fitted. The correct key was located almost immediately; the distraught *Direktor* released back into the community. The fun and games were over in less than ten minutes. On another occasion, the eldest pupils sprayed the teachers' cars with shaving foam, decorating them with cotton-wool buds and smarties. Eye witnesses said it looked quite artistic. The *Direktor* sent the culprits to the cleaner's stores to collect buckets and *Wischmops*.

It's the final lesson. I'm just circulating the Year Nine classroom, handing back the last test. Pausing here and there, I'm dispensing praise to recipients of *Note* 3 and over, while offering comfort and commiseration to everyone else. All of a sudden loud music booms out over the school's loudspeaker system.

It's David Hasselhoff's 'I've Been Looking for Freedom.'

My immediate reaction is to stop dead in my tracks and snort out loud. I've not heard this one-hit wonder since 1989. The pupils most likely have never heard it at all.

Penned by *Hitmeister* Jack White, the song had scored a mini-hit some ten years earlier for long-forgotten singer Marc Seeberg. But when reunification activists started demonstrating every Monday up and down the German Democratic Republic, White was already wooing the man who would take his tune to far greater heights. 'I've Been Looking for Freedom' was re-released the very week East Germans grabbed their hammers and started hacking away at the Berlin Wall. By the time the *Mauer* was reduced to rubble, Hasselhoff was everybody's darling. Alas, Hasselhoff's hit master failed to foresee one small thing – the higher you climb, the harder you fall. In the blink of an eye, East Germans found their own brand of freedom. They needn't look far – it lay just over The Wall behind the doors of the KaDeWe, West Berlin's giant temple to consumerism.

Whether the man from *Baywatch* singlehandedly brought down the Berlin Wall is a moot point. Fox News still seem to believe he did. Clearly, once everyone had found freedom there was little else to sustain Hasselhoff's career. Within three months he went from hero to zero.

But back to the classroom in deepest Lower Bavaria.

What on earth is going on here? All of a sudden, rather mercifully actually, Hasselhoff goes stone dead. He's replaced by the muffled sound of scratchy audio, followed by the highly-strung voice of a pupil: *'Achtung, Achtung!'* It sounds like he's had a microphone thrust into his hand and is being forced to make a public apology for some grave misdeed. Perhaps he's carved his name into a school desk or spoken to a teacher with chewing gum in his mouth. But no. He's calling all teachers to proceed immediately to the main reception area. I have no option but to follow the flow.

Marching up and down robed as Roman emperors and empresses, the final-year *Abiturienten* and *Abiturientinnen* have commandeered the entire main reception block. Armed with official-looking clipboards and bearing conference-style plastic name tags, the adolescents are herding us into what appear to be haphazardly organised clusters. Group by group we're then force-marched into the school gym which has been revamped into an enormous Roman Empire Olympic arena. Outgoing Year 13 pupils have evidently stopped at nothing to ensure their gag goes down on record as a classic.

Needless to say, this is no routine German school day.

Within minutes of being bundled into the hall, I'm standing underneath the stage, face to face with a heavily made-up eighteen-year-old. She's sporting a snazzy sleeveless under-tunic, skin-snug bust bodice and thigh-high laced boots. More Roman Temptress than Empress. Does it say Messalina on her tag?

My suspicions subsequently deepen. Without so much as batting an eyelid, she hands me a semi-circular slave's toga and orders me to strip down to the waist. When I hesitate, she digs her heels into the ground:

'Hosnn a ob, und an mid am Toga!

I'm to take my trousers off and put the toga on. I'm undressing so frantically that my left-hand shoe gets tangled up with my trouser leg. I tug madly but it doesn't budge. For a second, I'm left hopping around on the other leg like a deranged flamingo.

The scene has to be seen to be believed. As do the ensuing 'crowd-pleasing' spectacles. These take place under the watchful eye of Emperor Augustus, his gold-leaved throne dominating centre stage, with an amphitheatre-like Roman arena vying as jaw-dropping backdrop. Humiliating stunts include donning cycle helmets and warrior shields and parading around in circles. Then – in a sudden and surreal switch of roles – being animated to lie down sideways on make-shift sofas and fed grapes by Aquila and Atticus.

But this is nothing compared to what follows.

The speed at which we're about to run the gladiator's chariot race would make even Ben Hur quiver with fear and head for the hills. By now, having been plied with free *Bier* and *Brezels* by just slightly younger pupils dressed in *Dirndl* decked with frilly bodices and pinafores, we're probably no longer fully conscious of what we're being put through. Pummelled into

submission, we've become willing victims, attached to
each other with emotional super glue. After re-entering
the arena to an ear-popping mixture of wolf whistles,
cheers and storming applause, things start to go slightly
wrong. All I can remember is standing at the helm of a
skateboard, and mock-whipping a much older female
colleague who'd been roped in to towing me. The
impromptu showstopper ends with me veering off into
beer benches at the final bend.

Fearing fall-out from this fateful afternoon, I keep a
low profile, bracing myself for a *Shit Storm*. But a whole
week passes and, most curiously, not a single word is
said. As if the whole thing were just a mad dream.

We're just getting into our pyjamas, readying for bed,
when the doorbell rings.

Bea answers. There's a man standing on the doorstep.
He's carrying an air rifle.

'Is your husband there?'

'*Neeein*,' she lies, eyeing the weapon with suspicion,
'*warum?*'

It turns out the man with the gun is a *Jäger*, a local
hunter. I'd been jogging in the woods just above our
house earlier that evening and, apparently, I'd scared off
a herd of deer he'd quietly been tracking for two hours.
He's not particularly pleased.

Poking my head around the bathroom door upstairs,
I hear the following conversation in local dialect:

'Please tell your husband that if he really must go

jogging, he should be back home by 8.30 p.m. latest. Otherwise there will be consequences.'

'But that path through the woods is a public right of way. Anyone can use it. Whenever they want.'

'Not when I'm shooting deer they can't. Tell your husband that, OK?'

'OK.'

As the huntsman leaves, I hear him say *'Sagen Sie Ihrem Mann einen freundlichen Gruss.'* Germans generally delight in sending each other friendly greetings. But when these greetings are dispatched with firm emphasis on *friendly*, it's unlikely that they're ever meant as such.

The incident speaks volumes of how highly esteemed hunters are in Germany. Probably because obtaining a hunting license in this country is both difficult and costly. Weapon owners need to obtain special certification to bear arms, and this involves taking special courses and tests. Most hunting in Germany takes place on private agricultural and wooded land, such as just behind our house. Hunters pay thousands of euros to lease a shooting area for nine years at a time. Deer in Germany are seen as a pest. They love to strip shoots off saplings and young trees. Desperate to ensure their numbers are kept in check, foresters don't hesitate to revoke the license of hunters who fail to shoot a given number of deer each year. Even more severe are the fines which both foresters and farmers can impose on hunters. Recently a local hunter had to cough up ten thousand euros in compensation to a landowner, after wild pigs rampaged through the farmer's fields, leaving a swath of destruction in their wake.

No wonder our local *Jäger* is so protective of his stomping ground. But it feels funny being put under curfew in a country where *Jedermannsrecht* – the freedom to roam – is guaranteed by the constitution.

And what exactly did the hunter mean by 'there will be consequences'?

Early the next morning we experience a foretaste. I'm just about to walk out of the front door when I almost fall over a dead fox. Either we're living at rather closer quarters to wildlife than we'd originally anticipated or someone's playing a sick joke on us. Judging by the glazed expression in its eyes – muzzle more upturned in disgust than pointed with pride – it doesn't exactly look like this animal has crawled there under his own steam. He clearly drew his last gulp of breath well before landing dead under the doorbell.

Better not push my luck with the *Jäger*. From here on, I'll do my jogging before dusk.

Step Two:

Get into lederhose
and go with the flow

*In 2016, Statista Research asked
Bavarians if wearing lederhosen
at the Oktoberfest should be mandatory.*

54 % said 'Ja'.

White Roses and 'Auf Wiedersehen'

Back at school, meanwhile, there's been a *Notenkonferenz.* Logging onto the central *Notensystem*, I discover a riot of grades *Eins* and *Zwei*. Class 11B, whose test screw-up almost sparked a major riot, aren't going to believe their lucky stars when they discover everyone's suddenly passed with flying colours.

The *Shit Storm* I'd feared following the *Abi* prank seems to have blown over. Which means we can now busy ourselves with other distractions. Such as silly award ceremonies, poetry slams and rate-the-teacher surveys.

Queues at the photocopier and coffee machine have also subsided. Perhaps we're all producing fewer handouts and consuming more mineral water than coffee. It's certainly been a scorcher of a summer. For some, however, it's also a sad summer: Michael Jackson drops dead from a drug overdose. He's just fifty.

There's a fair amount of bereavement – both in the staffroom and out on the playground. Not that Mr. Jackson's demise touches pupils to quite the extent that it touches teachers. We had, after all, grown up with his music. What's more, unlike the pupils, we're old enough to remember the days when he was still black. I recall my very first smooch – possibly even a snog –

accompanied by 'Rock with you' at the school disco. But I also have slightly less happy Jackson/ex-girlfriend related memories. Like dancing all sad and solo to one of his chart-topping ballads. 'She's out of my life', wasn't it?

I have my classes draft an obituary for Jackson. It seems a good way of both paying tribute to the star and practising what Germans call '*If*-clauses Typ III'. Pupils contend with each other to produce the most hypothetical statement. They come up with ideas like 'If he had lived longer, he would have married Elizabeth Jagger.' Another pupil proposes 'He would have died from something else if he had not taken drugs.' Equally plausible, given his rather non-conventional lifestyle. The pupils are curious to find out more about Jacko. But this is 2009, several years before smartphones invade our lives. So, in the final week I send them off to the library PCs to google the late superstar. It makes a welcome change from watching *Mr Bean Goes Swimming* for the umpteenth time.

Although end-of-semester life is generally low-stress, dark clouds are already gathering on the horizon. The media is reporting a *Lehrerüberschuss* – a surplus of teachers. Clearly the first persons in line for dismissal are likely to be 'cover' teachers. Is this why, in the final week of term, the *Direktor* calls me into his office?

I knock apprehensively.

Standing at the *Direktor*'s doorway reminds me of my own schooldays. At the age of nine I was sent to the head's study to account for a broken window pane in one of the portacabin classrooms. We absolutely loathed these make-shift, make-do classrooms. In summer we sweated like stallions and in winter we froze to the bone. Alas, one Christmas I was made personally responsible for the icy room temperature after accidentally leaning against the window. Very gently, but sufficiently enough to shatter it. By sheer stroke of luck, the glass fell outwards not inwards.

The headmaster invites me in. 'So, Mister Howe,' he begins. For a moment, I wonder if he's summoned me for a nice little chat, possibly to practise his English.

'*Guada Obistreich, gell?*' he continues.

Good Abi prank? It could just be a harmless aside, but the tone of his voice is ominous. It's like he's holding me *personally* responsible for organising the whole mad caper. That *I* had been instrumental in triggering this disastrous chain of events. Was that it, I wonder? Was he proposing to present me with *Schadenersatz* claims from members of the crowd who I'd ploughed into on my chariot, that fateful moment as I spiralled out of control at the final bend? Worse still, would the name 'Messalina' come up?

Bitte, nein.

Just who had tempted whom exactly? I don't recall seeing any witnesses. If this ever came to trial, it would be her word against mine. And the end of my teaching career.

I start to sweat. Visions of being shackled up in chains and deported out of the country flash through my mind.

Only a second earlier it had almost appeared as if we were going to have a nice cosy end-of-term chat together, possibly even share a little *Schnäppchen*. I survey the potted plant on his desk, next to which stands a half-empty bottle. Was he intending to offer me some such liquid refreshment? I loathe the stuff. And yet I'd happily have accepted a drop, just out of politeness.

Yes, it could all have been so very *gemütlich*.

But then this crazy *Abi* prank had put a spanner in the works. It had provoked something akin to what Frau Merkel once charmingly called a *Shit Storm*. Why had I not seen it all coming? I'd had a whole week to clear out my pigeonhole, pack my bags and get out of town, for goodness' sake. Too late now. Game over. *End Geländ*, as Bavarians say.

The next few moments' silence feels like half an eternity, sitting there on the edge of my chair in the *Direktor's* cosy little alcove-like study, with its Biedermeier sofa and matching armchair, framed family photos adorning the walls and expensive-looking matchbox model Audi 8 Coupés lining the sideboard. Then, all of a sudden, the *Direktor* takes a deep breath. Releasing air through puffed-out cheeks, he breaks the news:

'Naxts Joar konn i Ihna grod drei Stund obied.'

He can offer me just three hours work next year.

The news is both bad and good. Bad because it's barely half a morning's work. Not quite one hundred euros after the tax man takes his cut. If this were just one class, they would probably expect me to turn up on three separate mornings. And yet it's good because I'd been expecting fate to deal me a much more brutal blow. For a brief moment I'm tempted to shake hands on the deal.

But that would be calling his bluff. He knows I know he's spoilt for choice when it comes to replacing me with a gorgeous-looking, freshly-qualified *Referendarin*. In fact, the 'crown princess' probationer is probably hovering in the corridor outside right now, waiting to be called in for interview.

Stepping up onto the stage that same day, I receive my goodbye gift – a white rose (possibly a peace offering?) amidst heavy applause. Yet this emotional moment belies a much less cheery development. The Ministry of Culture plans to shave a full year off pupils' mandatory attendance at *Gymnasium*. From the following year, with the introduction of a slimmed-down syllabus known as 'G8', the school will allow only those with the full qualification, the *Zweites Staatsexamen*, to teach the top classes.

As it turns out, the new-fangled school system is short-lived. Largely unworkable, it puts unnecessary pressure on staff and pupils to complete an only slightly shorter curriculum one year sooner. In 2017, schools pop champagne corks and rejoice as the Bavarian state parliament announces a return to the nine-year regime.

In sum, it's been a momentous year of ups and downs, a real rollercoaster of emotions, or *Wechselbad der Gefühle*.

The German expression aptly conjures up images of torture victims being waterboarded in a succession of scorching hot and freezing cold bath tubs. Writing for *The Weekly Telegraph*, I end my dispatch from *Deutschland* with an encouraging message to other would-be teachers in the expat community:

'Who knows, play your cards right at *Gymnasium* and you might even be entrusted with the top classes.' Tongue in cheek, I add 'But take care what you let yourself in for on leavers' day.'

The report appears a couple weeks later under the headline 'To Sir, with beer and pretzels.'

Cool Germany

In July 2018, *Focus – The News Magazine* conducts a 'State of the nation' poll. It calls on readers to list sixty reasons why they like Germany.

The publication is inundated with replies. So many in fact that the whole survey, headlined 'Bleib Cool Germany, lasst uns Deutschland nicht kaputtreden!' (Stay cool Germany, let's not bust our guts with silly talk) stretches to a six-page special. The issue literally flies off the shelves, selling out within 48 hours. The 'Sixty Reasons' make for a telling snap-shot of contemporary Germany. My favourites include:

'We have over 130 professional orchestras – more than any other country in the world.'

'We're one of the most generous countries in the world' (last year Germans donated 5.2 billion euros to charitable acts).

'We obediently sweep our staircases and pavements.'

'Our engineers and technicians build the best cars' (despite exhaust gas scandals).

'It's safe to assume you can drink the tap water' (bizarrely though, Germans don't. They prefer expensive bottled mineral water).

'We rose up from the ruins in 1945 to build a new, strong and democratic country.'

Most popular of all, however, is this response:

'We love our country because it's governed by a woman.'

Nice one. But how might Brits typically reply, if asked to comment what they most like about Germany? I imagine something like this:

'*Bier* and *Wurst* you'd almost put your life on the line for.'

'Bakeries with fresh baked bread.'

'Magical Christmas markets.'

'Industry that should be the model for our own.'

'Trains that run on time.'

À propos. Germans often pour cold water over our rosy-glow take on their country's rail network. Bugged out by regional services that rarely run on time, they point out that if you want to experience German punctuality and efficiency you have to go to Switzerland. Comparing Germany with neighbouring countries, the ZDF documentary *Ziemlich Beste Nachbarn* – Quite Best Neighbours (the emphasis being on *quite*) – recently reported that fewer than 76% of German trains have run on time over the past three years, compared to 90% of Italian trains. If that's true then it certainly crushes the cliché of unpunctual Italians.

While German punctuality might not be all it's cracked up to be – more about train trouble later – there's one area in which Germany still shines: open-air swimming pools. Outdoor public pools have been big in Germany since industrialisation in the 1920s. And all thanks to a social movement known as the *Lebensreform*, a group set up to promote a more back-to-nature lifestyle. Amongst other things, they championed raw and organic food, alternative medicines, disapproval of alcohol and public nudity.

Wherever you go in Germany, you're never far from a *Freibad*. The literal translation is 'free bath'. You do have to pay of course – but not that much. You can get into most public pools for less than five euros.

It strikes me that, unlike in England, where we tend to associate open-air pools with our worst childhood memories, German kids actually enjoy lessons at their local *Freibad*. Pupils obediently swim alongside track-suited teachers, armed with clip boards and stop watches. Good German discipline.

Another familiar feature of the *Freibad* is the *Schnell-Imbiss*. The leaseholder of the snack bar at our local *Freibad* is a colourful character called Pepe. Sipping at an espresso, the short and stocky Italian describes how he'd love to sell a wider, healthier range of snacks. 'But,' he says, pulling a wounded face, 'this is Germany.' Apparently, when he took the place over, he cooked fresh pasta every day. 'No one wanted it,' he continued. 'I had to throw most away. Now I stick to pizza, *Pommes Frites* and *Currywurst*. It's what Germans want.'

Pepe and I stand talking in the shadow of a giant chess set. The larger-than-life pieces are lovely to look at, but I can't recall anyone ever playing with them. They stand sole and forsaken, in stark contrast to a long line of hungry bathers queueing up for snacks from the kiosk. Most are busily ordering the sort of take-away staples which Pepe has just scrunched his nose up at – chips smothered with mayonnaise and ketchup and, perennial favourite, the *Currywurst*.

Few Germans are probably aware that they actually have the Brits to thank for this humble dish. Back in 1949, Herta Heuwer, owner of a food kiosk in West Berlin, was given ketchup, Worcestershire sauce and curry powder by British soldiers. Unsure what to do with them, she slapped the ingredients over a platter of grilled sausage. The legendary *Currywurst* was born.

When it comes to working up an appetite, burghers are almost spoilt silly with yet more bathing options. Our region alone boasts a swath of swim holes, almost all in shouting distance. As well as an Olympic-size pool skirting Pepe's tuck shop, we can hop between over half a dozen lakes on the site of former stone quarry – and an idyllic *Waldbad* in the middle of the forest. Visitors from the UK marvel at this broad network of open-air bathing facilities. Probably because there are relatively few in British cities. Greater London, for example, has only 15 lidos for a population of around 8 million. Munich, eight times smaller, boasts twice as many outside pools. Germany has over 7,000 swimming pools, the majority of which are open air. That's one pool for every 12,000 citizens.

Just looking around the pool here at Moaburg, the keenest swimmers seem to be those with most time on their hands – senior citizens. Clad in identical looking bathing robes and flip-flops, these so-called *Frühsportler*, or early-morning sportspersons, typically arrive at six, ready to rack up 50 lengths before *Frühstück*. Better not to stray across their lane. Foolishly, I recently did so, almost ploughing head-first into an elderly *Sportler* who appeared to be challenging the current world record in 100-m crawl. He was enraged, and rightly so.

Middle-aged Germans, on the other hand, seem more attracted to the *Freibad* by non-swimming pleasures. They just lie, read and nibble salty German savouries such as *Salzstangen*. And ogle whatever breezes by in a bikini.

Everyone, young and old, enjoys relaxing on the *Liegewiese* – a lovely green lawn alongside the water.

Green spaces are something else Germans do very well, in fact. And they're invariably uber-tidy. I have seen people here pick up litter – a paper tissue or a shop receipt quite often – and go up to the person who dropped it, say politely that they think they have lost something and give it back to them. Difficult to imagine that happening in England.

On one of the last days the *Freibad* is open this year it's still thronging with the usual *Frühsportler*. Having just notched up a dozen or more lengths before breakfast, I decide to pop into Aldi, just around the corner. I often park in the discounter carpark if I want to kill two birds with one stone.

It's already mid-September and there's an autumnal feeling in the air despite a very pleasant ambient temperature of 19° C.

Entering the supermarket, I notice that bargain bins selling off summery goods such as t-shirts, sandals and garden gear have all disappeared. No wonder – they'd been clearing out end-of-season stock at ridiculously low prices. German *Hausfrauen* love *Schnäppchen*, and have probably snapped everything up, storing their bargain buys away for the following summer.

But look what's taken their place. The bargain baskets in the middle aisle are crammed with Christmas clutter. Which is selling fast and furiously. Jostling for foot space, housewives are preparing to pounce on the last remaining packs of marzipan hearts. They're all fancily packaged in Christmas-tree shaped woolly stockings topped with a bauble or two. With late-summer sunshine streaking in through the supermarket's sizeable front windows all this doesn't feel right somehow.

Heat and hordes. It's too much for me.

Grabbing a pack of *Lebkuchen*, I charge towards the check-out. Aldi has a total of four pay desks in this store, yet rarely operates more than two at the same time. The queue for the only manned pay desk is slowly snaking down the central aisle towards frozen foods and Thursday's special offers.

On the way home, we call for bread at the local *Bäckerei*. German bakeries are a far more sensory experience than their British counterparts. Verging almost on the sensuous, they're more a hybrid of French *boulangerie* and *patisserie*, minus – alas – all the divine choux pastries. But what it lacks in sweet sensations, the *Bäckerei* more than makes up for in *Brot*, which comes in all shapes, sizes and varieties. While Brits pace up and down the supermarket aisle, undecided whether to go for brown or white, Germans can take their pick from over 3,259 different types.

Why so many? First, the country grows many types of cereal, such as wheat, spelt and rye. Second, German bakers are required to attain a very high standard in training, far higher than in most other countries. German bread culture even features on UNESCO'S 'intangible cultural heritage' list. *Deutsches Brot* is a craft, a staple food in its own right. German law, which bans shops opening on the Sabbath, graciously excepts bakeries. Burghers regard bread almost as a natural birth right. Heaven forbid anyone deny them their beloved *Sonntagssemmel.* There would be a national outcry, a revolution even.

All of a sudden, my thoughts drift from *Brot* to *Kuchen.* Pressing her nose and lips against the cake vitrine, my daughter leaves a string of dribble oozing its way down the glass. As if to apologise for the trail of drool detracting from the pastry display, I immediately feel obliged to buy more than just a loaf of crusty *Sauerteig* bread. But Tildy's already reaching out and fingering a *Zimtschnecke,* a sugar-saturated cinnamon twirl. Problem solved.

Choosing which type of coffee to go for, proves tougher. *Kaffee mit Schlagsahne* or *Milchschaum?* I eventually plump for whipped cream over foam. Squirting it into my beverage, Frau Lutzenburger, the friendly café proprietor, greets me with the customary *'Grüßi Gott.'* In passing, I mention the scene of mayhem encountered at the discounter. It's the bane of the Germans, she says with a sigh and flick of the hand. They fear if they don't get in quick enough when bargains are up for grabs, they risk going away empty handed.

That might explain why Germans rise at the break of

dawn – even on holiday.

Leaving the store, I deliberate whether to pop back to Aldi for a few more *Lebkuchen*, just in case they sell out by the weekend.

Christmas, by the way, is still three and a half months away.

Help from on High

'How's the new job?'

This message has just flashed up on my facebook wall.

It's from Claudia. A well-connected family friend, she'd helped secure me a part-time position, teaching English at an all-girls' school in Munich. It's my first time standing up in front of a class full of pubescent females. It's also a private Catholic school, which means that in everything I do, I'm answerable to a gaggle of nuns. On both scores I'm more than just a little apprehensive.

Scared out of my pants is perhaps a more accurate description.

Better not admit that to Claudia though.

'Ooh, not bad,' I shoot back, 'the nuns haven't eaten me up yet!'

I'd assumed this was a private dialogue. Suddenly I recoil in a flush of horror. My notification box is flashing up a dozen 'likes', half of which are from people I've never heard of. I'd foolishly failed to edit the privacy settings. Inadvertently, I've shared this confidential comment with my, her, and everyone else's friends. Worse still, someone's probably copied and pasted the whole lot onto the school's home page and the Sisters are presently poring over it too.

Although the job started three or four days ago no one's actually asked me to teach yet. But it's been fun sitting in on a variety of well and slightly less well-behaved classes, some of which – luckily maybe – I won't have to teach at all. Tomorrow, though, I'll give my first proper lesson.

Claudia likes my response. Posting a clapping emoji, she messages back:

'*Viel Glück!*'

Good luck. Yes, I'll need that.

Other commentators are less encouraging. Some even cautionary. Iris from Pfaffenhofen warns 'Things can only get worse, you'll see!', while Katinka from Krailling near Regensburg quips 'Hey Tim, just you behave yourself with those innocent *Mädls.*' Underscoring this with a trail of emojis, she adds 'or you'll have the nuns round rapping your knuckles!'

First thing I learn about these innocent *Mädls* is they're not quite the picture of purity painted by some of my social media detractors. I spend a whole afternoon sitting through a staff meeting in which the nuns proceed to lay down school policy for cracking down on the pupils' 'extra-curricular' activities online. Understandably ill at ease in this department, the sisters are slightly fuzzy on the details. But, from what I gather, some girls in the upper school have been topping up their *Taschengeld* by posting slightly inappropriate selfies. In places, presumably, which school management would wish they weren't so streetwise about. Luckily though no innocence minds are corrupted and no knuckles need to be rapped. My tenure under the sisters' prayerful eyes passes incident-free.

Well, almost.

There are just one or two unfortunate incidents. Such as when I dish out a grade four to a pupil, prompting her to burst into tears and flee the room. Before I can calm her down the rest of the class have followed her out into the corridor in a consolidated show of sympathy. Or possibly just to escape my vocabulary test. That's Class 8D, who are quite a handful – even by their own admission. On another occasion, I'm in the middle of handing out an assignment when the whole class link hands, in yet another show of solidarity. The peers pledge not to let go until I allow them to leave ten minutes before the lunch bell rings.

Higher up the school there's a run-in with a student who takes me to task for awarding her oral performance a mere *drei*. Like most pupils in Germany, she's expecting nothing inferior to *zwei*. It's another of my countless encounters with that typical 'Made in Germany' problem of *Notenstress* – the fear of poor marks. The result of which seems to be a constant state of pressure on pupils to meet teacher and parent expectations by obtaining good grades. Yet marking, as I'd already discovered in that *Notendrama* at my previous Gymnasium, can be merciless. Score margins prescribed by the *Kultusministerium* are often so tight that one small slip of the pen might easily make the difference between a respectable *drei* and a shameful *vier*. Expectations have hit such heights that, for many pupils, even a *drei* is considered disgraceful.

'Well,' I say, in a bid to placate her, 'perhaps it wasn't *such* a bright idea to perform perched on my *desk* like that.'

This rather risqué approach to delivering a formal presentation brings a smile to the faces of her Year Ten audience, but leaves her *Englischlehrer* rather less amused. Having observed how I tend to straddle my desk when teaching, she's clearly making an all-out effort to outsmart me.

Still, nothing prepares me for the outbreak that follows:

'Do you have a *problem* with me?'

She pauses before the word 'problem', underscoring it with a theatrical jolt of the head. Her long auburn mane is tossed back ferociously, rather like a startled stallion rearing up on hind legs. Then, with a haughty turn of the head, she clicks her heels and flounces off into the corridor. I'm left wondering whether it's actually *me* who's the problem. Perhaps it is. I make a mental note to stand well clear of my desk for the remaining lessons with this class.

Fortunately, it's not all about trying to dodge run-ins with challenging adolescents. There are friendlier pupils and lighter moments too. One Year Nine group is particularly polite right from the word go. They stand to attention each time I enter the room and always ensure that the blackboard is wiped clean, chalk stored away in receptacle and sponge squeezed and left to soak in sink. They often leave a little bouquet of fresh wildflowers on my desk, and sometimes even a little sweet or praline too. These girls sure know how to soften up their new teacher. They're the direct antithesis of 8D.

Occupying prime real estate in the heart of Munich, the private school is a mere stone's throw away from the Oktoberfest. When the festival starts in the second week of school, many pupils come to class dressed in *Dirndl*. The plan, of course, is to make a beeline for the *Fest* as soon as lessons are over. But, before dashing off, the girls in 9C have a surprise in store. Taking me to the back of the room, one of the pupils ties a scarf around my eyes and instructs me to spin me around 360 degrees. Blindfolded and totally disoriented, I then have to make my way back to the front. Mock-staggering, I tentatively grope my way forward. The girls squeal with delight each time I bump into obstacles such as chairs and desks, or trip over an errant schoolbag.

The reward for not falling flat on my face is a free beer stein. Which the girls, bless them, have already filled up for me. Guided the final few steps by two helpers, I pounce on the prize like a bird of prey. All I have to do now is drink it – still blindfolded of course. This makes the young ladies hoot with laughter as I attempt to connect mouth with beverage. After I've downed the last drop of brew, the class do a very German thing. Instead of cheering, they knock solemnly on their desks. With their knuckles. This, I learn later, is one of the highest marks of respect which a German can pay you. Mysteriously, nobody knows why the Germans prefer knuckle-knocking to clapping.

In the final week of summer term, shortly before my temporary contract is due to expire, Head Sister invites me into her study. It's another of those do-or-die meetings – top-or-flop as the Germans say – will or won't they encourage me to stay another year or two?

Just like that farewell dialogue at the grammar school, this one also starts favourably. And – unusual for Germans – with a burst of small talk. Handing me a cup of herbal tea, Sister smiles sweetly and asks if I take milk. When I politely decline, she shoots me a look of mock horror. Like most Germans, she seems to think all Brits take their tea white. I explain that health-conscious middle-class England is trending more towards herbal and green teas. Sister nods wholeheartedly, agreeing that such antioxidant-rich options are decidedly more nutrient for the soul.

The nun's next question, however, hits me like a freight train.

She wants to know if I've passed the *Staastexamen*.

I'd deliberately stayed schtum, lest she learn I'd been spending almost every waking moment outside the classroom swatting up for the state teaching exam. This was to be a gruelling three-hour test of my knowledge of Didactics, Linguistics and Literature – in both English and French. Yet none of this was quite so excruciating as the demands of English History. It felt like I was being tested on almost every single milestone from the Age of Dawn right up to the Third Industrial Revolution. While the rest of the house slept soundly, I'd burnt the midnight oil, torturing myself with minor incidents dating back to the age of the dinosaurs. All the while hoping against hope that I'd never actually have to stand up in front of class and teach any of this infernal stuff.

As if that weren't enough, I'd also been driving up to Regensburg University each week for *Nachhilfe* from a German post-graduate who was taking the exam too. Initially Hannah had refused payment for this extra tuition, insisting that being able to converse in English with a native speaker all the while was sufficient compensation. Poor soul, I don't know how she managed to keep so poised and patient. When it came to performing syntactic analysis on a medieval text, I really wasn't the brightest bulb in the box. I dare say Hannah was secretly wishing she might wriggle out of this reciprocal arrangement. Especially when, after several all-evening sessions, I was still questioning a basic phonetic formula halfway down page two.

Despite already holding a double honours degree in Applied Linguistics, this same subject was now stretching me beyond busting point. And, given she too was soon to sit these monstrous exams, sluicing me through them was probably the final straw for Hannah. I really hope she got through and is in a good place now.

But there's one verity I'd rather not share with Sister.

Halfway through the year my results had arrived. Hannah and I didn't dare utter the 'F' word in each other's company. 'F' stood for failure, of course. Ironically, I'd comfortably passed French yet flunked the English part of the exam. It was probably the Stone Age questions that stumped me. It feels strange, being allowed to teach French in Germany, but not English. I'd not spoken French for over a decade. Didn't it make more sense to teach my native tongue? I share this predicament with Sister, who listens sympathetically, intermittently nodding in acquiescence.

For a moment, sitting there together, sipping clove and cinnamon infusion from bone china cups, I'm optimistic that the school will employ me for another year or two. But then, almost as if donning a different hat, one labelled 'business', Sister suddenly frowns:

'Na, in dem Fall.'

'Ah well, in that case,' literally. While little more than an after-thought in English, the expression is much weightier in German. It usually signals ominous news. Gesturing with cupped outstretched hands, it's like Sister is saying 'shit happens.'

Hearing the harbinger, I frantically say a little prayer – a last-ditched plea that she'll extend my contract. As I do so, I fix my eyes on a crucifix hung over the latticed window beside a portrait of the Virgin Mary.

Sadly, despite Sister's sympathetic ear, buttressed by the Blessed Virgin Mary beaming down at us amidst floral-pattern curtains, divine intervention is strictly off limits. At least when it comes to earthly matters such as prolonging my contract. We shake hands, solemnly wishing each other every best for the future.

A year later, however, there's a surprise *coup de grâce*.

I'm offered a further position at a secondary school in Bavaria. Manifestly, my last-minute prayer for an extra year's employment had been heard in heaven on high. By some stroke of fate, or maybe just delicious irony, divine intervention strikes at the best possible moment. Not only is this another Catholic girls' school but it's another *Lohnsteuerkarte* job, which will pay my social security contributions. In Germany these are high. This is important to me, since by taking so much time off to study for the *Staatsexamen,* I'd suffered a heavy loss of regular income.

I warm to the place immediately. The atmosphere at the private *Realschule* in Regensburg is rather more relaxed than at the grammar school in Munich. I suspect that's because the youngsters here are under much less pressure to perform than at *Gymnasium,* where from very early on they're groomed to sit the *Abitur* exam – their admission ticket to university.

Founded under the name 'Institut der Englischen Fräulein', the pupils at the junior high are still quaintly known as *die Englischen.* I teach the 'English maidens' for just under a year, before hitting the same stumbling block as last time, and the time before: *Staatsexamen,* or rather lack thereof. This time though I'm better prepared for the let-down as the *Direktorin,* bless her, smiles and says she wishes she could have pulled some strings for me. But, naturally, she can't – her hands are ever tightly tied to the demands of the *Kultusministerium* and their monstrous state exams.

Still, once again I don't regret the experience. I don't know whether it's the calming influence of the nuns as they hover around the corridors, heads bowed mindfully in prayer, or possibly some other soothing spirits circulating the school, but the girls are all impeccably well behaved. They seem genuinely upset when they hear I'm going. I'll miss the lovable way they wish me 'Good mor-neeng!'

And here's another good thing about Catholic Bavaria. You can still pick up teaching work without passing the tough *Staatsexamen*. Providing you have a little bit of help from high places.

Beware of 'Leitungswasser'!

Although I'd been teaching just a stone's throw away from the heart of the fourth biggest city in Bavaria, I'd not bothered to explore much of Regensburg. Perhaps because I'd always regarded Munich as jewel in the state crown. Yet, as I later discover, this beautiful medieval city is the best preserved in Germany, and possibly in all Europe. Unlike Munich, Regensburg was spared the devastation of Allied bombings during World War II. The wonderfully intact and car-free *Altstadt* is a riot of winding alleyways, a treasure trove of romantic nooks and crannies dating back over two thousand years. It also has the highest density of bars and pubs per square metre in the whole of Germany.

Living halfway between Munich and Regensburg is like having two world-class cities almost on the doorstep. Which is why, whenever we have visitors from abroad, we try to squeeze in trips both to the state capital on the River Isar and the 'medieval miracle' cum pub paradise on the Danube. As we do one searing hot summer weekend in August with friends from London.

After enjoying a stroll around this world-heritage gem, marvelling at the 20 or more dynasty towers – the city's must-see Middle Age skyscrapers – we call in at a *Gastwirtschaft*. Along with beers we also ask for

Leitungswasser, or tap water. We're served a jug of sparkling water – presumably decanted from an Evian bottle, or similar. When I politely point out the mistake to the waitress, she looks a bit confused and disappears without a word. After a while she returns with a jug of 'normal' tap water and everyone is happy. The meal is lovely too. But, when the bill arrives, I notice they've added an extra six euros and ninety-nine cents for *Mineralwasser.*

The *Kellnerin* seems out of her depth with my questioning the error, so I ask to see her boss, the *Gastwirt.* We'd ordered mere *Leitungswasser,* I explain. We're not allowed to serve tap water, he retorts matter-of-fact. I'm just about to enquire if this is for public health reasons – unappealing levels of calcium deposits, maybe. But then I remember. This is Germany. Humour – Germans were recently voted the world's least funny nation – certainly isn't going to diffuse this issue. Instead, I ask in German: 'So why didn't the maid tell me that, instead of simply slapping expensive fizz on the bill?' After much discussion, or *hin und her,* the girl is instructed to give me a three-euro refund.

She hands it over with a scowl.

Leaving the restaurant, head hung in shame, I probably look like some piteous character straight off the pages of Charles Dickens. Talk about throwing the cat among the pigeons in the workhouse. The three euros in my hand feel more like rebuttal than refund. But how bizarre. Splash from the tap is readily available, without asking, in restaurants in some of the poorest and most expensive cities in the world – even in London.

You'd think a rich country like Germany would be able to offer its fresh, clean and safe-to-drink tap water free of charge too.

Why is it almost impossible to obtain a glass of complimentary tap water in restaurants here? The answer probably lies in the language. In English, 'tap' is generally a positive word. Anything 'on tap', such as beer or food, is readily available. Yet *Leitung*, the German word for tap, has nothing but negative connotations. Saying of someone that they have a *lange Leitung*, for example, is tantamount to calling them a dunce. A *geborstene Leitung*, likewise, is a burst pipe – the stuff of a German's worst nightmare.

Leitungswasser is clearly on a hiding to nothing. Literally translated as plumbing water, this sounds only a tad better than sewage. No wonder Germans turn their noses up at it, preferring to drink expensive bottled alternatives. In 2018, 1,374 billion litres were produced, the average German consuming 144 litres of still or sparkling. That's merely half as much as bottle-mad Mexicans drink, but a lucrative market nonetheless. From Aachener Kaiserbrunnen to Vulkania, German mineral water producers must be laughing all the way to the bottle bank.

As for Regensburg, you probably won't find a more beautiful historic city in the whole of Germany. It's certainly my favourite. But if I eat out there again, I won't be asking for *Leitungswasser*.

'Goodbye Deutschland'

Germany is envied the world over for its technical expertise, extensive public transport network and superbly functioning health and social security system. Best of all, it produces the planet's most drinkable beer. So good in fact that antipodeans think nothing of re-mortgaging their homes in order to fund a week-long binge at the Oktoberfest.

And yet some Germans go to great lengths just to get away from the place. Their efforts are centrepiece of the highly popular TV series 'Goodbye Deutschland'. This docu-soap shadows families who choose to turn their backs on one of the most successful economies in the world, burn their bridges and start from scratch abroad.

So far, I've seen only one episode. It involved an unemployed couple, five children and grandmother in tow, who recently headed off to Denmark. With neither money, nor foreign language skills, or indeed any plan of what to do when they get there. None of that sounds very *Deutsch* to me. Germans seldom have five kids. And they don't generally share the bathroom with granny and grandpa – not if they can help it at least.

Germans take punctuality and planning dead seriously. They rarely leave things to chance. *Risiko,* the idea that there might be an element of risk, is almost a dirty word in this country. Yet it's almost as if producers of 'Goodbye Germany' have gone out of their way to scour the country for what appear to be the most unprepared candidates. Having lured these poor souls on board they then seem to wish something dreadful to befall them the very moment they set foot on foreign soil. Recent episode titles include:

'Beer King banned from performing in adopted country'

'Biggest disaster of their life'

'Didi and Hasi come to blows over last *Brezel* in Barcelona.'

Clearly not all televised emigrants hit the ground running after turning their backs on Germany. And clearly not all can agree over who gets the very last pretzel stick on the Spanish mainland.

The whole thing has led to a heated debate over whether such TV programmes are encouraging reckless emigration just to boost their ratings. Fortunately, not all people leaving Germany appear quite as ill prepared and penniless as their television counterparts. An increasing number of highly qualified young people are upping sticks – in spite of a buoyant jobs market. The German media is ringing alarm bells – there's even talk of *'ein Brain Drain'*. Germans are great ones for using Anglicisms in place of uber-long German expressions. The German for 'brain drain' is, hold your breath, *'Die Abwanderung von hochqualifizierten Arbeitskräften.'*

Small wonder they prefer to use the English term.

My curiosity is piqued when I come across a report

on how this *Brain Drain* is being fuelled by students from Munich's renowned Ludwig-Maximilians-Universität. I'd taught a couple hours a week there recently, so this news confirmed what I already knew about the students' get-up-and-go approach. The LMU regularly tops the Times Higher Education rankings for German universities. And now many of these students really had got up and gone. The media has pounced on this leaking away of academic know-how with a vengeance, treating the phenomenon as a hot potato, or *'heisses Eisen'*. It sounds like a good topic for my next dispatch, so I contact the student magazine UNICUM to see if they're interested. Yes, they say, providing I can file the feature in German. Apart from my review of the Abba copy cats, I've not written at length in German since completing my final thesis for university over twenty years ago. Hopefully my *Deutsch* is still up to it.

I start by finding out what my own students have to say on the matter. Although many are currently out of town – summer holidays stretch well into October – I manage to scoop together a small group in *Schall and Rauch*. A typical student pub, it's exactly as the name says – noisy and stuffy. The postgrads have all just completed Jobline LMU, an EU-funded job-application course, which aims at improving the English language skills and prospects of graduates on the international job market. I'd helped run the course and to celebrate everyone passing we'd already knocked down a few litres each at this bohemian *Kneipe* in Schwabing, the heartland of Munich student life.

I invite each student to say a few words about their

career plans. For Nicole a move is imminent – her partner is being sent to Brighton. She plans to pick up work there too. Ingrid, an Environmental Science undergraduate, also has her sights set on London, where she hopes to learn more about typically British solutions to ecological problems. Thanks to Jobline LMU, her application papers are word perfect and grammatically impeccable.

Kornshulee from Bangkok, originally came to Munich to take a degree in Political Science, but doesn't plan on hanging around here too long either: 'There's simply more life in Asia – I miss it,' she says. I tell her it's all relative. Way out in Lower Bavaria we'd kill for just a fraction of that action.

All agree they'll first seek several years' work experience abroad, regardless of how well the domestic economy performs. Few seem bothered about long-term issues, such as missing pension contributions. The work-life balance seems to matter more.

'Life is too routine,' laments Andrea, 'here you just follow the rules and fulfil your life.' I'm tempted to point out that life could be a lot worse than that, but I keep quiet. Andrea, who has a double MA in Humanities, feels this is the downside of Germany's healthy economy and hopes to find work – and adventure – in Canada.

Another Business Administration student, Johanna, also believes it's harder for young people to realize their dreams in Germany. 'We're not as open-minded as most English-speaking countries. There are too many obstacles here.'

I nod in agreement.

No one around the table has journeyed quite so far in search of work as Hannah. When her contract with an architecture firm in Munich expired a few years ago she headed Down Under and landed work in Sydney. The 25-year-old Bavarian had no regrets about turning her back on Germany, where she toiled long hours on a low salary. She tells how she worked comparatively less Down Under and was promoted three times in just six months. That certainly raises a few eyebrows around the table. When somebody asks about pay, however, she grins back sheepishly. She recently returned to seek work again in Germany.

Back home that evening I write up my findings:

'Graduates going abroad with work experience can generally expect to earn as well as or even better than their German counterparts. The good news for the German economy is that the brain drain is only temporary. Most graduates appear not to be emigrating but only migrating.'

Shooting the report one last cursory glance, I mail it off to London. Job done, I stroll over to the fridge and grab myself a nice cool beer. I then go back to my laptop and proceed to write the whole thing up in German.

I soon regret not having conducted the whole interview in German too. The postgrads speak excellent English, but now I have to figure out how they would have said all this in *Deutsch*.

After binning half a dozen drafts of awkwardly phrased *Deutsch*, I'm still struggling. I've definitely gone overboard with the 'combos' – that typically Teutonic practice of piling together long words to produce even lengthier words. And much of the language sounds more like something out of a technical instruction manual than an entertaining news feature. Either way, the conclusion reached in both languages is clear. Few of my interviewees express desire to leave Germany for good. After submerging themselves short term in foreign cultures and living it up in sunnier climes, most seem happy to return to mundane but familiar Germany.

They'd be foolish not to. Germany has the fourth largest economy in the world and its cities are regularly cited as among the best to live in. Berlin, apparently, has now replaced London as default destination for the 'Big OE', the overseas experience typically undertaken by Aussies and Kiwis before they settle down with more 'serious' jobs back home.

Evidently, those German graduates who've spent time abroad are starting to see their rule-bound country from a totally different perspective. No wonder they just fix each other with a tired grin when I ask if they're up to speed with 'Goodbye Deutschland.'

Winter Wunderland

Expats and migrants are often smart at picking up local lingo and adapting to different climes and lifestyles. Yet when it comes to customs and conventions, grappling with the nitty gritty of daily life, they can easily come a cropper. I arrived in Germany able to speak the language fluently. But it took me ages to realize that a tersely uttered *'danke'* really means *'nein danke'*. Or that a long-drawn out *'neeein'* actually translates as *'ja'*.

It also took time getting to grips with the minutiae of German Christmas customs. I'd started to think of German *Weihnacht* and British Christmas as having become more or less identical: Winter Wonderland markets peddling sizzling sausages, chocolate-coated gingerbread and grossly over-priced hot spiced wine. Oh, and cheap and cheerful Aldi with its Christmas-tree shaped stockings topped with a bauble. Have I forgotten anything?

There are some small differences, of course. German *Kinder*, for example, find that if they polish their shoes and put them out on the eve of December 6 they'll wake up next morning to a boot full of sweeties – more about that in a moment.

But here's a surprise. And it's something you'll find nowhere else in the world: whole families crowding around the telly on New Year's Eve to watch 'Dinner for One'.

While Brits flop onto their sofas every Christmas and binge-watch world TV premieres such as 'Mission Impossible Six' it seems unfair that Germans have to make do with an old black-and-white comedy – in English no less – which virtually no one else has ever heard of. And yet 'Dinner for One' is massive in Germany. This 18-minute skit about an English baroness' 90th birthday celebration has run here each *Silvester* for the past 45 years. It's broadcasted loop-like on almost every single public TV channel. Think of the comedy's popularity as such: just as virtually every Brit can parrot-back Basil Fawlty's best lines from cult sit-com 'Fawlty Towers' – 'Don't mention The War. I did, but I think I got away with it!' – so too can almost every single burgher recite by heart the closing lines to 'Dinner for One':

Miss Sophie: 'Well, James, it's been a wonderful party!'

James: 'Yes, it's been most enjoyable.'

Miss Sophie: 'I think I'll retire.'

James: 'You're going to bed?

Miss Sophie: 'Yes.'

James: 'Sit down, I'll give you a hand up, Madam.'

Miss Sophie: 'As I was saying, I'm going to retire.'

James: 'Ya, ya. By the way, the same procedure as every year, Miss Sophie?'

Miss Sophie: 'The same procedure as *every* year, James.'

Just what is it about 'Dinner for One' that prompts millions upon millions of Germans to slap their thighs and howl with laughter every Christmas? Academic researchers point emphatically to the typical management structure of the country's 3.6 million small and medium-sized enterprises. They contend that the 'same procedure' punchline reflects the nation's desire for continuity and stability. For non-academics though, the secret of the sketch's success is a no brainer. It's Miss Sophie's come-hither response to her loyal butler's innocent enquiry.

This sexual innuendo delights Germans of all ages. The catchphrase has long entered their everyday vocabulary. It regularly pops up in newspaper headlines, advertisements too. It's as well known in Germany as *Vorsprung durch Technik* in Britain.

So much for Miss Sophie & Co.

Another thing that still puzzles me after twenty years in Germany is this whole Father Christmas business. Children here are gifted by either baby Jesus, known as Christkindl, or Nikolaus. I typically mix these characters up, mistaking them for one and the same.

I first encountered Nikolaus as a translator in Bonn. It was 6 December and we all turned up to find a chocolate effigy propped up against our coffee mugs. German bosses follow this custom every Advent, supposedly in honour of Bishop Nikolaus of Myra, famed for helping the needy around 325 AD. After his death, word of the gift-giving legacy spread, slowly transforming man and image into the modern-day, red-dressed chocaholic. The Christkindl, on the other hand, originates from Luther's time. Ironically, it was Protestants' attempt to de-bunk this whole Catholic celebration of Saint Nicholas on 6 December.

How lovely that Germans still embrace both figures, one historic, the other religious, rather than some beardy boozer celebrating Coca Cola. But, as we're about to discover, Christkindl and Nikolaus have a grim sidekick. And just like 'Dinner for One', he too is barely known outside Germany.

Only a week into Advent and we're in for a fright. Darkness is falling when a sudden thud at the front door makes us almost jump out of our skins. Peering out through the window, we spot the shape of a ginormous figure plodding up our garden path.

This devil-like horned creature is Krampus. Half Gruffalo, half Godzilla monster, he's probably the last creature you'd wish to open your door to on a cold dark night. Let alone beckon in and offer a piece of *Plätzchen* and glass of *Glühwein*. And yet that's exactly what we end up doing, once we've established his real identity.

In a tradition tracing back over 1000 years, Krampus' sole role has been to flag up naughty kids to Santa, before dragging them off to the underworld. That's what parents tell their kids, at least. Unofficially, he's just an uncouth guardian angel, scary enough to put the wind up you. Like some Simon-Cowell-type 'X-Factor' judge (German readers – just think big mouths from Modern Talking).

Fortunately, he's not alone. Accompanying him is Nikolaus, the absolute antithesis of the pot-bellied, larger-than-life All-American Santa. Tall and lanky, the Nikolaus outside our house looks more like the village priest. And since we booked him through the local church he probably is too. There's just one small problem. Only children who polish their boots the night before will find them filled with goodies. Another key Christmas tradition I'd missed. Sadly, our child's boots haven't been cleaned since around Hallow'een.

We come face to face again with Krampus and Nikolaus the very next day. It's the duo's annual appearance at the village *Christkindlmarkt* and I've just committed the classic yuletide blooper in the company of Bavarians – I've foolishly referred to Nikolaus as the *Weihnachtsmann*. Something only a Prussian would dare do. Well, it is all a bit chaotic and I'm trying to take a picture of Tildy shaking the old man's hand while an army of kids keep prodding me impatiently from behind. I can hear some of them quietly tut-tutting and one little boy politely corrects me:

'Des is doch da Nikolaus!'

Oopsi...

It's almost like Krampus is punishing me when he hands over his birch stick, the one with which he beats naughty children. *'Hoid moi guad fest,'* he says, motioning me to hold tight while the old man patiently plods through the meet-and-greet routine with his little guests. Some are not quite so little, actually. One girl must be pushing at least thirteen or fourteen. She's reaching over to shake Nikolaus' hand. It's something of a one-sided conversation with all the usual have-you-been-good, have-you-listened-to-teacher type questions.

Visibly embarrassed, the pubescent visitor is just nodding and giggling. Maybe she does still believe in the bearded benefactor, this is backwater Bavaria after all. Yet her eyes are clearly on the prize. She's spotted the free bag of sweets which Krampus is preparing to hand her.

After Tildy has encountered Krampus and Nikolaus a second time in as many days, sworn that she's been good all year, and collected her goodies bag, I slip off for a mulled wine. Snow's falling and it's icy cold. I notice some drinkers huddled under a patio heater. I'm surprised to see one of these contraptions in a small Bavarian village. Even Parisians have banned environmentally-fiendish outdoor heaters. Still, this absurd appliance provides much appreciated warmth. Hugging my mulled wine, I enjoy just standing there listening to snippets of conversation all around.

Although rather rough around the edges, there's something mellifluous and singsong-ish about Bavarian dialect. Yet one of my neighbours at the high table sounds slightly distressed:

'Mei Buidog schofft's den Hügl ned mehr houch.'

My tractor can no longer make it up the hill.

Uttered in English, this might be alluding to the speaker's sagging libido. Spoken in Bavarian dialect though, it's music to the ears. The three other mulled-wine sippers around the table show sympathy for the farmer's plight, offering practical tips and advice on how he might soup up his vehicle:

'Probier doch oafach moi de Kolbn und Dichtungsringe auszutauschn.'

Try replacing the pistons and gaskets.

This is *deutsche Weihnacht* at its best – heavenly sweet aromas wafting from mulled wine urns, the local infant school choir singing 'O Tannenbaum' and the haunting blow of hunting horns.

There's something almost spiritual about this fairy-lit *Christkindlmarkt*. It's almost light years away from a carol service we attend the following week at an international church in Munich. We belt out all the classics like 'We Wish you a Merry Christmas' and 'The Twelve Days of Christmas'. The latter comes with all the manic hand gestures, more befitting of a child's sixth birthday celebration. It's great fun, but decidedly more show than sacred, more party than piety. Especially when the choir mistress encourages us to leap up and down, jangling our car keys to the sound of 'Jingle Bells'. Something else you'll seldom see in a German church service.

The best *Gottesdienst* I attend is an international celebration on Christmas Day in Freising. This lively little town just north of Munich has taken in scores of refugees over the past year, so the Christi-Himmelfahrts-Kirche called on local migrant centres, inviting them all to a service in both English and German. A touching way of making these newcomers feel welcome and included in the community.

Just as I arrive, an ethnically mixed group are leading praise and worship up on stage in a very un-churchy way for Germans. They're swaying from side to side and clapping to the rhythm of 'Oh Happy Day!' There's a lovely mixture of French, Spanish and English carols. Much of the liturgy though is very German. The congregation rise to pray and sit to sing. For the Word of God, however, Germans rise in respect. As you might do when someone important enters the room. Singing is deemed less important than prayer and so they stay seated. German rationality over practicality. At the end of the service, cups of piping hot mulled wine are doled out from an enormous urn alongside the scene of the nativity. It's difficult not to love this church.

Back to Nikolaus and Christkindl. Unable to agree on which old man gets to gift our child, we strike a compromise. On *Heiligabend,* Tildy's pressies lie not only under the *Christbaum* but also in a bulging pillow case propped up at the end of her bed.

On New Year's Eve we turn into typical Germans. We zap through the TV stations, searching for one of the half dozen channels simultaneously screening 'Dinner for One'. Moments later we too are behaving like die-in-the wool Germans, slapping our thighs and squealing with glee at the saucy sketch.

Dusk is falling as the queue of passengers stretching all the way back to check-in grinds to a complete halt. Hardly surprising really, given we're into the week spanning Christmas and New Year. This is one of the busiest times of year at Munich Airport. Last Christmas, Spain actually overtook Germany as the *Bundesbürgers'* most popular holiday destination. Looking at this line, you'd think almost half the population of Bavaria were boarding for the Balearics.

We're also queueing to pass security control. And yet we're not actually flying anywhere at all. My family and I are booked onto a '*Lichterfahrt*', or 'nightlights trip', set to take a behind-the-scenes look at the second busiest passenger airport in Germany.

But half way into the ninety-minute tour and we're still stuck in a parking bay outside security control. One of our fellow passengers has been pulled aside by a man in dayglo jacket. She's now being interrogated about the contents of her handbag. Monika, our guide, livens up the wait with figures and fun facts. Her on-board commentary feels more like instructions from cockpit to control tower: 'Airport 28.5 km northeast of Munich. 34th busiest in world. 42 million passengers and rising. 248 plus destinations worldwide.'

Dodgy Handbag finally boards and we move off. The first part of the tour follows a stretch of periphery road also used by the public. Suddenly a black sedan hurtles past at breakneck speed, tyres screeching. We're in a 30-km zone. The vehicle must be travelling at least 70 km/h. Last-minute passenger, no doubt. 'Hurry up,' laughs Monika, 'your plane's boarding at Gate 20!' Next up, we're off public and onto private terrain. After courteously stopping to let a plane pass, our coach gently meanders around the 'apron', the area of the airport where aircraft are parked, loaded or unloaded, refuelled and boarded. It feels odd overtaking moving aircraft. When we suddenly pass a Boeing 777-220, I almost fancy the coach is readying for take-off too.

After a while I warm to our guide's curt yet comical commentary. As we roll past Satellite Terminal, an extension of Terminal One, Monika motions to a wide-body aircraft, noting 'Boeing 747-8. Destination Singapore. Lots of carrot juice on board!' This Boeing is second largest passenger plane in world. '1,500 litres kerosene and 10% extra,' continues Monika, adding '13-hour flight – long haul!' She points to a line of supply trucks parked up alongside. As from March 2018, the world's largest commercial passenger plane, the double-decker Airbus A380, is also set to fly from Munich. To deal with extra demand generated by the flagship, Munich Airport is hiring 1,000 extra flight attendants. Flashing a smile to two young girls in the front seats, she adds: 'flying sure beats working.'

A little further down the apron we pass a Lufthansa jet festooned with pictures of FC Bayern players and the world-famous logo. 'Carried our boys two years ago. Loved the deco so much we left it on!' By 'our boys' I assume she means FC Bayern and not her own sons; by 'we' I take it she means Munich Airport rather than her own family. But you never know. Monika's been working on the ground here for over 30 years. It's like she almost blends in with the backdrop. In an aside she tells us her best experience to date was a stand-by, last-minute trip to Hawaii. Underscoring the happy memory, she says 'and only 150 deutschmarks, ha!'

Monika is a font of facts and figures. She reveals that the airport has parking spaces for over 200 planes, yet they sometimes have to put a 'full' sign up at the entrance. Or that kerosene comes from the Greek word 'keros', meaning wax. It's also interesting to see the LG Skychef catering vans right up close as they dock onto the planes. The largest airline caterer in the world, LG supplies over 590 million meals a year. That's a mighty mountain of grilled chicken and shrink-wrapped potato salads.

We also learn why Berlin-Brandenburg Airport, BER for short, is taking slightly longer than the 13 years needed to build its Bavarian rival. Originally scheduled to open in 2012, BER is the second-most-expensive building in the world, costing over five billion euros more than originally expected. Almost half the tab has been picked up by German taxpayers; the remaining costs have largely been shouldered by the EU. Monika comments on the capital's white elephant as if it were part of a comedy routine: '800 building alterations already submitted to contractors. Ready by October 2020? I think not!'

Barely pausing for breath in her whirlwind commentary, Monika takes us back to better days, waxing lyrical about the 53 years when Munich Airport was located in the east of the city. Munich-Riem Airport, as it was known, closed down in May 1992, just a day before planes lifted off from the new Franz-Josef-Strauss Airport near Freising, further north. Hearing the name of its predecessor brings back memories of coming in to land there on a study trip in 1983. All that remains of this airport today is the monumentally-protected control tower, the head-end structure of the grandstand and a sign that says 'Abflüge'.

Our guide, meanwhile, is holding forth about the

'Berlin Blockade'. She's not referring to the Soviets' attempts to cut the capital off in 1948/9 but rather the city's *Flughafen* fiasco. I'm beginning to wonder if Monika's deliberately painting such a dismal portrait of the capital so that that we'll come away from the tour even more sold on Location Munich.

After the tour we call in at the *Winter Wonderland Market* where we go ice skating. Well, the rest of the family does. Last time I donned ice skates I hadn't been on the rink two minutes before colliding with a far more proficient freestyling skater. Falling flat on my buttocks, I suffered a minor compression fracture in my backside. I hobbled around in agony for several days, flatly refusing to see the doctor. This time I settle for the safer option of spectating from the side. But not before queueing up for *Bratapfel Glühweizen*, a hot wheat beer laced with cinnamon and fried apple. It tastes absolutely divine.

Heading home, bellies bulging with mulled wine and Nutella crepes, it strikes me that the Munich Airport experience is not merely about catching planes. Spanning two terminals, Munich Airport Centre – MAC Forum to locals – is accessible to non-flyers too. Visitors who spend money at the Winter Market are treated to free all-day parking. I do some quick mental arithmetic. We've forked out almost twenty euros on food and drink, yet saved far more on parking. Net profit in hand, I almost feel like punching the air in triumph and whooping 'Yesss!'

Booting up my laptop later on, I look to see what TripAdvisor has to say about the airport tour. There's nothing on the 'Lights Tour' but I spot a rather scathing review of the 'A380 Tour'. MiriamPastor85 complains that she could see the world's largest and most spacious passenger aircraft 'only from the bus'. She probably wished the driver would stop long enough for her to hop out and take a look inside the world-beating aircraft. Munich Airport, on the other hand, would probably wish customers book to fly on said plane rather than just gawp at it on a 14-euro bus ride.

That aside, Munich Airport seems to punch just about every other button. For ten out of the past twelve years it's been named Europe's best airport, and it's easy to see why. There can't be many other international airports which offer travellers not only ice skating and Christmas markets but also an onsite brewery in the shade of a chestnut-tree garden.

Rounding off my latest blog I wax lyrical: 'So if you're actually thinking of catching a plane, this could be the one airport in the world where you might just *prefer* to be delayed.'

Naked Pleasures

Having been instructed to strip off in a unisex dressing area, I've just showered in front of a horde of total strangers. I'm now squatting over a bowl of tepid water. Only inches away on either side are yet more total strangers. We're all stark naked.

This could easily be the stuff of life-long dreams. Or nightmares, for that matter. But no. I'm wide awake and this is for real. Glancing around at my neighbours, feet immersed in similar receptacles, my gaze falls on an athletic-looking thirty-something with chestnut-brown hair. All she's wearing is a pair of rose-petal sandals. Staring just a little bit too obviously, I become aware of someone prodding me in the side.

'Entschuidigung?'

I pretend not to hear. The prodding stops but the voice gets louder:

'Entschuidign Sie!'

Dressed in standard pale blue nylon tabard, multi-purpose spray cleaner in one hand, mop in other, the *Putzfrau* is signalling me to stand up and move aside. She wants to wash down the stone slab I'm sitting on. Previously all nice and warm, the hard surface now feels as icy-cold as the water around my ankles. My backside's shivering. I get up and wait while the cleaner fusses around the stone seat with her squirty bottle.

The scene's hot and sweaty. And it's one you'll find repeated all over Bavaria. The Free State boasts more nude spa landscapes than anywhere else in Germany.

With over 900 spas registered nationwide, a whole industry – and indeed cult – has sprung up around the business of wellbeing.

Take, for example, the cult of the *Sauna Meister*. You can actually study to gain this qualification, a title which carries every much respect in Germany as that of, say, qualified accountant or lawyer. Germans particularly value anything specialised and prefixed by the word *Diplom*. Not surprisingly, the *Diplom Sauna Meister* often has a copy of their certificate, neatly framed and proudly displayed over the cabin door.

Conducting proceedings at my latest visit to the sauna here at the Kaiser Thermen in the spa town of Bad Abbach is actually not a 'master' but a 'mistress'. And an attractive-looking one too. Introducing herself as Teresa, she begins the ceremony with a lecture on all the different heavenly scented oils wafting out of her bucket of lukewarm water. She then splashes the entire contents over chunks of glowing-hot wood atop of a giant stove. This invokes a chorus of *'oohs'* and *'aahs'* from the delighted assembly.

Having wished us all *'Frohes Schwitzen'*, or happy sweating, the *Sauna Meisterin* takes a towel by both ends and starts whirling and twirling it around in circles. The idea is to waft cold air into the cabin, an intricate process known as *Aufguss*, or infusion. 'Are you all happy?' she asks in broad Bavarian dialect. '*Jawoiii*!' replies a large-bellied middle-aged man slouched on one of the top benches, adding, 'When you do the *Aufguss*, Teresa, I'm always happy!' The comment provokes hearty laughter amongst my bench neighbours.

And then, all of a sudden, everyone falls silent. All eyes focus on an elderly man sporting a dwarf-like sauna hat. He's just uttered a word I'd never heard before. It sounds something like *Schleimer*. Is he implying the other male guest is a bootlicker? Striking back, Big Belly on top bench replies 'Charming! All I did was be nice to the young lady!' At this point the *Sauna Meisterin* wades in. Turning to Dwarf Hat, she says in mock chastisement 'You're the reason why nice men like him don't dare pay women more compliments these days!'

We all laugh again.

All told, the whole experience somehow feels more show than sauna. Working the room with her flappy towel, Teresa cracks jokes about the pain she's inflicting upon her captive audience. Still, it can't be too painful because at the end of the *Aufguss* we all offer up a cheery round of applause.

The applause could just as easily have been for the hilarious *Sauna Meister* joke I heard last time I visited this spa. It's the one about the American, Japanese and Irishman sitting in a sauna. The Ami gets beeped and, switching it to mute, says sorry, it's his pager microchip. The Jap gets a phone call, it's his mobile microchip under the skin of his wrist. 'Sorry,' he says, turning it off, and lying back down on the bench. The Irishman receives no bleep, no call; nothing. But being Irish he can do one better. He goes outside and comes back a few moments later with some toilet paper trailing from his behind. The other two glare at him. *'Would ye look at dat!'* he announces, *'oy tink I'm getting a fax!'*

The humour possibly loses a little in translation. But the *Sauna Meister* tells it so sweetly that everyone chuckles as they shuffle off to shower and briefly immerse themselves in ice-cold plunge pools.

Meanwhile, crouched over my stone slab, I'm shivering from toe to temple. Oh, and the girl with the rose-petal thongs has vanished. The slab, on the other hand, is now so squeaky *sauber* I can almost see the reflection of my own goose pimples.

I'm just about to refill my bowl with hot water when I hear the sound of a bell clanging. Next thing, bathers are starting to rise from the heated slabs and file past me in an orderly procession in twos and threes. They're all conversing in hushed tones, just like on a guided tour of a church. Unlike in a church, everyone here is trotting past stark naked. Well, except for flip flops.

Wondering if I might have missed something, I ask a passerby what's going on.

'Zum Aufguss gad's,' she replies, gesturing at a cabin a few doors away.

Jumping to my feet, I fall into line but lose precious seconds re-adjusting towel around waist. Finally, reaching the sauna shed, I pull gently on the door handle. I tug. It still doesn't open. Peering through the steamed-up window, I see swathes of sweating bodies bent over the benches. Suddenly the view is obscured.

An almost ghost-like figure is glaring at me through the steam-covered glass pane. Gesticulating wildly with his hands, the *Saunameister* is visibly indicating that I'm not welcome here.

That's odd. The *Schild* over the window says NÄCHSTER AUFGUSS 19:00 – next infusion at 7 p.m. The clock I just passed on the way had indicated it was a minute or so *before* seven. I'm on time, surely? Technically speaking, yes. Even allowing for minor discrepancies between the various clocks dotted around the sauna landscape. And yet, although bang on time, *punktgenau*, I'm still late. It's the sort of thing that can happen to you only in Germany. I'm being made to feel, at best, the *persona non grata*, and at worst completely ostracised. Rejected and outcast, while everyone else works up a nice little sweat inside the 32°C hot cabin. I'm just turning to go when a rather rotund woman wobbles up alongside me.

'*Zua spod. Scho zua. Ned ealaubt,*' she tutters.

Too late. Already closed. Not allowed. Why do Germans so love to censure each other in disjointed word pairs, as if calling off items on a shopping list?

No matter. I've clearly flouted the rules here. Arriving just on time, bang on seven, is simply not good enough. The *Sauna Meister* has every jurisdiction to deny me entry.

À propos rules and regulations in the sauna. In Germany full nudity is norm – any form of clothing is frowned upon. Brits and Americans typically squeam at the idea, particularly when it comes to sharing the sauna cabin with the *other* sex. Perhaps it's the definition of nudity per se, with all its explicitly sexual connotations, that gives Brits that extra special hot flush at 88 degrees. But really, it's no big deal. When I pitched up in Germany at the end of the nineties, I spent most of my first pay packet on membership to a state-of-the-art *Wellness Center* in Bonn. The highlight was something which Brits tend to associate more with red-light districts, flashing neon signs and swingers' clubs. It was a subterranean landscape dotted with steam rooms, thermal pools and jacuzzis. For me, this was a bit like stumbling into some futuristic Garden of Eden – scores of people lolling around like Adam and Eve, their bits and boobs dangling in all directions. From the get-go, I was unsure whether it was rude to consciously look – or indeed consciously *not* look. Until I realized how blissfully unbothered everyone seemed with how they looked. Yes, I did notice how 'well groomed' everyone was – men and women in equal measure. But it didn't seem like they were vying with each other in a beauty pageant. So I just went with the flow.

Sure enough, I soon shake off all remaining inhibitions. And the jumbo-size towel hiding my modesty.

Slowly – excruciatingly slowly, actually – the harsh Bavarian winter segues into spring. And while the sauna experience has been great for the bitterly cold months, both for health and mindset, I'm looking forward to getting outdoors into the fresh air again. With another week or two to go until college classes resume, I've just enough time to pen another report on expat life. After a bit of googling, I come across something very German – *Naktivism*.

Not without feeling a certain *frisson*, and instinctively getting up to shut my study room door first, I hastily do an advanced search on the word. *Naktivism* dates back to the early 1900s, when the German youth group, the *Wandervögel*, or wandering birds, hiked around the countryside, setting up camp wherever they found somewhere to skinny-dip. This prompted the idea of 'free body culture', and the creation of nudist beaches along the Baltic coast. But, scanning the *Naktivist* homepage, I also discover that they don't just strip off at the seaside. There's also a spin-off club – for naked cyclists.

The commissioning editor chortles when I run my idea past him:

'Nudes on sweaty saddles? Ooh, kinky. Give me 800 words and pictures. Can we get it by Friday?'

There must be demand for this sort of thing.

An email and one or two phone calls later, I soon find someone willing to be interviewed on the subject.

For a fleeting moment, I have this vision of some clothing minimalist turning up for interview wearing nothing but a suntan and smile. But, arriving on a vintage Dutch push-bike, he's fully dressed, bless him. Introducing himself as Richie, the naturist spokesman is a founder member of 'Nude Europe', an organisation which has been leading nude hiking trips in the Alps for almost 10 years.

Richie buys me a beer, which we enjoy at the Irish Pub just off Marienplatz.

'We're not afraid to challenge commonly accepted social norms,' he says.

Richie talks every bit like a German, dispensing with habitual expat small talk and cutting straight to the chase. He tells me he's from Bury St Edmunds, but frankly he sounds more Bavarian than British.

In between sips of *Weissbier*, Richie describes the latest craze. Almost every weekend during the summer some 20 men and women, aged up to 70, expose themselves to the elements – and curious onlookers – on cross-country cycling tours around Bavaria.

Founded three years ago in the wake of World Naked Bike Ride Day, the *Nacktradler* appear to enjoy being at one with nature. It's something local organiser, Alex von der Tour, is eager to point out when I phone him earlier in the week to start the ball rolling. Curious to learn what makes them do it, I ask:

'*Wozu soll es gut sein?*'

I regret my unintended directness almost immediately the question leaves my mouth. I'm beginning to sound like a typical German myself.

Oops, done it again.

Dead silence at the other end of the line. Perhaps he's already hung up. Finally, he replies in German:

'We do it for freedom.'

Alex sounds less like a seasoned nudist, more like some sort of political activist.

Just a moment, can't Germans experience that freedom just as easy by driving fast and furious on the autobahn? It's obviously a silly question to ask Alex. He doesn't exactly sound as if he rides around in a jazzed-up twin-exhaust Audi 5.

'Cycling nude in public, isn't that illegal?'

No, he counters. Apparently, the authorities prosecute only if members of the public complain: 'Some of our group have been fined, but only when out alone.'

Safety in numbers, no doubt.

In the pub, meanwhile, Richie is in full swing:

'Here in Germany it's another way of life. A lifestyle.'

My interviewee makes nudism sound as if it's something you can just pick up at every street corner, or order from Amazon by clicking 'Add to Cart'. Yes, 'things' do occasionally happen, he admits. I push for details. He describes how one member, out jogging nude in the woods, was reported by a woman who suffered shock after the surprise encounter. But such incidents are rare, he assures. Bavarian state television recently broadcasted scenes of the *Nacktradler* being applauded as they boldly biked along the promenade of Bad Tölz, one of Bavaria's swishiest spa towns.

The way Richie goes on to describe the group's grand entrance into the spa town, its sounds like they'd ridden in on a magic carpet. Following a rapturous welcome outside the *Rathaus*, they'd been awarded a Freedom of the City key by the burgomaster. At the very least, it sounds like something he's finally able to tick off on his personal bucket list.

'Most people we meet are either encouraging or curious,' my interviewee expounds. He recalls an elderly lady who once stopped to quiz them. 'Not about our nakedness, oh no,' he assures, eyes wide open and glistening, the memory flooding back, 'but because we were navigating a hazardously narrow forest path and she was concerned we might not get through.'

Oh, how adorable. Another case of 'only in Germany'.

Richie's favourite anecdote involves an oncoming cyclist, who was so distracted by riders in *puris naturibalis* that he ran into a signpost. I grin. It conjures images of scenes from Benny Hill. Balding men chasing maidens in bikinis or scanty nurse uniforms, not looking out and bumping into lampposts. The soundtrack must be 'Yakety Sax'.

'So then,' I probe, 'is this something that expats often get in involved too?'

Richie tells me that the only expat he recalls taking part in the nude biking experience was a U.S. exchange student. Apparently, she'd heard of the club on the internet and turned up spontaneously for a ride out to Kloster Andechs, a Benedictine monastery in the Alpine foothills. Richie has a far-away look in his eyes and almost gushes as he recalls the girl's one-off involvement:

'She was red hot on the idea. Really threw herself into it. And you know what she said when she left?'

'Go on,' I reply.

'They arrest you if you do it in America!'

I'm left wondering whether 'it' simply refers to naked cycling *per se.* Or whether we're hearing of something specific that happened along a leafy lane just around the corner from the Benedictines' pre-alpine bolthole.

Perhaps wiser not to press for clarification. '*Ja,*' he sighs wistfully, his voice all furry and sentimental, as if wishing to spin out the fond memory just a little longer.

'That was Bekki from Missouri. Red head. Gorgeous girl.'

Later on, I peruse the nude cyclists' website. I come across a picture of Bekki, diligently rubbing SPF 30 onto a fellow cyclist's back. She's surrounded by a group of gawking males.

I copy and paste the photo on Toytown, Germany's online expat network. 'What do expats make of this?' I ask.

Responses immediately start flashing up. Comments range from 'Gross, unhygienic' to 'Can we make this into a caption competition?' Not everybody appears to be taking my question quite so seriously. I shoot off some of these reactions to Richie. His reply pings back instantly. It's accompanied by a bold red exclamation mark. Isn't this the symbol you generally reserve for urgent, life-or-death messages? Maybe he's trying to tell me something.

'It's more hygienic not to wear textiles – clothes tend to rub against the saddle, provoking pains and causing sores in various bodily places.'

Fair comment. But what if a cyclist falls – is it not dangerous without protection? Richie's reply lands in my incoming box almost before I've had chance to hit 'Send':

'The risk is low, since the group doesn't go in for extreme heights and distances. But, since you have brought my attention to this matter, Tim, we might indeed consider donning knee and elbow pads.'

Okaaay. But then an alarming thought: 'What if it rains?'

Again, the answer pings back before I can count to three: 'Very pleasant. You dry out more quickly.' I can just imagine Richie perched over his laptop, rubbing his hands with glee as he contemplates the idea.

Back in the pub, we're trading thoughts about expat life in Munich when Richie, hearing his smartphone vibrate, suddenly sits bolt upright.

'Oh blast!' he exclaims, 'next appointment in twenty minutes. Sorry Tim, have to hop it.'

Crawling out of the cellar pub back into broad daylight, I blink to adjust my eyesight. As Richie steps down to untether his bike – difficult to imagine him choosing any other mode of transport to carry him to our meeting – I reflect on our alcohol-infused dialogue. What might my fellow compatriots make of naked cycling? Are they ready to embrace the 'bare essentials' of the idea? British attitudes to nudism are, at best, rather ambiguous. I'm reminded of a sign on a beach at Sandspit, on the South coast of England:

'NUDISTS MAY BE SEEN FROM THIS POINT'

That, I guess, could be taken either as a warning or invitation.

I'm heading in the same direction as Richie, so we walk a short distance together to the Viktualienmarkt, Munich's famous fruit and veg market. Richie wheels his bike alongside and, for a brief moment, it feels like we're two carefree students strolling home after a lecture. Then, thanking Richie for his time – and the cool brew he kindly bought me – I step out to cross the busy high street alongside the vegetable store booths. It's at this moment that I'm almost run over by a pale beige vehicle which suddenly swoops out from a blind corner. In a split-second reaction, I both absorb the shock and recoil back onto the pavement, suffering no more than a close shave. *'Sau kabd,'* as the Bavarians say. But I feel like cursing these dullish-looking taxis that are such a familiar sight all over Germany. Why can't they paint them in a colour you can see better?

Bright lemon might be a good start.

Which reminds me. Next week I'm doing what Germans like to call a *Fachschaftsausflug*. I'm taking students to visit one of Munich's biggest crowd-pullers. Centred, of course, around that classic German object of passion – the automobile.

BMW Hypnotised

'We'd like the tour in English, please.'

'You want the tour in *English*?'

The assistant taking my call on BMW Welt's 'Info Service' line says the word *English* as if I'd just made the most outlandish request. Perhaps she feared I wanted instant translation into some unidentifiable language barely uttered outside the jungles of Borneo.

'*Ja, genau.*'

Pause.

Sorry, but hadn't I just said I'm bringing a group of *German* students?

'*Ja, genau.* German students learning English.'

I'd got into the habit of answering almost every question with '*ja, genau.*' A sure-fire sign that I was already thinking and talking like a typical German. So how come we'd got our wires so frightfully criss-crossed?

Pause again.

'But they all understand German, that's their *Muttersprache*, yes?'

'*Jaaaaa,*' I confirm. But we'd still like the tour in English. I'd noticed on their press blurb that they offer all tours in English. All of a sudden, however, the line goes totally dead.

'Hall-oooh?'

No response.

'Ha-llo! Hearn Sie mi?'

Yes, she's still there. She just had to check with her superior about the price. Tours in English, she tells me, count as premium service. All told, an extra one euro per head.

This surcharge rather surprises me. Doesn't BMW use English, not German, as its international corporate language? Premium prices for standard service?

I could have chosen either the Compact, Creative, Discovery, Premiere or Intensive Tour. Instead, I go for the simple 'Classic' at six euros a head, English-language surcharge *inklusiv.*

And now I'm standing right outside the building they call 'The Mushroom'. I should probably be marvelling at BMW's rather quirky choice of architecture. Only it's nothing new to me. I pass the place every time I go to my classes at the *Hochschule.* And I've often wondered about the statement this giant, half-collapsed toadstool is trying to make. Inside it's a comic cross between Dubai Airport and space-age shopping mall. I'm no expert on modern architecture, but something here tells me that BMW Welt is more about experience than aesthetics.

Billed as 'Adventure and delivery centre', BMW's eye-catcher is ranked as Munich's third biggest tourist attraction, just behind the English Garden and, top of the pile, Marienplatz, the main city square. The motor manufacturer's popularity doesn't surprise me. Word is out that Germans love their cars more than their own children. And yet, rather ironically, BMW Welt feels like a giant playground for grownups who never really stopped being kids themselves.

Entering the futuristic foyer, I immediately spot my Tourist Management and Hospitality students. Clustered together in a tiny corner, every single head is hanging like a droopy flower. Nobody bothers to look up from their smartphone. Until I clear my throat, clap my hands together like a patriarchal Boy Scout leader and call out 'Okay!'

We're standing directly under a stunning glass-and-steel twin cone. Designed by the Austrian firm Coop Himmelb(l)au, BMW's 'carthedral' manages to support a 16,000 square-metre roof with only eleven columns. Given their full immersion in digital data, I wonder whether my students have cast even a cursory glance at the architectural genius of this structure.

We've been promised a behind-the-scenes peep at where customers pay a pretty premium to pick up their new vehicles. Constructed to mimic the interior of a 12-cylinder motor, BMW Welt is a showroom for some of the most flashy and costly vehicles produced over almost 100 years of company history. Such as the Phantom Rolls-Royce, price tag 450,000 euros. Our guide, or 'Ambassador' as they're called at BMW, is a student called Alina. She explains how 450 manpower hours go into building this work of art. And they clearly haven't skimped on accessories. Opening the passenger door, she slides her hand into a side pocket and pulls out a telescope-shaped case, out of which pops an umbrella. It's all very larger than life, and I'm half expecting James Bond to bound around the corner any moment, jump in and speed off in a cloud of exhaust fumes.

But no sign of Daniel Craig, alas. Instead, Alina leads us alongside a plug-in hybrid i8, which she describes as 'cutiful'. It's the first time I've ever heard the word used in connection with automobiles. Looking rearward, Alina points excitedly to the vehicle's fender, vent shaped like a reversed number seven. Stopping in her steps, she gazes in awe at the automobile, almost as if about to stoop on one knee and pray. For a moment, I'm almost tempted to do so too. Torn between saying a prayer that I might own one of these awesome automobiles myself one day, and quietly confessing to some imaginary cassock-clad priest posed prayerfully at the wheel.

Forgive me father, for I have sinned....

Heavens, this place really is pseudo-church.

I'm debating whether to stop and have my photo taken, when our guide ushers us around the corner into a mini cinema. We watch a flashy PR film on the BMW brand, all a bit *'mehr hui ois pfui,'* as Bavarians like to say. A roller shutter behind the screen rises to reveal line upon line of vehicles stacked one over the other. Just this moment a rack robot glides past, hooks itself up onto the car directly in front of us, and carries it off. This is one of around 100 vehicles which are united every day with their owners, and we're about to witness such an event. In BMW parlance it's known as 'premiere'.

Returning to the central concourse, we climb a walkway suspended between six floors and a filigreed steel-glass-skin roof. Next moment we're surveying a stage-like and dynamically twisted ramp. With up to 170 cars being handed over here at peak times, Alina explains this is where the customer 'deflowers his baby'. It seems a rather odd way of describing the process of clambering into a just-purchased vehicle. Almost as if she's about to raise and wiggle her forefinger to underscore the sexual innuendo. But no. Pointing to three persons standing at the top of a Las Vegas-like staircase, she says 'Look there.' We watch how a nearby low-roofed sedan-like hatchback suddenly starts revolving, remote controlled by the BMW ambassador accompanying the amorous couple.

Customers can book whatever 'premiere package' they wish, says Alina, all depending how deep their pockets are. 'Little extras' include rose petals strewn over a ribbed bonnet, a sea of balloons falling from the rafters, and – for those seeking a fun way to propose – a wedding ring stashed away in the glove compartment. Alina assures us that this practical combination of *Auto und Frau* happens quite often. I look around, almost expecting someone in denims, crisp white shirt and jacket – classic German-man style – to go down on one knee, rose stem between teeth. No such luck, sadly.

German males typically reserve their greatest passion for cars. Maybe things are slowly changing. But today, at least, it's still a case of suitors going for gearshift over girl.

Having asked my students to review BMW Welt as part of their course work, I've already looked at comments other visitors have left at TripAdvisor. These range from 'Petrol-head must' and 'Classy, efficient, unpretentious' to 'Too much capitalism.' One visitor proudly describes himself as 'BMW hypnotised.'

After the tour I notice that Alina is in no hurry to go, even though she's finished bang on time. Just like a good German. So, lingering a while longer, I enquire about her job. She tells me she's working as a 'BMW Ambassador', to help fund her Business Administration studies. I enquire whether she can afford to drive around in a pricey BMW. 'But of course,' she replies matter-of-factly.

Then, all of a sudden, she leans towards me slightly, grins mischievously and whispers conspiratorially:

'BMW drivers get more action of a *non*-automotive kind than drivers of Mercedes or Audi.'

She mouths the word *'non'* deliberately slowly, widening her eyes as if roping me into some dark secret. Sensing that I'm not altogether sure whether this is just chirpy banter or something more specific, Alina snaps back into a more formal tone. She goes on to explain that two thirds of all cars driven in Germany are German. In stark contrast with just one in seven cars on the road in Britain being 'British'. Or at least manufactured on British shores.

Perusing the exhibits afterwards, it hits home how much the three German premium brands are at pains to outsmart each other in the battle of words. Compare, for example, BMW's claim to produce *'The Ultimate Driving Machine'* with Audi's own words of unbridled wisdom: *'Truth in Engineering'*. Such statements are so milk and water, you can't really argue with either. It's all too like for like, tit for tat. No wonder BMW have struck out with their ostentatious mushroom-like edifice, sticking it up just a mile from the middle of Munich, right next to the

Olympic Park. It's like cocking a snoot, flicking a monstrous V-sign at their closest rivals. What other reason could there be to throw 500 million euros of private money on such a pile? Here in Germany, architectural structures of such a size are typically funded by the public purse.

What I like most about this place is that there are no hidden charges. You can sit in and 'sample' all BMW's production models without any pressure to buy. Freebies are unusual in a city like Munich, where you have to pay like sin for just about everything, inclusive of going for a pee. Still, should you wish to splash out and go for a spin, show-room models are on hire from 75 euros an hour.

It's tempting.

After waving my students off, I quietly slide behind the steering wheel of the latest Mini Cooper Hardtop.

I'm suddenly disturbed by a cheerful Chinaman touting an uber-large zoom lens, asking if I'll take his photo. No problem. He's delighted when I hand him back the camera and practically purrs with pleasure as he scrolls through the shots I've taken of him. '*Veerry* good, yes, *veerry* good,' he hums. But then he starts pointing his lens at me. He wants my picture too.

That's it, time to go.

Writing up my blog for the day, I note that BMW Welt is not selling cars, but *lifestyle*. Of both automotive and *non*-automotive nature, to coin Alina's playful expression. For me, cars have always been about getting from A to B at minimum cost. Function over frills. I drive a Mitsubishi Space Star, for heaven's sake. The thought of measuring my status in terms of the vehicle I drive doesn't appeal. And yet for once, just once, I'm slightly overcome by the glitz 'n' glam of all these awesome dreams on wheels. *'Designed For Driving Pleasure.'* Yes, I remember now, that's the other slogan which had struck me as rather weird. Alina has since disappeared back to her ambassador's restroom, but she'd probably contend, eyelids all aflutter, that it's one of a *number* of pleasures. It's hard not to get carried away, surrounded by all these lovely models. On balance, I'm not sure whether it's the lustrous vehicles or the lusty tour guide that have been steadily working their charm.

Whichever way, I too have become BMW hypnotised.

Toytown

When it comes to English-speaking clubs, expats in Munich are spoilt for choice. Specialist groups cater for just about every activity you can stab with a stick. From crossword-puzzle solving and toast-mastering to 'zero-waste zealots'. There's even a meet-up called 'Bitch and stich'. Moaners and groaners are welcome, says their website, but it does help if you can also knit.

To date, we've been involved with only one of these groups, The Munich Wanderers. Initially they made us feel quite welcome ('We go hiking every Saturday. Wanna tag along?'). But camaraderie soon turned to indifference. And, when others started to simply ignore us, we began to feel like the fifth wheel on the wagon. Several times we were all together when, all at once, the rest of the group did a disappearing act. Halfway through a ride on a ferry on the Ammersee, for example, I popped into the gents just below deck. We were supposed to be going to the other side of the lake, still half an hour away. I came back up to find everyone, without warning, had just disembarked at a stop in between. On another occasion, we were relaxing at a beer garden together and I went over to the serving hatch to fetch another *Weissbier*. When I returned, the benches they'd been huddled together on were all deserted. Sitting in the shade of a chestnut tree, Bea looked rather lonesome. 'Where are they all?' I asked. 'Uuuh,' she responded, shrugging her shoulders, 'they just got up and left.'

That was the last time we took a trip with the Munich Wanderers.

We'd got to know the Wanderers through a platform called Toytown, which claims to be Germany's largest English-language online community. I'd wanted to unsubscribe from the platform, but must have hit the wrong button, because instead of drying up, the emails start to pour in with a vengeance. Each is an invite to join yet another of Toytown's abundant 'special-interest' groups. Curious as to whether we might have a little more luck with one of these, I arrange to meet the man responsible for creating the expat community.

We're sitting on the top floor of Café Glockenspiel enjoying *Kaffee und Kuchen* and a sweeping view of the Marienplatz. James, or 'Editor Bob', as he's known online, describes the 'dark days' when Munich's 12,000 or more expats were crying out for a forum to exchange messages and arrange meetings. Licking latte froth from his top lip, James recalls how he set up such a platform. Launched in 2002, Toytown Munich is funded mostly by advertising. Relocation agencies and doctors are particularly supportive.

Heart of the community is the chat forum, which 34-year-old 'Bob' moderates full time. He describes how around 1,000 of the site's some 30,000 regulars – including Americans, Brits, Canadians, Irish, South Africans and Aussies – gather here daily to share news and organise social events.

It's not unusual for topics to attract several hundred responses. This happened to me when I invited feedback on my very first website, one that I'd built from scratch on a site called *wetpaint.com*. I spent weeks on end working at it when, really, I had far better things to do.

Such as earning a living.

Reactions to my efforts were blunt but honest. My website, which one expat commentator compared to 'a sixth-form schoolboy's clumsy attempt to impress his girlfriend', ran for six months or so, before mysteriously disappearing. A little later, seeing that the domain 'Know Howe for English' was still free, I did it properly, outsourcing the job to our friends Claudia and Ralph, professional webmasters.

Taking to the Toy Town chat forum on another occasion, I posted a query on my favourite comfort foods from the UK. 'Anyone know where you can buy flapjack in Munich?' 'Sure,' some joker replied, 'the flapjack shop is on the corner of Amalienstrasse. Right opposite the Treacle Tart Store and Spotted Dick World.'

Ha, if only.

While enquiries in the regional forum are generally of an organisational nature, such as 'Where can I find a babysitter?' and 'Who can offer my daughter flute lessons?' discussions on the Germany-wide forum can cover almost anything. His favourites, James tells me, are 'How can I make myself laugh at German humour?' and 'What should a lonely wife do while her husband's away?'

Bet that last post received plenty likes.

'Nicest thing about Toytown Germany,' says James 'is that it's less about chat and more about arranging meet-ups in real life.' The most popular ones, apparently, pursue a passion for curry nights and 'impro' comedy.

So, is there such a thing as a 'typical' Toytown user?

'Absolutely,' nods James encouragingly. He describes rank-and-file members as 20-to-40-year-old office workers 'with time on their hands.'

I grin. Just wait till German employers hear that. Still, it probably explains why the most popular time for online meet-ups is weekdays, just after lunch break.

Stabbing at a slice of *Sachertorte*, I tell James about my experience with the Munich Wanderers chapter of Toytown, how they'd jumped ship, leaving me in the lurch on the lake.

James snorts.

'Ha, I've never heard of *that* happening before. Unless they were just trying to dodge the ticket inspector.'

Then there was that other strange experience with The Munich Wanderers. It involved a fair deal of nudity and voyeurism. I choose not to tell Editor Bob about this. Probably because we're sitting next to two elderly British tourists. Draped in cheap plastic anoraks typically worn by Brits abroad come rain or shine, the dear old dames are busy sipping milky Earl Grey tea. And deliberating whether or not to order another helping of *Sahnetorte Schwarzwälder Art*.

The following experience is the closest I'll probably ever come to being pursued by a paparazzi.

We were on an excursion to the Tegernsee one

sweltering hot summer's day a few years back. Stopping at a nice little bathing area with jetty and picnic area, a few of us slipped into the water for a cool-off. We didn't have swimwear with us, so went in '*oafach so*', as Bavarians say. We had great fun frolicking around. But, as I leapt around waist high in water, I noticed one of the 'Wanderers' had his camera cocked at the lake. He was clicking away as if his whole life depended on it. And it didn't look like he was just taking pictures of the delightful panoramic view. As we came out of the warm water, he was still touting his camera. It was trained directly at me. When it came to continuing the hike, the guy suddenly disappeared, camera and all. We never saw him again.

Yes, it's fair to say the Munich Wanderers attract decidedly odd types.

James is anxious to show me that his rank-and-file Toytowners are different. He suggests we meet at the beer garden social this coming Friday.

'Look out for the pink stonker,' he calls back over his shoulder, as he heads off towards the *U-Bahn* and I make for the *S-Bahn*.

Roll on Friday. Entering the Augustiner Biergarten punctually at six o'clock sharp, I discover a 10-strong gaggle of even more punctual expats, all huddled under a giant pink balloon. James is right; Toytown expats are typically aged between 20 and 40. There's just one thing James hasn't mentioned – tonight is Ladies' Night. And, judging by their very business-like, almost identical outfits – knee-length black skirts paired with wide-spread-collar shirts – it looks like these ladies have piled in straight from the office. Either that or they're dab hands at 'partner look'. Brooding on the ladies' lovely attire, I'm suddenly distracted by a gentle gyration in one of my trouser pockets. Something's definitely trying to make its presence felt.

Ha. My mobile of course. I'd switched it to buzz only.

It doesn't help that I'm wearing a pair of multi-pocket trousers. I finally find the right opening.

'*Jaaa, hallo?*'

It's 'Bob'.

'Sorry, stuck in office. Chasing deadlines. Catch you later.'

I grin again. 7 o'clock on Friday evening and this Englander's still not done for the day. His German office mates have probably spent most of the afternoon lazing on the *Balkon* or jogging ten laps around the Englischer Garten.

Pocketing the phone, however, I suddenly feel self-conscious. Bob's left me in the lurch – one male amongst a mob of expat lady look-alikes. The token gent.

Some of the ladies are already tucking into charcoal-grilled *Steckerlfisch* – fish on the stick that tastes so toothsome in beer gardens. They're all quaffing Pinot Grigio – an odd choice of drink for a *Biergarten*. But then this is up-and-coming Westend, the new *schikimicki* part of Munich. Anyway, they're quite a cheerful crowd who soon give me the feeling I've just made ten brand-new friends. We're having great fun. So great, in fact, that I lose all track of time. Until I pull out my smartphone to see if there are any more messages from 'Bob'. And realise I have just 13 minutes to catch my Passau-bound express from the *Hauptbahnhof*.

'Y-*aaa* n-*aaa*t c-*aaa*m*iii*n' to B*aaa*bo*oo*lo*oo*vskys?'

I look up to see a freckle-faced redhead. Immaculately groomed and manicured, she's every bit the quintessential Californian. Her Valley Girl accent, with all those delightful elongated vowels, sounds like Cher in very slow motion. The sort of speak that heterosexual Englishmen might find hard to resist. Think Prince Harry falling for Meghan Markle.

And now it's working its way with me too. In between Pinot Grigio-fuelled *Prosts*, we'd already exchanged a few sneaky glances. But I'd stopped short of actually speaking to her. Perhaps I was simply willing her to initiate a conversation. American females are supposed to be good at that, aren't they?

'Naaah, home,' I retort, slipping my jacket on.

I immediately regret turning down an invite to Bolovoskys, one of Munich's top night spots.

'See you here ag*aaaiii*n then?'

'Ahhm, maybe,' I waver, glancing at the time again. I'd love to, but it's a three-hour round trip to this meet-up. Probably easier just to meet up online. When I suggest exchanging virtual identity names, Freckles' eyes light up:

'Hey, I'm Bahoo.'

Darting for the exit, it strikes me that I haven't disclosed my own online identity.

It's 'knowhowe'.

Bavarian Home Lovin'

Anywhere fortunate enough to bear the title 'The World's Largest Continuous Hop-growing Region' would be foolish not to make a noise about it. Especially when the local cash cow is commonly known as 'green gold'. And yet, curiously, it's not the precious hop crop that first strikes most visitors to the Hallertau. Passing through, you'll more likely see roadside hoardings promoting *Titty Twisters* and *Bumsdis.*

Titty Twisters and *Bumsdis* are farmyard parties staged in villages with unpronounceable names. Losing our way home one day, we stumble on such an event near a place called, I think, Oberschweinshaxlbächerl. We stop to ask for directions outside an enormous marquee in the middle of an empty field. I peep inside. The tent is heaving with adolescents rocking to and fro, trancelike expressions etched upon their faces. The way they're lunging from side to side, it looks more like they're mounted on springs than beer benches.

Just what were Lower Bavarians thinking of, calling their parties *Titty Twisters*?

Search me. But one thing's clear. Nothing makes them happier than assembling under colossal circus-like tents, jumping up onto wooden benches and rocking from side to side. Squashed together like sardines, and all swaying in robotic synchrony.

The next striking thing about the Hallertau is the music they play at these events. Google key words like 'Niederbayern Party Hits' and you'll not find one single recent hit. Or, for that matter, any yodellers or alpine horn blowers. Top of the pile, it turns out, is a number by Neil Diamond. Everyone in the Hallertau – young and old – knows the refrain *Wo-ho-ho, good times never seemed so good*. And, when it comes to *Hands, touchin' hands, reachin' out, touchin' you,* they know exactly what's expected of them: hands stretched, they flutter their fingers in mid-air and form a human pyramid. Like members of some strange sect, willing the Holy Ghost to move among them.

That very song is playing right now. But I'm at neither a happy-clappy church gathering nor a reunion of the Neil Diamond Fan Club. I'm attending *Sommerfest* at my daughter's kindergarten. Huddled up on beer benches in a giant tent, we're being jollied along by a pop duo with the unpronounceable name of Leidlfestodorreiba. 'Where are you all, children?' asks the lead singer. Rows of hands – adult hands, actually – shoot up excitedly. This is the cue, apparently, for everybody to clink beer mugs together, jump up and down on beer benches and break into a chorus of 'Sweet Caroline'.

Yes, everybody.

Seriously. Go to any *Titty Twister* or *Bumsdi* and you'll find not just adults but also bench after bench of teenagers singing along to songs from the early seventies. It's difficult to envision Mr. Diamond exerting such an influence on British adolescents.

What is it about these tunes that makes so many burghers, regardless of age, slap their thighs and swing from side to side, as if under some David-Copperfield induced hypnosis? My friend Matthias is doing it as well. I ask if he likes this music. 'Actually not,' he says in perfect English, 'I'm more into rock.'

Beware of any German who makes out they hate those cheesy yet awfully catchy tunes they call *Schlager*. They're living in denial. Germans typically wrinkle their noses at *Schlager*. And yet they sing along to them with such sonority that even the Vienna Boys' Choir would be impressed.

Matthias is dressed like a veritable Oktoberfest male model. He's wearing lederhose, knee-high cream-coloured socks and Haferl shoes. All that's missing is a green felt hat with a shaving-brush type feather tucked down the side. His wife and five-year old daughter are clad in very pretty dirndls. As if to apologise for their folksy outfits, he adds 'But this here is different. Local tradition. We have *Stimmung*, good feeling, you know.'

He's used another of those typical German words with no direct English equivalent. *Stimmung* roughly translates as 'mood', 'atmosphere' or 'vibe'. But that only touches the surface. *Stimmung* is more about an internal and external state of mind. It reaches deep into the soul. Originally it was used to describe the tuning of a music instrument. The idea, therefore, is that if all parts of your life fit nicely together in a harmonic way, your *Stimmung* is good.

All in all, the 'state of mind' – a dubious expression

in English, almost as if we're questioning these individuals' sanity – looks *sehr gut*. Suddenly, however, Matthias jumps up and disappears. Nature's call. Must be all that beer. Sixty seconds later, however, he's back, and beaming all over. 'Got it from the barmaid!' he grins, waving a pen in the air, as if it were a magic wand. Then, grabbing a beer mat, he starts to sketch something vaguely similar to a line graph. 'Look,' he says, joining two axes with a bold 45-degree arc, 'the level of willingness to sing and dance rises parallel to the level of alcohol consumed.'

All at once we're into probabilities, time scales and statistics. It feels more like we're in a college lecture theatre than kindergarten beer tent. Holding up his beer mat, Matthias gently rotates the impromptu chart a full circle, carefully studying it from various angles. It's as if he's willing the blueprint to suddenly reveal a startling new dimension to his theory. Putting it aside, he takes a gulp of *Weissbier*. And, with froth-coated lips, proceeds to explain how oldies and *Schlager* unite people of all different ages and music tastes:

'You can have a group of different nationalities, all with different tongues. And music is their universal language.'

And with that, as if duty-bound to practise what he preaches, Matthias hoists his tankard and proceeds to swing to the sound of 'Sweet Caroline.'

Oh boy, hit alert. They're playing *that* one again.

Every year during Oktoberfest, German radio stations – no doubt with a little encouragement from one or two major breweries – speculate which songs are set to fuel the greatest amount of alcohol consumption. Perennial favourite, it seems, is 'A Prosit'. On a typical Saturday at the Fest, oompah bands play this drinkers' anthem up to 80 times, during which roughly 24,000 litres of beer are guzzled. And that's just in *one* beer tent alone. There are 14 large main tents; each packs in up to 11,000 people.

No wonder the Germans' official beer drinking anthem sweeps the board every single time. Yet the success of the second most played Oktoberfest hit may come as a surprise. 'Take Me Home, Country Roads' definitely didn't start out as a boozing song. John Denver wrote it as a tribute to Mother Nature. Originally released in 1971, the tune topped the charts in North America yet flopped in Europe. Normally that should have been end of the road for 'Country Roads'. But in 2001, Hermes House Band gave the song a playful twist and sent it rocketing to the top in Europe too. It's been a sensation at beer festivals ever since. From the very opening line – 'Almost heaven, West Virginia' – virtually everybody, young and old, grabs their litre *Mass* and starts rocking from side to side.

Puzzled, I turn to Matthias for an explanation.

'The lyrics are simple to sing along to – even when we're punch drunk, we can rattle off 'Country Roads' just like parrots.'

Singing like chatterbox birds when you're three sheets to the wind? Ah, good old Germans.

I tell Matthias this probably says more about their desire simply to work up a thirst rather than any special affinity towards the late country and western musician.

But it might at least explain why these oompah bands rattle off the same set of songs at every single gig. As I look around, everyone's tapping their toes to the tried and tested sounds. Some parents have even started to 'schunkel'. Slowly and sluggishly, they're swaying to the beat, as if under a state of hypnosis. Others are doing a little hop, skip and jig, as they hover between bar, beer bench and child's play area.

To learn more about this very Bavarian phenomenon, I call up local singer songwriter and bon vivant Maria Reiser. Hailed as the inventor of *Yodelpop*, Maria defines her style as *'Bavarian home lovin''*. This seems a strange way of describing a genre of music. To Brits, *home lovin'* sounds more like tripping down to Homebase on Saturday morning, pushing around a trolley piled high with rolls of wallpaper, replacement light bulbs, mulch for the flower beds and so on.

My yodelpop friend actually lives just a few streets away, so getting together should present no problem. But, as with most locals, it's often difficult to arrange a meeting at short notice, or *kurzfristig*. The word smacks of spontaneity – something Germans feel innately ill-at-ease with. Burghers baulk at the mere mention of anything that's *kurzfristig*. Even when it's just a question of getting together for coffee, they end up fixing a specific time, day and venue months in advance.

Clearly, I'm already conditioned to behave like an uber-organised German. Pulling out my diary, I flick through dates over the forthcoming month. Business-like and purposeful, I fire suggestions down the phone:

'So Maria, how about next Friday afternoon?'

'*Na, sorry, do heb i Prom.*'

She's rehearsing. Giving her annual *Benefizkonzert*, or charity show, at the local retirement home.

'*Null Problem,*' I say, entering the fund-raiser in my diary. Then, trying again, I suggest Wednesday in two weeks. Rather tentatively I add 'mid-morning maybe?'

'*Na, do bin i im Studio.*'

'*O-kaaay.*'

Ha. I'm already saying this word like a German. Long drawn out and overpronounced. Almost sounding as if it's *not* OK. Barely recognisable in its original Anglo-American form.

Then, dismissing Wednesday lunchtime offhand, I try for the week after:

'*und foigende Woch übahabt?*'

Maria is probably already shaking her head again. Blow it, I'd been pegging all my hopes on that following week.

I'm about to throw the towel in when I suddenly have an idea:

'*Du, Maria?*'

'*Ja, Tim?*'

'*Bisd du heid namidog frei?*'

'*Bassd scho.*'

So this afternoon it is then. All sorted.

Within the hour we're relaxing out on the decking, sipping sea buckthorn tea and listening to her latest single 'Glabbelwirt'. Maria is wearing a dirndl, of course. The costume comes complete with brightly embroidered bodice, black skirt and pink and white striped apron. It's very eye-catching. Quite kinky in fact.

For Brits, think 'farmhouse chic' – upcycled potter's smocks and plunging necklines. But not really the sort of thing you'd expect a thirty-something hipster to show up in when the invitation's simply for tea and choc-chip cupcakes. Maria, like many other young Bavarians, seems to delight in dressing up in garb which originated as working clothes for farmhands and servants.

Chances are, any non-German dressed like that in England would be viewed with deepest suspicion. Or it would just be assumed they were auditioning for the stage version of 'The Sound of Music', awaiting their cue to launch into 'Edelweiss'.

How did this traditional German clothing, or *Tracht*, suddenly become trendy? Maria describes how some ten years ago fashion designers started putting a modern twist on the traditional outfits. Delicately embroidered wide skirts and aprons, for example, were made brighter in colour and bigger in size. 'The cleavage has also grown much wider,' grins Maria, gesturing at her own. She doesn't actually say so, but I suspect young ones are dressing up like this for just one reason – to turn each other on.

Maria has brought along some lovely *Kandiszucker*, a sort of rock candy, something I've come to associate less with rainy summers at the British seaside and more with winter *Gemütlichkeit* in Germany. That's the typical German 'feeling' of cosiness and contentment. It's like *coorie* to the Scots, and *hygge* to the Danes. Dropping a lump into her tea, she describes how it's all part of a back-to-roots trend, which begun in what she calls the *Sommermärchen* – the fairytale summer in which

Germany staged the World Cup. Even more telling, was when they – hitherto unheard of – started draping every available surface area with red, black and gold flags. 'This patriotism, a sort of longing for local traditions, became a go-to movement from around 2010,' the songstress explains. 'The icing on the cake was winning the World Cup four years later.'

Maria tells me how Germans' newly found patriotism and reconnection with oldy-worldly clothing also goes hand in hand with their longing for '*Geborgenheit*'. 'This is something Germans have always been into, particularly in times of unrest. It's all about surrounding yourself with homey, cosy things. Things that warm your heart.'

Maria's own heart bumps to the beat of Beyoncé and Keith Urban. Yet she too confesses having a soft spot for Diamond and Denver.

Back at the *Kindergartenfest* they're playing 'Sweet Caroline' once more. It's almost like it's on a loop. Before I can slip off undetected, I'm being grabbed and pulled into a pyramid of interlinked hands.

All of a sudden, it's the interactive part where we have to sing *wo-ho-ho* and raise our hands and fingers in the air. But this time it feels different – it's actually quite fun. Matthias and Maria are right. The music, motions and traditional costumes do create a sense of togetherness, the feeling of belonging to a local community. A communal feeling which transcends all ages.

Once again, this scene under the kindergarten canvass underscores current music trends in the rest of

Germany.

But when it comes to the crème de la crème, it's not Neil Diamond – not even Beyoncé or Rihanna – who pack the greatest number of burghers into the arenas. The hottest *Schlager* star in Germany today is Russian-born Helene Fischer. Virtually unknown outside the German-speaking world, the 34-year-old in cropped top and lederhose warbles about unrequited love and heartache. In *Deutsch*. *Natürlich*. Fischer, whose texts are oft mocked as screensavers for the middle classes, has sold over nine million albums – more than any other German artist ever.

How extraordinary. While the rest of the world trends towards English-sung lyrics, Germany is heading in the other direction and embracing its own language instead. Asked why they prefer listening to songs in *Deutsch*, adolescents just laugh and say it's because at least they can understand them.

Truth is, these *Schlager* stand for what Germans of all ages crave for most – *Stimmung* and *Gemütlichkeit*. Because, when it comes to ramping up the feel-good factor, these cheesy melodies really do hit all the hot buttons. Take, for example, Helene Fischer's latest hit 'Wenn du lachst':

> *When you laugh, you hush my eyes*
> *When you laugh you banish every fear*
> *When you laugh it's like a day at the seaside*
> *And it's clear to me that I always want to stay with you*
> *When you laugh, when you laugh.*

Their music taste may well lag forty odd years behind what the rest of the developed world considers contemporary but, by eschewing English music and plumping for *Schlager,* young Bavarians are keeping local traditions alive and kicking. As the band plays on, I'm also singing along to these tunes, swaying to and fro like locals. I probably look every bit the knee-slapping Bavarian.

And, as we start fluttering fingers and linking hands again, I can't help enjoying it too.

Wanderlust

How come visitors from abroad often know more about tourist attractions on our own doorstep than we do ourselves? We recently had friends from Poland to stay for the week. Since we had to work, we left them to their own devices during the daytime. During which they visited Legoland, Rothenburg ob der Tauber, Neuschwanstein Castle and Bayreuth. On the fifth day they were so exhausted, they crashed out at the local *Freibad*.

They looked quite baffled when we confessed that, apart from the local pool, we'd not been to a single one of the places.

There was no excuse of course. These world-beating attractions lie virtually in our backyard. Take the mountains, for example. We live just ninety car minutes from the *Voralpen*, the foothills of the Bavarian Alps, but I can count on just a few fingers the number of times we visit them each year. Living north of Munich, we'd long kidded ourselves that the mountains were too far away to make it there and back in a day. In reality, having reached Munich in less than an hour we're already halfway up the hills. Well, almost. The Alps are actually so close to Munich that they creep up on you, springing into view long before you join the Salzburg autobahn that tenaciously snakes around the Bavarian capital. Several years ago, Bea and I flew over Munich in a four-seater Cessna 150. One moment we were passing over the Marienkirche, the city's landmark church. I bent down to adjust my seatbelt. When I looked up again, we were already cruising over the snow-sprinkled Alps.

It's time we started discovering more of Bavaria. Starting with the Alps.

Pulling a 1:50 000 map off the shelf, I splay it out on the floor. Bea, bent double over her i-pad, is already thumbing through Google Maps, mentally measuring out distances. To watch us, you'd think we're gearing up to trot half way around the globe.

'Got it,' says Bea, suddenly looking up from her device, 'we're off to the Leitzachtal.'

The following weekend, as we hurtle down the autobahn to Leitzach Valley, these snow-capped mountains suddenly leap into view. While still almost 100 km away, they appear tantalisingly near. Towering majestically on the horizon, the jaw-dropping alpine scenery reminds me how lucky we are to have world-class hiking and ski regions almost at our doorstep. All of a sudden, taking a 270-km round day trip to the Alps feels just like a short hop, or *Katznsprung* as Bavarians say.

We're in good company. According to the Deutscher Wanderverband, almost 40 million Germans – more than every second burgher – go hiking either occasionally or frequently. And just over 17 million regard trekking as a major leisure activity. They've certainly got plenty open space to pursue their

Wanderlust. Germany's forests, mountains, rivers and coasts are home to 200,000 kilometres of hiking trails.

The walk we've chosen starts and ends at Fischbachau, a pre-alpine village crammed with picture-perfect houses decorated with so-called *Lüftlmalerei.* These colourful frescos depict traditional local fairy tales or religious scenes and adorn countless homes in Upper Bavaria. One such brightly painted building particularly catches our attention. Splashed over its facade is a life-sized painting of a harp player. But it's no normal harpist. This one's an angel and it's straddling a Harley Davidson. We're just gawping at this slightly unusual fresco when the owner suddenly appears through the side gate. My instinctive reaction is to apologise and quietly move on. But before I can do so the man is beckoning us over.

'Wo kimmd ihr ha, wo gäd ihr hi?'

Where are you from, where are you going to? We tell him we're doing the Leitzachtaler Bergblick – a 14-km loop trail along the River Leitzach, over meadows and through woods. It'll take us right back to where we've parked, just opposite the eleventh-century Friedenskirche Maria Schutz, the oldest church in the valley. What's unusual about our conversation though is how talkative this man is. When you first meet Bavarians they're usually quite reserved and uncommunicative. This one is quite different. Talking nineteen to the dozen, he's already telling Tildy and her friend Simona jokes. 'Why do Red Indians do this?' he quizzes, holding both hands flat above his eyes, as if scanning the horizon. Nonplussed, the girls shrug.

'Because if they did this,' he reveals, cupping hands around eyes, 'they wouldn't see anything!'

The thermometer's nudging 20 °C – ideal temperature for a mid-summer hike. Any cooler up at this height and we'd need jackets; any warmer and we'd probably be dripping with sweat. Yet dipping our toes into the River Leitzach we get a shock. The water's ice cold. No great surprise really – its source lies 200 metres high in the Alps. We stop for sandwiches and coffee at a splashy *Wasserfall*, the crystal-clear water shimmering in the morning sunshine as it tumbles over the rocks. '*Papa schwimm!*' the girls chant in unison, daring me to strip off and plunge into the glacial water. A hardened swimmer, I'm usually the last one to say '*nein danke*' to a nice fresh dip. But there's no way I'm leaping into this water. It must be a good 10 °C cool. Crossing a bridge which leads us away from the river, we enter a small village. Every single half-timbered cottage with its flower-box-filled balconies looks like something straight off a *Milka* chocolate box. One of these gingerbread-like houses has a sign on the garden gate warning:

'*Vorsicht, bissiger Hund!*'

The vicious dog's possibly taking a siesta. But, more likely, it simply doesn't exist. Germans often put up such signs just to scare off nosey passersby.

Just past the village we spot a cherry tree leaning over the pathway. Its branches are so heavily laden they're almost snapping under the weight. The fruit is squelchy, gloopy, overripe, and absolutely divine. Drooping right across our path, it's crying out to be picked. We hastily fill our sandwich boxes, cramming in as much as we can.

Continuing the hike with heavily stained hands, we're just passing a small *Gastwirtschaft* when we notice, a little higher up the hill, a group of farmhands loading piles of wood onto a gigantic bonfire. It's the second or third bonfire we've seen today. On the café terrace, meanwhile, half a dozen waitresses dressed in dirndl and chunky-heeled doll shoes are flitting around, busily decorating tables and clambering up stepladders to hoist up bunting and fairy lights.

I bounce up to one of the pigtail-braided waitresses. With eye-popping cleavage struggling to contain itself inside a mercilessly tight bustier top, she probably embodies every foreign male's ideal of the quintessential *Fräulein*.

'*Tschuldigung, ist was los?*' I ask.

Is anything happening?

It's a silly question and *Fräulein* shoots me a lop-sided look as if to say 'Are you having a laugh?'

I should have known. It's 21 June, the longest day of the year and this isn't the last bonfire we'll see today. They're being lit all over the mountaintops to celebrate summer solstice. Alpine folks traditionally believe that these *Sonnwendefeuer* will ward away evil spirits. Originally a pre-Christian custom, the Catholic Church 'hijacked' the heathen practice by turning it into a celebration of John the Baptist's birthday which falls just three days later. Ever since, the fires have been known as '*Johannisfeuer*'. In recent years, dare-devil youngsters have started jumping over the glowing embers in the belief that this purifies their souls and protects them from illness. Apparently, the more people who leap over the red-hot cinders, the more purgative the whole process. Couples crossing over the fire hand in hand are said to signal that a wedding is on the way.

A little further on we suddenly spot, dotted around a meadow just above the path, a group of wooden sun loungers. Each curved lounge chair is wide enough to seat two to three persons. It's the sort of furniture that wouldn't go amiss in the relaxation room of an exclusive wellness centre. And yet quite a common sight in Bavaria – expensive furnishings dumped in the middle of nowhere. 'If only we had one of these at home in the garden,' sighs Bea, flopping onto a luxury model.

Oh, if only. Actually, they're so cosy it's tempting just to stay put and quietly forget the rest of the walk. But then reality bites. We've still got another half dozen kilometres to go.

These final six kilometres feel almost twice as long. The kids have already slowed down to a crawl. Fending off relentless pleas to carry Tildy piggyback, we pass a small chapel. A snowy-haired man has just locked up the building and is pocketing the keys. *'Grüßi Gott,'* I say, in typical Bavarian greeting style. I ask him for directions to the nearest *Wirtshaus* and, pointing to the tired kids, enquire how much further to Fischbachau. *'Ooch, gar net so weit'* – not far at all – he says, gesturing across the fields towards a group of buildings clustered around an onion-shaped church spire. He also recommends a local hostelry which does good food. But before I can thank him in local dialect *('vagelt's God!')* he's jumped into a car and pulled up alongside us. 'I'll drop them off at the car park,' he offers, beckoning the kids to climb in as he revs up the engine. Simona's mother manages to hop in too. But only just.

'Uuuh, have we just done the right thing?' questions Bea, as we continue the walk on our own. Quivers of doubt suddenly cross my mind too. Standing sentinel by the chapel gate just a moment ago, the man had looked so trustworthy. 'Oh, they'll be there at the carpark, you'll see,' I say cheerily, seeking to reassure her. Sure enough, arriving back where we'd started out five hours earlier, Magdalena and the girls are waiting for us safe and sound.

Well *almost*.

Having tenaciously trekked over a dozen kilometres of undulating pre-mountain track, Simona is suddenly hobbling around on one leg. Larking around on a bench in the carpark, she'd managed to fall off and sprain her ankle.

Still, Bea and I had been lucky to enjoy probably the most stunning scenery of the whole hike; plateau-like terrain with wide-sweeping panoramic vistas of the Mangelfall mountain range, the eastern part of the Bavarian Alps. Looming up straight ahead of us we marvelled at the Wendelstein – at 1,838 metres the highest local peak. We'd been up there once by cable car. The mountain top boasts a cosy restaurant, meteorological station, ginormous solar energy system and stunning views far into the Austrian province of Tirol.

When we turn up at the Café Krugalm, the place recommended by the man at the chapel, we discover they're no longer serving full meals, only snacks. Taking our drinks orders, the waitress scurries off to the kitchen to see what food she can fix us. We're expecting just sandwiches and soup at the very most, but it turns out that Germans' idea of a mere snack is nothing less than a full-blown feast. Soon we're tucking into wagon-wheel sized pizzas, piles of crunchy side salads and mouth-watering *Kaspress Knödel* oozing with Pinzgau Beer Cheese.

But it's the *Kuchen* that really steal the show at this mountainside eatery. Pinned up over the kitchen door, a notice reads 'Cakes don't make you fat, they simply straighten out the creases.' Inside, a massive table stretches from one end of the room to the other. It's crammed with cakes which, as the maid proudly announces, are all *frisch gebacken* – baked daily. Spoilt for choice, I'm torn between the *Gedeckter Apfel-Mandel* and *Versunkener Kirsch mit Joghurt.* Both look irresistible.

Unable to make my mind up, I plump for rhubarb-and-yoghurt *Torte*. With a big blob of *Sahne*, whipped cream, of course.

'Grüßi Gott!'

I've just been greeted by half a dozen beaming assistants, all lined up and standing to attention. For a fleeting moment I feel like a member of the Royal Family, about to amble down a line of dignitaries all eagerly waiting to shake hands and exchange a pleasantry or two.

I almost blurt out 'Oh, and what do *you* do?'

And then I get a closer look. Each one of them is identically dressed in crisp white polo shirts, flowing gowns and clog-like footwear. Perhaps it's a team of personal trainers. As if any one of them might suddenly dash over, bend down and harness me onto some imaginary body building apparatus. V.I.P. treatment similar, maybe, to that bestowed upon Vivian in *Pretty Woman*. The scene in which she's helped in and out of shoes and skirts by a dozen fawning salespersons.

What bears all the hallmarks of an upmarket fitness centre or a scene from the movies is actually nothing of the sort. I'm in a perfectly 'normal' German chemists.

Customer service in German pharmacies is second to none. They make such a fuss of you, it's almost as if going in there to fix an ailment is something pleasurable. And, despite the throbbing pain in my left leg, I'm experiencing the pleasure right now.

My knee hasn't felt right for a couple days. I'd completed the 14-km hike last weekend without a single bruise or blemish. But, ironically, I'd managed to sprain my ankle early the following morning while boarding a train for Munich. From the far side of the car park, I could see my train pulling up. The *Parkplatz* at Freising is ginormous and linked to the platform by tunnel and several flights of steps. I was worried I wouldn't make it. A typical situation in which you know what you're doing won't do you any good, yet the short-term alternative – missing your connection – overrides far more painful outcomes. Bursting into an Olympic sprint,

I'd somehow managed to catch the train, slumping with a huff, puff and wheeze onto a seat in the end carriage. By Friday afternoon, however, my condition is such that I'm literally on my last legs. I can barely walk.

With doctors' surgeries already deserted for the weekend, I've no choice but to seek out the nearest chemists for some instant pain relief. German pharmacies are like nothing you'll ever see in the rest of the world, where a chemist's nowadays is usually more like a pop-up 'prescriptions counter' – at best an afterthought in the corner of a crowded supermarket. Here, however, every single store is unique. Our local *Apotheke*, for example, devotes shelf upon shelf to personal hygiene products made from hops: deodorants, shampoos, face, toe and nail creams. Even the corn plasters smell of beer.

Limping into the pharmacy at Marienplatz, Munich's central square, I immediately feel like I'm entering the Promised Land. Smiling assistants tip their caps to me, as a chorus of *Grüßi Gott* (literally 'God greet you') echoes around the store. This is red-carpet treatment before I've so much as spoken a single word.

But then I suddenly spot an elderly lady uber-laden with *Kaufhof* shopping bags looking as if she's just about to faint. A pharmacist, quick off the mark, manages to break her fall, and with the other arm intuitively grabs hold of a chair onto which she flops with a thud. Over in the corner sits another customer, a bald gentleman with a pretty apothecary leaning over him. I may be mistaken but, from where I'm standing, she appears to be massaging his thumb. Before I can do a double take it's my turn to be served.

I ask for a bandage, explaining I need to apply it straight away. The shop assistant produces some scissors and waits patiently as I, holding up the rest of the queue, clumsily cut off a piece and start binding it round my troubled knee. Seeing my difficulty performing this standing up she apologises for the lack of chairs, gesturing to the elderly lady sitting with shopping bags and the bald gentleman, who really does look like he's being thumb massaged.

Having regained full consciousness, the fall-prone *Frau* is now remonstrating about there not being a single store in the Bavarian capital to sit down and rest. I'm about to contend that central Munich, with its high density of cafes and bars, surely has enough seating to fill the Allianz Arena several times over, when I suddenly find myself agreeing – nodding like a Chihuahua dog bobbing from a car rear-view mirror. Whoever invented the expression 'shop till you drop' certainly hadn't envisaged the disastrous implications of collapsing in a German supermarket.

Semi squatting on the floor, one leg tucked behind the other like a dying crab, I struggle to bandage my leg up as best I can in the circumstances, wishing away the crowd of curious onlookers squeezed into line right behind me. My gaze drifts from the sales assistant, who's grinning as if to say 'We don't get this sort of thing happening every day,' to the woman recovering on her chair, still holding forth about the lack of seating in Munich stores.

Gathering up my medical supplies, I ease myself back

up onto my legs. Then, parade-waving to a line of white-gowned assistants, I hobble out and off into the crowds on Marienplatz.

My Lederhose's loose

I'm at a local folkloric evening – *Hoagarten,* as it's called in Bavaria and Austria. The atmosphere is exuberant, the beer tastes almost better than ever. And yet I immediately feel like a fish out of water.

I'm the only one in lederhose.

Believing lederhose to be *de rigeur* at such an event – thigh-slapping Bavarians don't dare wear anything different, do they? – I'd dashed out earlier and purchased the appropriate attire. Bavarian men typically buy only one pair of lederhose in their whole lifetime. And males make no bones about ever washing these garments. No matter how much beer they manage to spill. Sloshing booze over your lederhose is equally *de rigueur.* There's a folk saying that goes 'Only greasy lederhosen are good lederhosen.' On just the few occasions I'd worn my expensive leather outfit, I'd already spilt copious amounts of beer everywhere. And, lazy bones, I'd made no effort to wash it out either. Quite by accident I too now look like a brazen Bavarian.

But I'd not reckoned with one or two sticking points. Firstly, kitting myself out in traditional attire had cost an arm and a leg. When a Bavarian goes out and buys his lederhose, he doesn't just purchase knee-length pants with suspenders attached. He invests in the whole *Tracht*; from chequered button-down shirt and Tirolean-style jacket right down to dark-brown leather loafers and knee-high cream-coloured socks. I'd ended up shelling out around a thousand euros for the whole works. The only *accessoire* I'd foregone was the wide-brimmed felt hat with mandatory feather tucked down the side.

The other problem was my lederhose *per se*. They were far too big. With ugly beer stains spanning both sides, and, embarrassingly, a yeasty-smelling splotch right over the crutch, there was no way the shop would exchange them. Like or lump it, I was stuck with the ill-fitting costume. Forever.

That said, the folk music at this *Hoagarten* is just great. The acts have such delightful names: Hopfawinkl-Musi, Haglmo-Musi, Schmankerl-Musi, and – I love this one – Bladlbeisser. In between performances, Deputy *Bürgermeister* Frau Langwieser who's been roped in as Master of Ceremonies, tells jokes and animates the audience in broad Bavarian dialect. Luckily, I manage to understand most of the wisecracks, and join in the hoots of laughter with the predominantly pensioner audience. At every punchline I notice how they lift their shoulders up and down when they chortle. As Bavarians of a certain age tend to do when they find something particularly hilarious.

Much of the humour, which seems to involve either priests, pubescent altar servers or drunken *Polizisten*, strikes me as rather risqué for Catholic Bavaria. My favourite joke, however, involves none of the above job descriptions:

Plumber repairs vet's toilet. Job done, he demands 600 euros. '*Whaaat*?' gasps vet, stunned at the cost of just half an hour's labour.

And then: 'I don't earn a third of that. Not even for a full hour!'

'Ha, funny you should say that,' replies plumber, 'when I was a vet I didn't either!'

The joke strikes a familiar chord. Just a few days earlier we'd also been grossly overcharged by such a tradesman. He'd replaced our front door lock and demanded a hefty €807. For barely ten minutes' work. Soon after, we discovered that he belonged to a mafia of 'emergency locksmiths' operating through a call centre in Essen. Craftsmen in Germany are usually highly regarded, particularly if they're a *Meister* in their metier. We'd automatically assumed that the locksmith was charging the standard rate. But not this one. Foolishly, we'd paid on the spot by credit card swipe. These extortioners typically have criminal records, and yet recouping the money in such circumstances is like getting blood from a stone. Glancing around at my snowy-head neighbours, I see yet more shoulders move up and down as they chuckle at the joke. Some are exchanging knowing nods too. It looks like I'm not the only one around here who's fallen foul of the locksmith scam.

Just then my friend Horst arrives with his girlfriend, Sabine. It's good to see Horst again. We met through a local *Tauschbörse*, an exchange platform. Horst was offering to do odd jobs around the home, I was rendering my expertise as a translator. We didn't swap services but we did enjoy a good natter over a *Mass* or more. Looking for a family hairdresser, Bea and I found one on the 'platform', and traded a few jobs in return for some very acceptable haircuts. Shortly afterwards, however, quite a few of us quit the 'club'.

Germans are keen and quick to share. Probably because they regard this as a way of reducing consumerism and ultimately good for the planet. But they draw the line when it comes to lending two specific things – their vehicles and their wives.

Fortunately, my spouse was safe. It was my Mitsubishi Space Star which a fellow member couldn't wait to get his hands on. The first time Wolfgang requested the car I was willing to help out; he wanted to take his family to a wedding somewhere they couldn't reach by public transport. But I put my foot down when, the following Sunday, he requested my car for a family picnic. He even had the audacity to ask if I'd include both him and his wife on my driving insurance policy. End of exchange. Actually, I don't think the guy was offering anything in exchange at all.

It's nice to stay in touch with others though, and I often see Horst ambling around town. As Schmankerl-Musi strike up again, I turn to him and quip: '*Des Liad hom mia scho kabd*' – we've already had that song. Horst looks at me baffled for a second or two. As if I've posed a brain teaser. Then, getting the joke, he smiles and gently prods me in the ribs. But it's true, many of these German drinking songs sound identical. As if they're all a variation of just two or three tunes.

After the show Horst takes me back stage to meet his musician friends. One, a pretty girl called Karoline, has just given the most magnificent of solo renditions on the harp. As I admire her beautifully crafted instrument, she asks:

'*Du bisd doch Englanda, gell?*'

How can she tell I'm English? All I've said is '*Grüss Di.*' The only thing that gives me away are the ill-fitting lederhose. She's pointing to my bare knees and grinning.

Karoline then poses that question which Bavarians typically ask when encountering anyone with a foreign accent:

'*Wia kimmsd noch Bayern?*'

Note the question. It's more a matter of what they *don't* want to know.

Not 'Where are you from?'

Not 'How long have you lived here?'

All they're asking is what the heck you're doing here. In Bavaria, of all places.

What a no brainer.

Seriously, why *not* Bavaria? After all, according to state broadcaster B24, in 2018 over 18,000 Brits were naturalised in Bavaria alone. That's more than a sixth of Brits in the whole of Germany. The state offers employment in abundance – and generous benefits if you lose your job. Germans typically work fewer hours than in the UK and enjoy some of the longest paid holidays in the world. Yet they still manage to produce more. Their health and social care system is exemplary. And as for *Bier*....

Karoline's still waiting for me to respond.

Yes, what did bring me here? I'm tempted to grin and give a literal reply: a plane, of course. But Bavarians often draw a blank when you pretend to take them literally. They don't spot the joke. They're expecting you to say you're here either because of work or *'da liab weng.'* Most expat males tend to wash up in Bavaria because of a woman.

Raising my glass, I smile and say *'da Bier weng.'*

Step Three:

Recycle and Retune

*Germany currently leads the world in
recycling 68% of municipal solid waste.
It also leads the world in annual consumption
of two billion coffee capsules.*

Not a single one is recyclable

Bravo, you've saved 13 trees

When it comes to being green, Germany's track record seems second to none. Just think of all the trouble they go to separating their waste into so many different colour-coded wheelie bins. So, when the VW diesel emissions scandal rocks the world in 2015, we're all gobsmacked. How could a nation of tree huggers pull off such an impudent stunt?

Although VW initially try to hush-hush the affair, chief executive Oliver Schmidt is eventually incarcerated for conspiracy to defraud the US government and his role in 'Dieselgate'. Turning to my blog, I write: 'We're sold this idea – by industry and media alike – that Germany is world beater in clean, environmentally friendly technology and sets standards for the rest to follow. Suddenly it turns out that America has much stricter environment laws – and they're smarter at catching cheats too.'

Flashback to 2008. I'm teaching 'Ethics' to Business Studies students as part of their compulsory English course. The big news story of the day: the Siemens scandal. The telecommunications company paid million-euro bribes to 'friendly' officials in Nigeria, Russia and Libya – in return for lucrative contracts. Little did we know back then that Volkswagen was cheating customers, dealers and environmental authorities on a far grander scale.

Standing outside my local VW dealer, I almost feel like going in and crying out 'You frauds!' Naturally I don't. This is Germany. Still, the whole episode has got me thinking about wider environmental issues here. Does Germany's image as recycling *Weltmeister* still hold water, I wonder?

Where better to find out than at the local *Recyclinghof*. With a turnover of around €50 billion, waste management is serious business in Germany. And so too is waste theft, it seems. *'Schauen Sie mal'* – see over there – says site supervisor, Helmut Gschlössl, pointing to a vandalised container in the corner. Thieves have struck again. They've made off with PCs and heaps of other electrical goods. I begin to wonder whether this is indeed a recycling yard and not some branch of Media Markt.

While Britain landfills around 75 per cent of its waste, Germany sends a hefty 68% to the recyclers; each individual collecting an average 322 kilos of recyclables per year. Less than one per cent of the remaining refuse ends up as landfill. Rubbish separation is not compulsory. You could save yourself both time and trouble by bunging everything into just one bin. Some expats probably do. Most Germans, however, baulk at the idea. Love of *Ordnung* – a combination of orderliness, tidiness and properness – goes hand in glove with the rationale of sticking to rules come what may. Surveys show 90 per cent of *Bundesbürgers* relish sorting their household waste. They treat it as a national pastime.

From my experience of sidestepping neatly-piled bright yellow bags in our cul-de-sac, none of this surprises me. One of my colleagues even takes time off work solely to sort and prepare rubbish for designated collection days.

Ever since 1991, when a recycling company called Duales System Deutschland was set up, Germans have meticulously sorted their rubbish into four colour-coded bins. Brown is *Bio*, or organic, yellow is for plastics, blue's for paper and grey for everything else that will squeeze into the bin. That leaves just *Sperrmüll*. Interestingly, very little of this 'bulky waste' actually ends up at the dump, since many second-hand dealers tour the neighbourhood, claiming anything of commercial interest. Unlike pinching from the recycling yard, this practice is perfectly legal.

I washed up in Germany in 1998 with very little idea about recycling. When my hairdryer broke, for instance, I simply bunged it in the bin. I soon learnt a lesson from my German neighbours – not *all* waste is junk. Electrical items go to the recyclers, not into 'waste' junk, stupid.

Unwittingly, I'd committed my first *Umweltsünde*, or environmental offence. Note how the word 'offence' in German is 'sin'. That's very telling of how seriously Germans take rule flouters. I was a sinner. From now on, my neighbours – one of whom had reported me to the *Polizei* – would be watching me with eyes like a hawk.

'Environmental sins' are actually so rare in Germany

that they make local headlines. While my own little *faux pas* didn't quite attract media coverage, more serious cases, such as fly-tipping, certainly do.

An almost full-page spread in our local *Hallertauer Zeitung* describes how an observant *Jäger* recently spotted a 'sinner' tipping bags of building rubble in his forest. The hunter noted the perpetrator's vehicle and filed charges to the police. There are several pictures of the illegally dumped rubbish shot from various angles. On one photo the hunter can even be seen posing alongside with his .357-caliber air rifle.

I recently called on our Munich friends, Anna and Tom, who gave me a proud tour of their cellar, piled high with colour-coded bins. Plastered all over the cellar wall are dozens of charts; dates of each collection are highlighted with virtually every colour of the rainbow. Half a dozen or so dates are marked up for each month and Anna can effortlessly recite every one off by heart. What strikes me even more than Anna's photographic memory is the sheer detail and precision of her recycling programme. Listening to her describe the whole system blow by blow feels a bit like being briefed by government intelligence on state contingency plans for surviving nuclear fallout. I'm rather overwhelmed by it all, quite frankly.

No wonder Anna and Tom have it so well sorted, literally. The recycling ethic is inculcated from earliest age in Germany. At kindergarten, toddlers barely out of nappies receive instructions on how to sort waste into four categories. They are able to recognise these waste colour codes even before they've drawn their first ever rainbow. Recycling later on broadens into a cross-curricular topic, particularly in English lessons. I've lost count of the number of classes I've delivered on global warming, the dangers of deforestation and the drive towards sustainability. And – this really amazes me – pupils never seem to grow tired of the topic. They soak it up like sponges.

Having not missed a single collection date and remembered to take waste poisons and toxic liquids to the local fire station for collection every fourth Friday, there's only one more thing to do – head down to the local *Trödelmarkt* and sell your very last piece of unwanted junk.

I've good reason to be proud of my own efforts on the green front. Hanging on my study room wall is a framed certificate. Sent to me by my 'green' electricity company 'naturstrom', it begins:

'Herzlichen Glückwunsch Herr Howe!'

The utility company is congratulating me on my having bought 3,031 kWh of natural electricity from 100% renewable energies. The document states that this will save the environment 1,212 g of atomic waste and 1,443 tons of CO_2. It's the equivalent of saving 13 trees. I have absolutely no idea how they worked that one out. Are we talking about big or small trees? Christmas trees even? I don't think anyone really knows. And I'd certainly rather not know how many trees they sacrificed to produce these pretty certificates.

Still, the mere fact that 'naturstrom' went to all that trouble of issuing me with this certificate speaks volumes on how much German businesses value a clean environment. And how good they are at persuading customers to contribute to the noble cause by purchasing from them and not their rivals.

I've just been browsing naturstrom's website. I can feel quite proud of my 13 trees. Their average customer is saving merely 6.21 a year.

'Perhaps we can all learn a thing or two from the Germans,' I conclude in my latest dispatch to *The Telegraph*. Yet shortly after filing the report I learn from the Federal Environment Agency that the highly acclaimed 68% recycle quota merely refers to the amount of waste delivered at recycling and composting plants. The total amount actually recycled is closer to just 20%. The rest is simply incinerated. Worse still – jaw-dropping for a nation that's usually so particular and precise about everything – roughly 40-60% of recyclables are incorrectly sorted before collection. It's what the industry labels *Fehlwürfe*, or 'misthrows': plastics aimed at the 'yellow' bin, yet landing in 'grey' instead.

The German eye, celebrated for its *Gründlichkeit*, or precision, is not all it's cracked out to be.

One of the most practical things about German homes is that they usually come with a cellar. They're a God-send, when it comes to somewhere to store all your recyclables for the once-a-month collection. As well as for depositing everything you no longer need but just haven't the heart to part with. A sort of halfway house between Ikea shelf and rubbish bin. A dumping ground for procrastinators and the undecided. Maybe also for expat teachers who simply can't part with their old school stuff.

Clearing out my own cellar the other day, I stumble across a battered bag. Smelling a furry sort of mildew growing out of the zipper, I almost gag. And yet I'm loathed to bung it in the bin with the rest of the junk.

The holdall had schlepped piles of teaching aids all over Europe. Flying back from the UK, I always packed my bag beyond bursting point. The bulk largely consisted of stockpiled radio and TV recordings, newspapers, magazines and posters. Just about anything I could lay my hands on to add a hint of quintessential 'Very British' to my lessons.

I was ferrying far too much around even before baggage restrictions kicked in. This led to countless close shaves with check-in staff at Bristol International Airport. It was always something like 'Well sir, you *could* just be over our limit,' and 'We *would* normally have to charge you.' I loved how they used all these conditional expressions because the underlying message was that while rules were rules, they were willing to turn a blind eye. Seeing the words 'Cash-strapped Teacher' written all over my forehead, they probably took pity on me. Bless them. I once had to redistribute diverse tapes and videos all over my body. I might even have had one stuck down a trouser leg. But never once did I have to pay a single penny on excess baggage.

Delving into the bag, I pull out a pair of handcuffs. I'm extremely reluctant to bin them. Particularly after enduring all those embarrassing questions at baggage screening. On one occasion, I almost ended up on a national register of offenders. The holdall had been whisked away for closer examination and I was led out of security control into a behind-the-scenes interrogation cubicle. To be honest, I was more fearful about having the cuffs confiscated than missing my flight back to Germany.

After several hushed conversations on his mobile, the bemused official turned to me and said 'We've decided not to prosecute, sir. You're free to go.' Handing back the cuffs in a sealed transparent bag, he added with a wink of the eye, 'Enjoy your teaching aid!'

I managed to make it to the boarding gate just in the nick of time.

Ever since, I've used the schackles again and again in class. Younger pupils particularly like clamping each other in irons.

But the cuffs' impact on adults should not be underestimated either. Most recently I used them at a workshop for teachers. The topic was how to make roleplay more challenging for pupils. It was called *Wos scho wieda a Roienschbui?!?* I figured giving it a Bavarian title would add a bit of novelty value.

And how.

When there were no more free seats in the classroom at the Pädagogisches Institut in Munich we had to haul in extra furniture from next door. *'A Disch und no via Stühle!'* I could hear the organiser calling to her assistant as I paced the corridor. With another table and four more chairs finally in place, I proceeded to make my grand entrance. And it certainly was grand. But not exactly conventional. Tugging a pair of tights over my head, I burst in brandishing a toy pistol, hollering 'Hands up! Keep still everyone, this is a hold up!' The teaching colleagues, who were just quietly settling into their seats, looked on aghast as I staged a mock bank robbery before attempting to pull the ultimate punch in audience participation – I made them empty their pockets of all valuables. Huffing and puffing under the weight of my bulging booty bag, I then beat a hasty retreat. But not before binding and gagging two participants and abandoning them in a corner as they struggled to undo my tricky constrictor knots. To add further authenticity to the *Spiel*, I had the *Direktor* of the Institute turn up, faking horror and confusion at the ensuing chaos. He duly encouraged the participants to write a short description (in English, naturally) of the offender, before whipping out his smart phone and pretending to call the police.

As my pièce de résistance, I re-entered the room, posing as a detective investigating the incident for Interpol:

'Can someone please describe the criminal to me?'

As participants rose to leave at the end of the session, I overheard one of them say '*Wos hod des fia oan Zweck?*'

Rough translation: What was the purpose of all *that*?

Boy, do Germans just love asking that question. When it comes to questioning purpose, German boasts an almost endless array of expressions. For 'why' alone, there are at least four options:

Wieso? Weswegen? Wozu? Weshalb?

And, ever increasingly, the very short and straight to the point *Grund?*

'Reason?!'

Germans clearly have a knack of making simple questions sound like matter of life and death. Perhaps it is too. No wonder two of their most popular adjectives are so frequently compounded – *lebenswichtig*, as important as life, and *todernst*, as serious as death (or *bierernst* – as serious as beer – in Bavaria).

They use these words with abandon – almost as frequently as Americans bandy around the expression 'enjoy!' It's always struck me as strange that you'll seldom find a single one in any 'useful' phrase book of German for foreigners. Probably because only Germans are expected to use them.

I once asked a Bavarian why they are so fond of the expression *'Wos hod des fia oan Zweck?'*

'Tim,' he replied, 'here in Germany we are *very* practical. Everything in life has a sense of purpose, a reason. And we need to know the reason. The *Begründung*, you know.' He threw in this German word as if talking about something sacrosanct. The *Begründung* as the holy cow of logic. As if no further justification or clarification were required. *Fait accompli.* Registering the blank look on my face, he expounded 'Because with no sense of purpose there is no reason to do something. And so we let it be.'

He spoke in a syrupy voice; the soft tone sort adopted by an elderly gentleman whose youngest grandson has just enquired about the meaning of life. I couldn't help smiling and thinking how awfully sweet.

Back to the roleplay training. In their feedback at the end of the day, some teachers said they *quite* liked my activities but weren't actually expecting to have to do any roleplay themselves. How very bizarre. This was, after all, advertised as a 'Hands-on Workshop'. Were they expecting to keep their hands in their pockets?

Yes, *Wos hod des fia oan Zweck*? Sometimes I feel like asking that question of the Germans too. Particularly when it comes to *Fasching*, the time of year when they go absolutely bananas.

Carnival is just a week away. But first I have to attend an audition.

'Achtung, you're eight octaves too low'

'*Oh guad!*' whoops Vroni in thick dialect, '*mia san ganz schee vui Weiber!*'

Unsure what she's saying, I flash a quizzing glance at Nicole, who's just introduced us both. 'She's pleased you've come,' Nicole translates, adding 'most of the group are women.'

Beaming from ear to ear, like she's just been reunited with a long-lost twin, Vroni really is pleased to see me. Save for one or two men skulking in the shadow of the stage, everyone here is female.

Vroni is director of The Wolperdinger Singers, 'Wolpis' for short, a local a-capella group. I saw their concert in a neighbouring village last weekend and enjoyed it so much that I'm attending Wednesday night practice. Germans take their singing societies dead seriously. There are over 10,000 choral societies in Germany, and Munich alone boasts over 200 such choirs. These include special line-ups for policemen, postmen, sailors and even a group by the name of Bad Mothers.

Cutting straight to the chase, Vroni questions:

'*San Sie soprano, tenoa oido bass?*'

Am I soprano, tenor or bass?

Ha, good question.

'*Tja,*' I blub, '*irgendwo in da Mitte...?*'

Somewhere in the middle.

If this were an audition for a TV talent show, the jury would already be gunning me down. The flunker buzzer would whir and I'd be whisked away through a darkened exit. But Vroni doesn't seem at all alarmed that I can't even determine my own voice range. Brushing all doubts aside, she ushers me between soprano Claudia and tenor Markus. And then presents me to the rest of the fifty-strong group, who respond with a warm round of applause. They haven't heard me sing yet, of course.

We warm up with some voice-tuning exercises. Vroni leads with '*ooooh!*' '*aaaaah!*' and '*jaaa!*', which we have to repeat, holding our voices fever-pitch high, as long as possible. I soon start to enjoy it, even though it feels like a throwback to schooldays. A mixture of full-school assembly and tough P.E. tuition. Sport à la a-capella. But the only things moving here are vocal cords. Next up, we're into the Udo Jürgens classic 'Aber bitte mit Sahne' – a celebration of the Germans' love affair with everything sweet served with a blob of whipped cream. Suddenly I feel Markus prodding me gently in the ribs. 'You're eight octaves too low,' he whispers. To be honest, I'm actually relieved. I rather feared I'd gone in the opposite direction – falsetto style, Bee Gees and Co.

Suddenly our choir mistress halts us in full flow: '*Stopp!*'

Apparently one of the tenors is striking all the wrong notes. Vroni's not looking at anyone directly, but it's as plain as day who's out of key. I don't dare look up or around, fearing I'll see everyone staring at me. I almost feel like curling up in fetal position, hugging my knees and whimpering.

The mortifying moment eventually passes and after a while I finally start to hit my stride. Until suddenly, during a Scandinavian song with the chorus *Seidamadei doo dooo*, it's Claudia's turn to prod me. '*A doo is zua lang,*' one *doo* is too long, she giggles. Which immediately sets me off giggling too. A few moments later Vroni calls us all to order once again, announcing we're finished for the night. I heave a huge sigh of relief. It's been fun but I don't think I could have carried on with that too much longer.

Afterwards there's nibbles ('finger food' for Germans) and *Sekt,* or sparkling wine — a couple members are celebrating birthdays. I'm just standing at a high table, chatting to my new colleagues when, all of a sudden, several of them burst into song. It must be a surprise performance for the birthday children. But they're singing something a little more demanding than 'Happy Birthday to you'. And not everybody's singing either. Only the top tenors, actually. It feels like I'm part of a flashmob everyone's party to except for me. A bit like Mr Bean in the scene where he's in church singing with no hymn book, and can only join in one and a half words – *Hallelujah, lel-ujah!* I don't even manage that. Totally out of my depth, I gently slide sideways and edge backwards until out of sight.

And then I do a runner.

Gasping for breath outside the building, I begin to

wonder whether this is something I can seriously sustain week after week. The previous day I'd browsed the Wolperdingers' website; they perform concerts almost every month throughout Bavaria and beyond. Was I up to that? More to the point, were they up for me? I'd hit all the wrong notes, flunked flashmob and made an inglorious exit. The audition had been an unmitigated disaster.

As we drive home, however, Nicole encourages me to join them all at the next meet-up:

'It's on Shrove Tuesday in Abensberg. We're marching in the *Faschingsparade* and stopping at every pub along the way. You'll love it.'

The pub crawl certainly sounds fun. But what clinches it is when Nicole assures me I won't have to sing this time. Not one single note. High or low.

'Perfect,' I answer, 'I'll be there.'

Chaos and 'Ordnung'

Fifty individuals all identically dressed in black silk pants and red tunic tops. Surely it can't be too hard to spot such a conspicuous bunch of revellers in a town of just 13,000 inhabitants? We've even synchronised watches and fixed a precise meeting place, time and day. This is Germany – nothing's left to chance. After scouring every nook and cranny in Abensberg, however, there's no sign of them anywhere.

I might have guessed. *Faschingsdienstag* is a byword for 'state of exception'. Anything goes and nothing is normal today. Nor had it been at all normal the day before. As is tradition on *Rosenmontag*, 'wild' women had stormed the town hall, taken the *Bürgermeister* hostage and proceeded to run through the streets kissing any man that took their fancy. And then, just to amuse the bystanders, they'd snipped off the scarves of any other innocent victims who happened to cross their path.

Today the wild girls' gang seems to have been joined on the streets by the entire population of Abensberg. The chaos is compounded by revellers from my own town. Roughly half the population of Moaburg, some 14,000 souls, have descended on Abensberg too. After painting their own town red only yesterday, it looks like my fellow burghers are hungry for a whole lot more.

The short journey from Moaburg to Abensberg takes ages. Tildy and I get stuck in a horrendously long traffic jam. Swallowing us up just outside our home town, it spits us out at an enormous carpark on the outskirts of Abensberg. We then run around the *Stadtmitte* like distraught sheep, trying to track down fifty silk-panted singers.

In a desperate bid to disguise myself as best (and cheaply) as I can, I go as a swash-buckling pirate. Tildy's dressed as Princess Elsa of Arendelle.

Clearly, revellers haven't exactly gone overboard with original costumes. The streets are awash with buccaneers and royalty-fiving each other. We're all sporting identical outfits snapped up from last week's special offer at Aldi.

We finally discover my a-capella colleagues fine-tuning their vocal cords and ready to break into song in *Franz Schwarz*, the town's largest bakery. Fortunately, it's a big store. The fifty-strong group just about all fit between window display and counter. After we've sung our hearts out for five minutes Frau Schwarz doles out 50 or more *Krapfen*, delicious sticky jam donuts typically eaten at *Fasching*. It turns out the singers had already called in at half a dozen bakeries earlier that afternoon and at least as many pubs too. Everywhere they went, they'd been treated to free food and alcoholic sustenance. I think it's fair to say that by this point not only were their bellies bursting full but they were pretty inebriated too.

What a sight – 52 a-capella singers in comic costumes blocking the entrance to a bakery, all stuffing themselves with iced donuts. And all nicely documented by as many smartphones. Before you could say the word *Fasching* those pictures would be plastered all over Pinterest.

Where does this whole *Fasching* thing – also known as 'Fifth Season' – come from? The word *Fasching* dates back to the 13th century and is derived from the old Germanic word *vaschanc* or *vaschang* – the last serving of alcoholic beverages before Lent.

That's funny. I've been searching for *Fasching* on Wikipedia, which makes no mention of gustatory sacrifice. The online encyclopedia defines *Fasching* as 'a public celebration and/or parade combining some elements of circus, masks, and public street party.' Describing how people wear masks and costumes on many occasions, it concludes 'these joyous activities, allow them to lose their everyday individuality and experience a heightened sense of social unit.'

Ha, love that bit about 'heightened sense of social unity.' A euphemism, no doubt, for a raised level of alcohol in the blood. Truth told, for several weeks a year Germans abandon all sense of sobriety and, to put it bluntly, get thoroughly washed up and wasted. Considering the antics of some burghers, what we've witnessed with the Wolperdinger Singers on their booze-fuelled crawl through Abensberg is very small schnitzel.

Historically, *Fasching* was a special time when ordinary citizens could put on masks and make fun of the nobles without fear of reprisal. And this year the outfits, which some revellers started donning as early as mid-November, seem wilder than ever. But, as they clamber out of their sweat-filled cow or donkey costumes at the end of today's parade, I suspect most Bavarians are secretly elated it's all over. Mad-cap capers out of the way, they can finally return to the *Ordnung* which characterises their lives for so much of the rest of the year.

So much for hijinks in the 'fifth season'. To survive the relative 'normality' of the rest of the year, there are just a handful of short phrases you need to know:

Das muss sein – that must be so.

Das darf nicht sein – that isn't allowed.

Ordnung muß sein. Order must be. Literally.

And – having unreservedly obeyed all rules – *und das ist gut so.*

You'll hear these expressions all the time here. Germans somehow intuitively know what they must and must not do. Saying that something 'must be' or 'isn't allowed to be' justifies everything. No further explanation is required.

Germans not only keep a tight rein on themselves – they're also quick to reprimand others. And, as I already discovered by binning my broken hairdryer, it's from disciplining each other on waste disposal that they seem to derive greatest pleasure. What is it about waste management that excites Germans so much? After two whole decades living cheek by jowl with the Germans, I'm still no wiser.

Interestingly, when neighbours chastise each other, whatever the issue, they seldom do so face to face. Usually anonymous, gentle reminders are typically left as written notes. I've had neighbours plaster these all over my different coloured container bins. I'd often come home from work to find a trail of post-its all up the garden path.

Funniest note I ever received was after parking my Space Star in a terrible hurry. Skew-whiff and half hanging over the kerb, it was nonetheless no great obstacle to either traffic or pedestrians. I came back to find some smart so-and-so had stuck a memo on the windscreen, saying something like 'If you have sex as badly as you park, you'll end up with a stiff neck too.' Disposing of the note in the nearest recycling bin, I couldn't help thinking what a charming way Germans have of connecting two totally unrelated activities.

Orderliness and civil obedience (and public chastising when rules are disregarded) go hand in glove in Germany. And yet, for all their civil spit and polish, when it comes to health, Germans appear prone to sicknesses only sufferable in Germany. Take the classic *Kreislaufstörung*, for example. Common sense says this is just a euphemism for 'to feel woozy'. A slight discomfort at most. Yet dictionaries typically translate it as *'functional circulatory disruption or collapse'*. That sounds like the sort of chaos you might cause by entering a roundabout in the wrong lane. Clinically, it evokes images of being hooked up to a life support system with just a 50-50 chance of survival.

Yet Germans will announce they've been struck by *Kreislaufstörung* without batting an eyelid. This regularly happened at the truck translation department where I was employed in Munich. Typical Monday morning German-English dialogue as I pass my workmate in the corridor:

'Hey Ulli, where's Klaus?
'Oh, der hat 'Kreislaufstörung.'
Heavens, Klaus has collapsed.
Is he in intensive care?
Then the cent drops. It's *only* that again.
'Ach soooo, alles klar.'
All clear, thank goodness.

As sure as eggs is eggs, Klaus was back in the office the very next day, swaggering about how he'd upset his bloodstream by climbing out of the shower too hastily. Bottom line: his life hadn't been on the line.

Germans clearly have a fixation with anything that might remotely trigger circulatory problems. These can be the most mundane of activities, from tying their neck scarves too tightly to simply waking up before hearing the alarm clock.

Who and what exactly is fuelling this fixation? German lifestyle magazines definitely shoulder some of the blame. A recent edition of 'Cosmopolitan', for example, offers a full double spread of bona fide tips. Half is devoted to a 'Secret Orgasm Map' which offers creative suggestions on how to prolong a *Lustpunkt*, while the opposite page hands out *'Top Tipps'* on boosting the peripheral circulatory system. Presumably the two activities are closely connected. One tip suggests readers stimulate their system by taking a hot/cold shower sequence at regular intervals, before rounding off the day by beating their backs vigorously with a birch-wood stick.

Altogether, *Kreislaufstörung* seems a perfectly acceptable excuse for throwing a sickie and spending all day pampering yourself. Especially as the German public health insurance system generously reimburses any circulatory-incurred expenses. Sickie-throwing Germans gulp in horror when they hear how faking illness in Britain can get you fired.

It works both ways, naturally. Things that are merely frowned upon in some countries are strictly forbidden in Germany. Such as crossing the road on foot at the red light, or *Ampelmännchen*, even when you're in the middle of nowhere. I have to confess doing this myself when no cars are around. This inevitably provokes Germans into tut-tutting and reminding me what a bad example I am to kids. Perhaps I am. But at least I don't skip work with *Kreislaufstörung*.

Given their love affair with obeying rules, coupled with a propensity to coerce others into complying too, it's almost as if Germans are hardwired to behave properly. No matter how trifle the situation. Take, for example, the 'divider'. It's what separates one shopper's items from the next at the supermarket checkout. This totally baffles me. I mean, who decides who puts this 'Next Customer Please' thing up between each other's shopping? Is it the customer in front or behind? It always seems hit and miss as to who does it first. And if someone else puts it up first, should you thank them or not? Then comes the embarrassment of failing to place the object first, and pretending not to have seen it. I envy Germans who keep their cool in face of such a dilemma. They innately know when and where to place the 'divider'.

When safely in place – German legislation, not the divider thing – is formidable. Law making in this country is most creative when it comes to curtailing citizens' fondness for frolicking around in fancy dress. If there's one thing I've learnt from the recent *Fasching* festivities, it's this: misbehaving yourself at carnival is par for the course. Yet behave inappropriately any other time of the year and you pay big time. The punishment for turning up at a meeting or demonstration in a mask or false nose, for instance, is a hefty fine or 12 months imprisonment. That's the so-called *Vermummungsgesetz*. It pays to know and respect rules like this.

But not even the most hardwired Germans can possibly know every single rule in the statute book. When I moved into my first flat near Dachau, I put up a satellite dish to watch the BBC. I was just tuning into News at Six when my landlady burst in. '*Es ist verboten*', she announced, demanding I take the dish down. I politely reminded her of the German Civil Code, which charters the right of every foreigner in Germany to watch television in their own language. '*Ach so. Alles in Ordnung*,' she replied. For a while everything remained 'in order'.

Until the day we tried planting a small shrub in the

garden – without permission. That really is *verboten*.

Law-loving Germans are, by nature, also risk-avoidance Germans. They leave absolutely nothing to chance. As I discovered recently, when I happened to peep over the garden fence. My *Nachbar*, Herr Schluddelmeier, was going around shaking tree branches *before* raking up the leaves. Apparently, it's *verboten* to let leaves on lawns pile up any higher than five inches. Presumably Herr Schluddelmeier had no wish to repeat the whole exercise each time the wind whooshed.

À propos nature, while Germans love their trees and forests, they appear engaged in a permanent battle to tame them. The other day I happened to pass my other neighbour, Frau Schnitzlbaumer. She was sweeping leaves from her section of the pavement. Nothing unnormal about that, of course. But it's what she said as we proceeded to greet each other that made me smile:

's is a Katastrophe.'

The semi-traumatised look on Frau Schnitzlbaumer's face as she gazed up at the offending tree suggested it really might be a catastrophe.

It seemed the nursery which sold her the vegetation had failed to warn her it would produce quite so much foliage. Anxious to either keep the rogue leaves at bay or possibly even beat them into submission, she'd been down on hands and knees and scrubbed her stretch of sidewalk spotless. So squeaky clean that you could probably eat your supper off it.

Well, as they say in Bavaria, *'Oadnung mua sei.'*

Order must be.

Same Procedure every Year

Germans take enormous pride in being straight forward and logical. Yet much of their lingo is anything but. Contradictions abound. Especially when it comes to compound words: *Handschuh* – shoe for your hand? No, glove. Or *Kummerspeck* – grief bacon, surely? No, actually it's the flab gained through eating comfort food. Only Germans could have a neat little word for such a condition. Not to forget the highly visual *Arschgeige* (literally 'arse violin').

My personal favourite is an oxymoron to boot: *Wahlpflichtfach*. I teach quite a lot of these 'optional-compulsory' subjects. But while English is technically optional, students have no option. They must do it. International Business Studies or Tourism Management, for instance, typically include such a foreign-language component.

Luckily, students generally appreciate that English skills will benefit them in their chosen career and are willing to work at the subject. They gracefully grin and bear it – '*guade meane zum bösn schbui*', as Bavarians jovially say. Ironically, teachers without a permanent contract have to grin and bear it too. A whole army of freelance teachers, myself included, have no guarantee that their contracts will be extended from one semester to the next. If a college is cash-strapped, the first to suffer are always *Lehrbeauftragte*, or assistant lecturers. Sometimes this means hello and goodbye within just three or four months.

Same procedure *every* year.

Following a series of such jobs, I'm offered a fixed two-year position at a leading Catholic university. I seem to be magnetically attracted towards Bavarian church-funded colleges. I end up spending two years at this one.

One of my first duties in Ingolstadt is to help a colleague invigilate a 'test'. We've just instructed a fresh batch of first-year Business Studies students to spend 90 minutes writing an essay entitled 'My career to date and my plans for the future'. 'It's to give us an idea of your academic writing level,' The Professor announces. He then mumbles something about grabbing a coffee and disappears for an hour or so, leaving me alone to 'test' the writing level of some 100 students. Afterwards we collect in the scripts and wait till everyone leaves the lecture theatre. Having stacked the papers into a neat and tidy pile, The Professor takes them, holds them above the waste rubbish basket for one split second and then lets them drop into the bin with a theatrical thud. My jaw drops in disbelief. The academic hasn't given the work one single cursory glance.

'Err, ahm, aren't we supposed to be correcting and grading these essays?'

'*Ach wos!*'

He dismisses the idea as if I'd just suggested we slip off secretly to the store room and snort illegal substances together. With a flippant chuckle he adds 'I never bother reading them anyway, ha!'

What troubles me about this remark isn't that we've wasted the students' time, making them write an essay all for nothing.

No, something far worse.

It's that the waste paper hasn't gone into the recycling bin.

At the strike of noon, my colleague disappears into his office for the rest of the day. Meantime I give my first proper lesson. I'm quite impressed how the students are all sitting there one minute before starting time, pens poised and ready to write.

The students immediately demand a full run-down of what they'll be examined on in the end-of-semester tests, and how points are distributed over each of the four main skill areas. As they sit there, scribbling away, it crosses my mind that I've not even introduced myself. Instead, I spend the first half of the lesson lecturing on examination procedure. I also talk about the importance of attending classes regularly. 'Make sure to get a doctor's certificate if you need to miss more than two classes' I tell them. This prompts one student to announce that she can only attend half the course as she's *becoming* a baby. When I flash her a surprised look, she corrects herself: 'Sorry, I mean I'm *getting* a baby'. 'Oh', I reply, playing along, 'are you adopting, buying it online?'

Germans typically mix up *get* and *become* (which sounds like 'bekommen'– to get). They're probably further confused by the way the two words often mean the same thing in English – take for example 'get/become rich' – which Germans translate with 'werden'. But, as we laugh about this student's blooper, it strikes me how arbitrary language can be on top of all this. I wonder if saying *having* a baby really makes any more sense than *getting* a baby?

At the end, the students do that very German thing – they knock solemnly on the table. Reminded how the girls in Munich did this too, I ask one of the departing undergrads why they display their appreciation by knocking rather than clapping. His reply: 'We use one hand to acknowledge teachers while the other is busy.' On their smartphone, I imagine. Orderly, disciplined and time-economical. *Deutsch* to a fault.

Having been desperately keen to start bang on time, at the end of the lesson it turns out that the students expect to be released equally *pronto*.

By now it's almost quarter past five and I'm good to go too. I can hear the clackety-clank of what sounds like a cleaning trolley creeping along the corridor. Moving towards the way out, I stop here and there to flick off lights still burning in completely deserted classrooms. It's something I've got into the habit of doing wherever I teach at the end of the day. No doubt to ease my every-growing green conscience. But there's something else bugging me after living ten years in environment-friendly Germany. If I'm to beat the cleaning ladies, I need to act fast. I glance nervously from one end of the passageway to the other, wondering if The Professor is still lurking around. He better not see what I'm about to do.

While the cleaners are busy emptying bins at the other end of the corridor, I enter the examination hall and strike out. Reaching into the waste paper bin, I pull out the pile of students' scripts and quietly transfer them to the recycling bin.

Sunday without Supplements

A typical cold and gritty-grey Sunday in wintery Bavaria. For most burghers it's a day to enjoy relaxing with family and friends. Relaxing nice and quietly, of course. Germans baulk at the mere suggestion of noise on a Sunday. Neighbours frown if you so much as sweep leaves or clip the garden hedge. And you'll get the look of death if you venture to mow the lawn or wash your car with a high-power pressure hose. Strictly speaking, Germans aren't supposed to clean cars at home at all (get caught hosing down your vehicle any day of the week and you risk stumping up a fine of 100,000 euros). Not that Germans remain totally idle on Sundays, of course. They typically spend the day doing noiseless activities such as strolling through the woods and sweating in the sauna. Not to forget hunkering down at home with the whole family over *Kaffeklatsch,* a combination of coffee and chitchat, all served up with giant slabs of mouth-watering gâteau.

As much as I love the family side of Sunday, I also rather enjoy spending part of the day all on my own. Just me, an extra brew out of the cafetière and a British newspaper. Hard copy, of course. There's something rather special about the smell of fresh newsprint from home, particularly when it comes complete with all the supplements.

I'm making that last bit up, of course. While British papers like The Sun and Daily Mail are available in most German cities, they seldom arrive until the day after publication. And *without* the supplements.

Yes, those shrink-wrapped specials such as glossy lifestyle magazines and coupons for free choc-chip cookies from Waitrose & Co. Where did all those goodies go to?

And another thing. Front page, top right of most international editions, it says 'Printed in Europe'. What's the big deal? All British, UK-based newspapers sold in Europe are printed here, surely. Unless they've outsourced the job to another continent.

While Germany is one of the largest magazine markets in Europe (nearly 6,000 journal and magazine titles jostle for space on the newsstands), papers generally play a far less significant role in forming public opinion here than they do in Britain. Sunday newspapers are practically non-existent in *Deutschland*. Germans really do prefer to spend the day relaxing with loved ones (and their must-have *Kaffee und Kuchen*) rather than curled up on the sofa perusing the papers.

As for the dailies, serious ones like the *Süddeutsche* tend to be painstakingly long-winded and hyper-convoluted – you almost need a university degree to follow them. Reports invariably run for several columns before they reach the verb – the big reveal as to what the whole thing is actually about.

Then there are the ridiculously uber-parochial local papers, with headlines as exciting as a Deutsche

Telekom wake-up call from Verona Feldbusch. Recent local news headlines have included *Traktor bleibt im Graben stecken. Feuerwehr rückt aus* (Tractor gets stuck in ditch. Fire brigade to the rescue), *Vandalen zerreissen Wahlplakat* (Vandals tear up election poster) and *Zimmer mit Warmwasseranschluss finden immer mehr Abnehmer* (Rooms connected to supply of warm water increasingly in demand).

Talk about living in a desirable area. But nothing tops this headline grabber:

Gestohlene Brieftasche taucht ohne Inhalte wieder auf.

Stolen wallet pops up minus contents.

Maybe I'm missing something here. But surely, if a stolen wallet actually manages, despite all odds, to find its way back to the owner *with* everything still inside, then isn't that a lot more newsworthy than a wallet which is turned in completely empty?

Back to British newspapers. Whenever we're expecting visitors over from the UK, I always shoot off a mail with a gentle but firm plea – '*Please* bring a paper!' Apart from providing an early-morning sidekick to coffee, British newspapers generate a wealth of teaching material. One of the teacher workshops I offer – *English through the News* – looks at lots of different ways in which you can exploit newspapers in lessons.

Pupils are often surprised when I return from England laden with piles of papers, dishing them around the class rather like you would lollipops at a kid's birthday party ('So, anyone not got one? Oh, *here* you are!') Admittedly, newspapers perhaps aren't the most obvious form of media for capturing hearts and minds of Generation Y. The other day though, just out of interest, I had my class of graduates quiz each other to see how many of them actually read news the 'old-fashioned' way. It turns out that two students read newspapers regularly.

'Woah,' I replied, genuinely impressed. 'And do you both read the *same* one?'

'No,' they answered, 'we both read a *new* one.'

Munich Goes 'grün'

Of the 530,000 foreigners living in Munich, the largest single majority is made up of Turkish men (around 40,500). That's followed by Greeks (ca. 26,000) and Croatians (approx. 24,000).

You need to scroll much further down the list to find the number of Brits – some 6,000 – in the city. Still further to find any reference to the Irish.

And yet, when it comes to celebrating National Day in their adopted home of Munich, this small contingent of expats manages to out-trump us all.

As for the English and St George's Day, perhaps less said the better. Most would probably struggle to pin even an approximate date on the dragon fighter's big day. April? May? June? Whatever. It's unclear why St George's Day isn't a public holiday in Britain. Some say we stopped celebrating when England and Scotland unified at the end of the eighteenth century. That probably tells you more about our relationship with the Scots than anything about our own identity.

17 March, and I've joined in Irish celebrations this year at the behest of the Munich English language teachers' organisation, Melta, of which I've been a member ever since arriving in Munich twenty years ago. Once again, the organisation is joining the mass procession which

marches a mile down Ludwigstrasse, the Bavarian capital's grandest thoroughfare.

Curiously, for as long as I can remember, I've made up all manner of silly excuses for not being able to go. Things like 'Oh dear, nothing green to wear', and 'Wait, do I *really* like Guinness..?'

But this year's different. I'm determined to go. That means registering attendance online the day before and ensuring there's a train connection that will land me in the centre of Munich – *pünktlich* and with plenty *Pufferzeit* to spare before midday march-off. Living out in the Hallertau, the trip needs planning with almost military precision.

The planning pays off and everything goes perfectly. First of all, the train's exactly on time. That's no given or *Selbstverständlichkeit,* when you're reliant on Deutsche Bahn for getting you from A to B. And then the weather. After a week of blustery wind and showers, the sky has suddenly turned navy blue, it's 21 °C and *sonnig.* As we set off down the car-free street, Joan from Limerick hands me a fistful of tokens for free Guinness at the after-parade party. Oh, and a green Leprechaun hat with a giant mock shamrock sticking out of the top. Do the Irish really wear these daft things? Someone's also given me a small flag to wave. It seems we're not just promoting our teachers' organisation but also Ireland's most popular dairy produce.

Although Melta has officially been part of the parade for just eight years, some members can remember when the event began in the mid-90s. According to Randy, back then it was just a small procession and the marchers literally had to plead with police to hold back the traffic and let them pass through (*'Wir wollen hier unbedingt durch!'*). Evoking images of Merkel assuring everybody that the migrant crisis would sort itself out, that characteristically German word *unbedingt* speaks volumes. *Wir schaffen es, unbedingt* – we'll manage, come what may.

No fear of getting waylaid by traffic today. The *Polizei* are practically rolling out the red carpet for us. With a record 1,500 marchers representing 62 clubs and organisations, Munich has become the biggest mainland European celebrator of St Patrick's Day outside Ireland.

Ninety minutes later and the dozen-deep crowd cheer us on as we cross the finishing line at Odeonsplatz. But, as we pause for a breather, I spot one small problem. Only Randy and I are still bearing the banner. What's up? Looking around, I realise all our female colleagues have just disappeared.

It turns out they've headed off to secure ring-side places to see Johnny Logan. For me though, the lure of *Freibier* weighs heavier. I spend the following half hour queueing to claim my free Guinness from the *Deutsch-Irische Freundschaft* tent. By the time I finally catch up my colleagues just around the corner, the legendary Irish crooner's already launching into 'Hold me now'. I quite liked the song first time round. But, thirty years on, the title almost has a ring of desperation about it. More plea than proposal. And judging by the expressions on some of my neighbours' faces, I suspect the audience reaction is 'No Thanks.'

Some of us might remember Logan as a cutesy twenty-something year old, Hugh Grant hair mop flopped over forehead. Today's beer-bellied, snowy-haired Logan looks more like he'd rather jettison his whiter-than-white image, jump onto a Harley Davidson and speed off in a cloud of dust. Savouring another sip of Guinness, I close my eyes and prefer to picture the singer performing in his heyday. I imagine him fighting off hordes of hysterical girls swarming the stage, screaming for hugs. Opening my eyes again, I can't help noticing an elderly man propping himself up against a high round table. Resting his belly on the bar-stand, he drains the remains of his Guinness and groans *'Ja, ja, jaaah!'* It seems odd how, when spoken like that, such a positive word can sound so negative.

Logan, meanwhile, is joined on stage by a full band. Grabbing hold of a guitar, he starts strumming more traditionally Gaelic tunes. Such as 'Irish Soul' and 'The Wild Rover'.

But wait, what's he saying?

'I won the Eurovision Song Contest three times.'

No Johnny. I've just been googling you and you only won it twice. But what's another year, anyway? Maybe you're imagining a hat trick of wins after that triple Guinness you enjoyed earlier on.

Just as well nobody else out there's fact-checking.

How odd though. I could swear 'The Wild Rover' was a dye-in-the-wool Irish song. But it turns out everyone around here knows it as 'An der Nordseeküste' by Klaus and Klaus, the North German duo who topped the charts over thirty years ago dolled up in dappy sailor suits. So here we stand in the shadow of an Italian Renaissance-style palace, swaying to an ageing Irish pop star belting out a Prussian seaman's song. And, to cap it all, the mostly Bavarian audience is absolutely loving it. Only an Irish man could pack a punch like that.

Evening falls, and, bowing to the Emerald Isle, central Munich goes green too. Verdant lights are beamed up and down major landmarks, including the Olympia Tower, Hard Rock Café and Molley Malone's. But, this time, sadly not Allianz Arena. World renowned for its innovative stadium-facade lighting, the stadium is bathed in blood red. Having pandered all weekend to the Irish, Munich city fathers are pulling the plug out when it comes to *König Fußball*. FC Bayern are playing Mainz 05.

I'm no great football fan, but FC Bayern's 6-0 victory feels like a befitting end to an all-round perfect day. And a great warm-up for next year, when Munich is set to stage its 25th Paddy Party.

Step Four:

Hold on like Hell,
Swing and Sing 'Ein Prosit'

'Prosit' is not a German word at all.
It's actually Latin.

Gripes and Groans

Everyone who takes my 'optional-compulsory' English courses has to write a conventional letter. As well as having them display their motivation and suitability in a job application, I get students to complain in writing. Not that they need too much encouraging. Most do so with gusto.

Asked why they so love to complain, Germans will usually respond with a no-brainer look. Better instead to ask *what* they most like to complain about. The answer is usually *'Alles!'*

They're not exaggerating one bit. Remonstrating about almost everything is par for the course in Germany. A formidable *Volkssport*. Despite the country's perpetually booming economy. But hearing Germans gripe, you'd think they were in the grips of a recession. Revealingly, one of their most frequent grievances is that their complaints aren't taken seriously enough. All this is borne out by a recent report in *Spiegel* magazine, which concludes that whining, bitching and moaning ranks as top national pastime in the land of Goethe and Schiller.

There's a lovely column called *'Quengelzone'*, or moan zone, in the newspaper *'Die Zeit'*. Each instalment focusses on a topical 'pet peeve', something that

Germans particularly enjoying whinging about. My favourite describes how Germans willingly pay through the nose for anything labelled *natural* or *ohne Chemie* – without chemicals. And yet they're world champions when it comes to buying chemical *Wunderwaffen* at the pharmacists. And, of course, complaining when said substances don't always do what they're supposed to do. Such as combatting natural nuisances like wrinkles on your face, grey in your hair, and hair where it both should and preferably shouldn't be. Seriously, if you can understand German, Markus Rohwetter's weekly moan 'n' groan column makes for entertaining reading.

When it comes to complaining, no one manages to get quite so fired up as the Germans. And no more so than about their once highly revered, now commonly derided state-owned railway company, Deutsche Bahn.

It's always puzzled me why Germans, renowned the world over for their *Genauigkeit*, or painstaking precision, seem so challenged at making their trains run on time. One of the most commonly heard announcements on railway platforms is *Verspätung durch technische Störungen* – delay due to technical disruption. 'Technical' can mean anything from defective rolling stock to *Streckenbelegung* (rail lines occupied by train ahead) or passengers attempting to yield the ghost by jumping onto the tracks. My favourite delay was one which generated the news headline *Lippenstift auf dem Gleis*. The lipstick wasn't *quite* on the lines, of course. Some prankster had disrupted the Munich-Pfaffenhofen service by running their *Lippenstift* between the train doors and they'd stuck together like superglue. It was no big deal, yet Pfaffenhofeners were complaining about the issue ages after the joker had been served his sentence of community service.

It clearly doesn't take much to rustle a German's feathers. Despite what rose-tinted surveys say. A poll conducted in 2017 by the German Institute for Economic Research, for example, suggests that satisfaction levels are at their highest since German reunification.

So why do Germans get such a kick out of expressing displeasure so loudly and frequently? I put the question to a group of graduates. One student described it as a 'personal survival mechanism – a way of soothing the soul and establishing togetherness'.

Soul soothing? Being at one with each other? It reminded me of Matthias at the kindergarten party, gushing about Bavarians experiencing 'togetherness' through music.

'We complain like you Brits make small talk,' the student explained, 'it fulfils the same purpose.' She told us how she'd been in a restaurant recently with some friends when a customer at a neighbouring table had come over to complain. Pausing a moment, to make sure she had everyone's attention, she continued: 'They said we were laughing too loud.'

We all howled.

Bizarrely, despite the national obsession with complaining, Germans rarely kick up a fuss in restaurants. The other day, for instance, I went out for lunch with some colleagues in Munich. We were served drinks immediately but must have waited a good ¾ of an hour for the first dishes to arrive. When food finally appeared, it came in dribs and drabs. Some of us were already finished by the time others were only just taking their first bite:

'Mind if I start?'

'Oh, please do' (mouth already watering).

'Really?'

'Yes, really. Do go ahead.' (subtext – 'a bite of your salad leaf would tide me over though.')

A lovely picture's been doing the rounds on social media. It's a message on a restaurant table in the U.S.A. left by some dissatisfied customers. Written in ketchup it says 'We waited 30 minutes. No service.' I can't envisage anybody plucking up the courage to do that in Germany. When it comes to no-nonsense complaining about poor service, the Americans seem to have just the right attitude.

All this begs the question why Germans love to complain about some things yet not others. I raise the issue of lousy restaurant service with my friend Petra. Hands on hips, she counters mock theatrically, 'Oh, we *do* complain. Don't say you haven't noticed. For bad service we give no tips.'

Petra describes how Germans thrive in a culture geared to ensuring everything goes right. Germans, she says, are so scared of making mistakes that they'll move heaven and earth to ensure everything goes smoothly. 'We are perfectionists. We have high expectations of everything.' Eyebrows knitted warily, she adds 'but that brings problems.'

Petra's right. It's almost as if Germans go around looking for problems. As if they secretly relish things screwing up for a change. Anything that shows slightest sign of being wonky warrants a *Reklamation* or complaint. Life would be so boring if everything were to run like clockwork, as in Charlie Chaplin's *Modern Times*. Petra evokes this image of the silent movie star, comparing him to the typical Bavarian *Mecka*, or 'moaning minnie'. She describes him as over-fifty male, beer stein clutched between cupped hands and constantly bemoaning the woes of the world. Just like little men such as Chaplin, he too strikes back when life deals him a rough blow.

It's an interesting thought.

Popular comedian Dieter Nuhr nailed it recently when, in his comic end-of-year review, he critically observed:

'It's been another great year for us Germans. Salaries up, prices down, economy's growing. And how do we respond to all this good news? We whinge about the bad weather!'

If Germans sometimes come across as being uber-negative, it might just be that they place more value on structure and stability. Bavarians epitomise this outlook on life, which probably makes them particularly prone to complaining.

Fortunately, they can fall back on a plethora of public platforms from which to air and share all their moans and groans. One of the most popular complaint forums is a regional TV show called *Jetzt red i*. Bavarians commonly use this expression when someone's been waffling too long and they should shut up and give others a chance to speak. The show champions itself as 'open forum fighting for consumer rights.' The impression it gives is that the public-at-large can air their grief about whatever they wish. In rural Bavaria, however, this process invariably boils down to just one thing – farming communities giving politicians a piece of their mind.

To give the show credit, it tries very hard to stand apart from populist-style talk shows à la Jeremy Kyle. *Jetzt red i* yo-yos back and forward between burghers and a panel of bureaucrats linked by satellite – usually fronting some flood-lit landmark, like the Bundestag or the Brandenburg Gate. The politicians are supposed to offer up a sympathetic ear to the electorate's grievances and promise to deal with them.

Ho, if only.

I once watched this programme on satellite at home in England, so presumably you can see it everywhere from Aberdeen to Zagreb. In one edition, which I'll never forget, an irate farmer protested about local male pigs being injected with drugs to put the brakes on their sex drive. Surely all men eating this meat risked losing their 'manhood', didn't they? I can't imagine the politicians took him too seriously but at least it made for entertaining viewing.

There's great excitement in our local community when news spreads that the show is coming to the neighbouring village. Although I can't help detecting a sense of envy-tinted resentment too. Steinbach is a lot smaller than our own village. Yet it boasts something we don't have. The recently built *Hopfenhaus* seats 200 persons. Any more than 70 guests and our *Sportverein* starts having to turn people away. Not wanting to pass up the opportunity, I go along too. I'm intrigued to hear if there are any grievances which my fellow villagers feel the urge to vent on public TV.

Even though I arrive in good time, every second chair is already draped with a coat or handbag reserved German style. It feels a bit like the Beach Towel Brigade are out in force. You know, when you go on holiday and wake up every morning to find that a certain nationality has already bagged the best deck chairs around the pool.

Finally, I manage to grab the last remaining seat – a wobbly bar stool. A policeman straddles an equally rickety high seat alongside. He tells me in excellent English that he's a community liaison officer, responsible for visiting schools and youth clubs.

'Ooh, how very interesting.'

I probably sound like some pre-school mistress lavishing praise on an infant's messy attempt to paint by numbers. But it also reminds me of my own schooldays, when policemen would typically bring their sniffer dog into assembly and show us how they train them to catch criminals.

'Do you take your dog along with you?'

'Actually no, we teach kids how to surf the internet safely.'

'*Ach sooo.*'

The programme lasts only 45 minutes and is over before it really gets going. By the time I've finally attracted the attention of the waitress and ordered an *Apfelschorle,* the closing credits are rolling. Celebrity presenter Tilmann Schöberl is waving and wishing us

'Servus mitanoind, ois Guate!'

He'll be glad it's all over.

Sliding off my stool, I join a fellow villager. Thomas was one of six 'lucky' locals chosen to ask the politicians a question. His own query had almost made me snort. Poking a gentle gibe at Brexit, he'd wanted to know why the Brits always demand – and generally get – extra sausage. And that's not the only thing bugging Thomas. He reveals that the programme's claim to give everyone a fair chance to speak is nothing short of farce: 'We held a village committee meeting last week and chose six questions. Then we drew straws to see who asks them. We had to send our questions to the programme producers, who forwarded them to Brussels.'

So much for spontaneous complaints forum. I suspect most locals in the audience just want to show their face on TV and wave to family and friends at home. Later that evening I post a picture on my blog. It shows me perched on pedestal. Speech bubble: 'Hi mum!'

Jokes apart, I feel fired up enough to complain too. I'd love to respond to the outrageous complaint about Brits demanding 'extra sausages', yet there's absolutely no chance they'd ever let me do so live on air. Most likely I'd be speedily dispatched with *Hausverbot*.

I don't bother checking the local newspaper's headlines the following day, but it's probably something like *Über Hundert Bürger finden den Weg zur Live TV Sendung* (Over 100 citizens flock to live TV show). Yep, that's how exciting it gets in this outpost of Lower Bavaria. Just imagine, however, the alternative headline: *Böser Brite kriegt Talk Show Hausverbot* (Bad Brit Banned from Talk Show).

That really would have made for a nice and spontaneous complaints forum.

When all's said and done though, migrant and expat life's all about adapting and assimilating. And there's an effective way of dealing with gripe-and-groan Germans: simply listen, nod in half-hearted agreement and enjoy another delicious *Bier*.

Fernweh

(or the grass is always greener...)

'Hello again. If you wondered why I've not been jaunting around in my lederhose recently it's because I was time-outing Down Under. When I get down to deciphering all the notes scribbled on the back of old maps there'll hopefully be a book out too....'

That's the latest from *http://howesout.blogspot.com/*. I start this blog when we set off on a three-month sabbatical to New Zealand. It's our last chance to do this before Tildy, just turned five, enters full-time compulsory schooling the following autumn. Travelling from December to March means I hardly need miss any classes at college. It's the time of year students disappear for *Winterferien,* that lovely long break between Christmas and Easter. A perfect opportunity to escape Bavaria at its coldest. The last we see of winter 2014 is the ice-skating rink and atmospheric *Weihnachtsmarkt* at Munich Airport, where we sip mulled wine and crunch on *Ausgezogene* – deep-fried yeast apple pastries, typical of Bavaria and Austria. *Ausgezogen* means pulled out. Which was just how they were traditionally made – pulled out over the housewife's knees to leave the centre thin but the rim thick. They taste absolutely divine. It's heartening to think that when we return mid-March it should be at least 10 °C warmer.

Carrying on, I write: 'I'd love to share my experience with you. I do school and college presentations and am happy to give a slide show and talk if I'm in your area. Contact me!'

Good, I reflect, shutting down my laptop. That should keep the bank manager off my back a bit longer. While living the life Down Under I'd almost forgotten what it feels like to have to work for a living.

During our adventures in the 'Land of the Long White Cloud' I'd been for an informal job interview at a rather nice girls' school in Hastings, North Island. 'Stay in touch,' said the headmistress as I leave, 'we might have something for you.'

That was back in January, with temperatures bobbing around 22°C. It seems strange, almost unreal, being back in snow-bound Bavaria – still in the throes of winter. Hauling a pile of thermal underwear up from the cellar, I begin to daydream. Just imagine spending the Bavarian cold season living and working Down Under, 'popping' back to Europe only to escape 'bleak' midwinter in the Southern hemisphere? You'd never really have to experience coldness *per se* again.

Mulling this over, I blog: 'Not a day goes by without me thinking of New Zealand.' And, dreaming of the laid-back lifestyle, I moot: 'We have long discussions with our bed & breakfast hosts on the pros and cons of life Down Under. David, our expat host in Takaka, South Island, compares living in New Zealand to the temptation of forbidden fruit. 'You taste it, go away a bit but always want to come back for more.'

We'd seen only a very small part of South Island, but we'd already tasted enough 'forbidden fruit' to make all three of us hungry for more.

It feels funny. We'd always regarded our home in deepest rural Bavaria as way out in the sticks – almost a good hour's drive from any decently sized town. Until this trip to New Zealand, of course, where just about everything feels out of the way. Would our stays at the end of countless dust tracks, often hours away from the nearest sizeable settlement, change our view of what it means to 'live out on a limb'? And could we actually see ourselves 'giving it a go' Down Under? A case of eschewing 'Dream Deutschland' in favour of 'Destination Down Under'?

Stepping out of the front door into a frosty mid-March morning I sense this could be a conundrum.

We do of course gradually settle back into the daily routine here in Germany, and life in the northern hemisphere in general. But I don't stop missing sea, sun and sand – in that order.

A few weeks after we return home, I spot the following news headline: 'Living overseas is good for your health, wealth and happiness'. It's the findings of a 'happiness rankings' survey, in which not only New Zealand, but also Germany has come out near the top.

The newly appointed editor on *The Weekly Telegraph* probably spotted this survey too. She's just sent me a long list of questions about whether I think being an expat is good for my own happiness. Maybe she liked my article on expats living the good life Down Under.

But more likely I'm just another number on her list of expat contacts. Under 'cc' I count the names of 42 other expats.

Still, it does the ego good to get these requests. Another is from the BBC Breakfast Show. They're doing a report on the stop-and-search policy currently operated by security forces at the Oktoberfest. The research assistant has left a message on my mobile which I don't pick up immediately. Before returning the call, I rehearse a neat little commentary. I mention our New Zealand friend Holly, currently travelling through Germany, who was also at the Fest. She'd just announced on facebook how she'd snuck out a mug or two. It almost sounded like a confession. Something she might even be willing to turn herself in for. But, when I query whether or not she'd been searched at the gate, she shows little sign of remorse:

'Security frisked me and still didn't spot them!'

Holly clearly holds the bragging rights.

I call the BBC back. Too late – the assistant has already tracked down another dozen or so Brits in Bavaria. It seems there's no shortage of expats willing to offer up soundbites in return for a 30-second fame slot on nationwide television. Still, it's nice to know they'd seen my *Being British in Bavaria* blog and deemed me an expert on all things 'Made in Munich'.

Replying to the *Telegraph* request, I give it to them warts and all: life in Germany isn't all *Bier* and skittles. Monthly advance tax payments and health insurance contributions make a big hole in earnings. Yes, I confirm, there is generally plenty work, but no guarantee it will still be available several months later. I cite my own example of having to renew contracts with colleges every semester. But, I add, the plusses greatly outweigh the minuses. Most noticeably when it comes to climate and lifestyle. Balmy Bavarian summers mean regular meet-ups with friends at shady, beer-rich gardens and free music street festivals. Alpine mountains and lakes, within a two-hour drive of my home, also beckon.

Scrolling down the list, their closing question makes me smile:

'Do you miss anything?'

'Yes,' I reply, 'British humour and TV.'

Brits and Germans have a completely different approach to humour. Especially when work is involved. British humour is all about accepting that life doesn't always go *pico-bello* and being able to laugh about it. Germans, on the other hand, take the view that they already have everything *unter Kontrolle*; that all is *in Ordnung*. And, if not, then steps are being taken to rectify things. 'Nobody is perfect, but we are working on it,' as Baron von Richthofen famously said. Add this nationally-held notion of being (almost) perfect to the concept of *Ordnung* and it becomes crystal clear that it is not humour but hard work that puts the average German ahead of the pack. Henning Wehn, Germany's self-appointed comic ambassador to Britain puts it in a nutshell:

'We like a laugh too. But we laugh *after* work is done.'

And not *instead of*, right?

As for British TV, for a couple years we're able to pick up the Beeb & Co. It's just like home from home. Until one evening when we tune in, looking forward to the latest episode of 'Grand Designs'. Instead of enjoying cutting-edge, open-plan interiors and beautifully landscaped gardens we're confronted by fuzzy nothingness. It's the ultimate wipe out – every single British channel is gone. Britain had simply switched off the satellite which broadcasted all its best free-to-view channels to central Europe. The word 'Brexit' is on everybody's lips, votes are soon to be cast. Could this pre-emptive move be taken as a portentous sign maybe? We grieve over the loss for a few days, as an almost funereal atmosphere descends upon our BBC-less household. Fortunately, we've since come to terms with a choice of German-only channels.

Hold on. Did I just say the word 'choice'?

No disrespect, but 'choice' is probably the last thing that German-speaking TV really offers. With one exception maybe – Friday-night talk shows. Witty, insightful and always thought provoking, German public TV, especially the regional channels, does this programme type superbly, covering a wide variety of both topics and interviewees – not just celebrities.

When the *Telegraph* feature goes online, I'm dismayed to see they've omitted something I'd praised to the sky: nationwide availability of value-for-money food. Because when it comes to what the Germans call *Preis-Leistung*, you always know where you stand. Pay a certain price and you can expect a certain quality. And when it comes to getting more bangs for your bucks, I've always felt nobody does it better than Aldi.

Some German shoppers might beg to differ there. The

type who are often first to complain whenever half of Aldi's checkouts are *geschlossen*. Even when the place is packed with punters. Other customers, usually the discerning type, eschew the fruit and vegetable shelves in favour of more fresh and natural produce at farmers' markets.

Still, most Germans agree that certain items at the discounter, such as organic dairy products, and no-name brands of essentials (coffee, pasta, toiletries...) are almost impossible to beat for price and value.

What I love most about Aldi are its *Sonderangebote* – those great twice-weekly special offers. On my latest post blog I rave about 'Taste of Britain' at Aldi as from tomorrow. 'Just look at the lovely line-up!' I announce, gazing gooey-eyed at the tantalising images on the discounter's website. Heading the line-up are salt 'n' vinegar crisps, fish 'n' chips, baked beans and Quality Street toffees.

'Certainly not the healthiest food to dig at the discounter,' I observe, 'but then whoever said that British food is good for you?' The rhetorical question provokes one or two critical reactions. Taking me at face value, Chrissie from Eching replies '*Niemand hat das gesagt.*' Technically speaking, she's right. No one ever said that. Franziska in Fürstenfeldbrück, meanwhile, makes no bones about where she stands on the matter: 'Lovely line-up is something else.'

Obviously, when it comes to English comfort food you can't please everybody. This deep-grained aversion to British cuisine is widespread amongst German adolescents. Many claim that our foodstuffs are uber-sweet and actually rather ghastly. Those who have done a school exchange to England often regale the class with shock-horror stories of force-fed diets of stewed beef, mutton and overcooked cabbage. Most of these anecdotes seem to end in dice-with-death encounters. The victim is typically driven at break-neck speed to A&E after suffering food poisoning from their guest family's 'Sunday Roast'. Once bitten twice shy, most young Germans successfully manage to escape further close shaves with British cuisine by reverting to drip feed from McDonalds.

Given Germans' innate distrust of British food, I'm slightly puzzled why Aldi is putting on a 'Taste of British' week at its 1,600 stores in South Germany. And why just the South? The North's being deprived British Baked Beans at an unbeatable 49 cents a tin. Or is it simply being spared? Most likely, the discounter is relying on some 100,000 home-sick expat Brits in Germany to boost sales this week.

Like most British kids, I was brought up on a diet of 'comfort food' such as 'Spotted Dick' and an instant dessert powder called 'Birds' Angel Delight'. Whenever these ghastly concoctions were served up at school, I habitually came home with dried blobs smeared down my blazer sleeves. We believed that all this sweet and sticky stuff was staple diet until we started travelling abroad, to countries like France, Italy and Germany, where *Hausfrauen* tend to cook much more from scratch, with fresh ingredients. Still, they do have rather more time: a whopping 40% of German women are at home most of the day.

Fortunately, not all British food is quite so ghastly. Somerset Maugham observed that in order to eat well in England, one should eat a cooked breakfast three times a day. It's true, the 'Full English breakfast' is generally rather good. What's not to like about bacon, sausage, eggs, beans, and fried tomatoes. No wonder Aldi's British Baked Beans come in a range of tantalisingly tasty sauces, including BBQ, curry and chili.

First day of 'British' week and I'm head of line when the doors of our local discounter are flung open at 8 AM sharp. Striding down the aisles, I feel like a child let loose in a candy shop on pocket-money day, gazing in wonderment at shelf upon shelf stacked high with sweet treats. This sheer range of choice is almost intoxicating. Most of it's confectionary you don't normally find in Germany: flap jack, caramel slice and – wow – chocolate-coated crunchy crisp bites. Overcome by a wave of nostalgia, and totally abandoning my better judgement, I reach out for one of my absolute childhood favourites – peppermint choc chip cheesecake. The package instructions state that the mouth-tingling product is best savoured 'slightly chilled so that the chocolate ganache topping is still hard and crunchy.' They even suggest sprinkling it with cracked sugar cane for enhanced flavour.

After leaving the Aldi cake in the freezer overnight, I take it out to chill for a while before tasting. Fearing that adding optional candy cane might be going over the top, I smother it with ganache frosting instead. Having gone to so much trouble, short of actually bothering to bake my own, I promise myself this 'taste of Britain' will be absolutely irresistible. But I'm in for a shock. The confectionary is more than just nice and sweet – it's sickly sweet.

In truth, it's probably no more saccharine than any other cheesecake or similar desserts I've ever fed on in Britain. After two decades of adjusting my palate to German cuisine, more savoury than sweet, I must have forgotten how sugary most Brits love their 'puds'.

What will South Germans make of all this? I round off my blog on 'Taste of British Week' musing 'Maybe, with Aldi's help, we can get the Germans to love British food after all.'

Aldi's 'Taste of Britain' has done more than just evoke nostalgic memories. The crunchy crisp bites even pull out an old filling. But one thing's clear: Germany has Germanised me – and my taste buds. This time I shalln't be going back for second helpings.

Learning to 'Prost'

Dienst ist Dienst, und Schnaps ist Schnaps.

This age-old maxim probably started out as a warning not to mix business with pleasures of a liquid variety. But tech is trump and these days it seems more like a call to unshackle ourselves from work-related mobiles and messages after a day at the desk. Recent surveys reveal that over 88% of gainfully employed Germans are contactable outside office hours. Clearly, the maxim is falling on stony ground, as we increasingly blur boundaries between work and play.

I'm lucky to teach in a college that actively encourages mixing business and drinking pleasure – right down to the last drop, literally. Students follow courses in brewery technology and get to test the final product too. Our campus at Freising is home to Weihenstephan, the oldest brewery in the world. The company claims to have been brewing here for nearly 1000 years.

Kloster Weltenburg, a delightful Benedictine monastery-meets-brewery on the banks of the nearby Danube, claims to be older still. Weltenburg alleges that Weihenstephan's claim is based on a forged document from the 1600s. Still, not many universities are blessed with their very own state-of-art brewing facilities, and students at Weihenstephan can enjoy both in-house brewery and beer garden just a short hop away from their lecture theatres. This week my undergrads wrote their final exam. Deciding where to go and celebrate afterwards seemed a bit of a no contest.

It's a lovely warm evening and I'm looking forward to a cool brew – or two. Scaling the flight of steps separating exam hall and beer hall, my colleague tells me how, after sharing a couple beers together, his students sometimes ask 'Can I say *you* to *you*?' Walter says the second 'you' in a slightly husky voice, suggesting a far deeper level of familiarity. It's a very German dilemma – unsure whether to address someone formally with *Sie* or informally with *Du*. Grown-ups might go all their working life calling each other *Sie*, before retiring with a typical arm-linking, tankard-clinking ceremony (so-called *Bruderschaft trinken*), in which they solemnly pledge to call each other *Du* for the rest of the lives. Small wonder that Germans view drinking to closer friendship as *bierernst*.

Last in line, I simply grab what I guess everyone else is ordering – the classic litre. After all, as the saying in Bavaria goes, *A Moas muss sei* (literally, a litre must be). But, as I struggle to gulp down the final suds, I notice how most students are nursing just half litres – and drinking *verrrrry* slowly.

Life's so unfair. When you're young you can handle beer easily (young Germans can down a litre or two without batting an eyelid). But when you're studying you can't afford the full fling. So you go halves with a mate. Then when you're older you can afford to up the ante, but you just can't handle the quantity. That said, the average German manages to drink around 106 litres a year. Almost twice the amount consumed per capita in Britain.

Musing these statistics, I feel like raising a glass to Bishop Korbinian for kickstarting mass-scale production of 'holy' brew. But perhaps we should also toast the inventor of the *Radler*. Part-brew, part-lemonade, this incongruous mix is probably akin to blaspheming about the Pope. For pious Bavarians, at least. Less devout Germans who enjoy *Radler* will point out that Germany's best-loved thirst-quencher was 'invented' by Franz Xaver Kugler, the possibly most famous pub owner in German history. On one particularly hot Saturday in 1922 he was busy serving hikers at the Kugler Alm beer garden on the outskirts of Munich when he suddenly ran out of beer. Some 1,300 cyclists had turned up *unangemeldet*.

Heading over to the students with my *Mass*, I can't help smiling at the thought of a thousand or more thirsty cyclists showing up unannounced at a *Gastwirtschaft*. As with all sporty Bavarians, they were crying out for a nice cool beer after pedalling like the crackers since the break of dawn. So Kugler seized on a bright idea. In the cellar he had several thousand bottles of lemonade lying around. He just couldn't get rid of them. Customers obviously preferred his beer. So, what did he do? He mixed the beer and lemonade 50-50, proudly announcing that he'd invented this drink especially for the *Radler*, or cyclists. The pragmatic innkeeper reasoned that anything too alcoholic would impair their ability to cycle home safely. Needless to say, he got rid of every single drop of surplus fizz.

That's the German version of how *Radler* was invented, at least. Brits fervently contest the story. They maintain it was Englanders who invented the drink some 200 years ago, serving it to troops as something called shandy.

Whether *Radler* or shandy, the beverage is a great thirst quencher and highly civilised alternative to a straight brew. There's just one sticking point. Dispensed in litre mugs, *Radler* looks just like real men's beer. Who's not to know? Not surprisingly, when you splash out on a big *Bier* you might just get handed a *Radler* by mistake. It's happened to me once or twice.

As we relax on the terrace overlooking the 'green campus' (so called not just because of its green technology courses but also the whole site, beautifully bathed in a sea of greenery), it's the students' turn to teach me a lesson. I learn how to '*prost*'.

The golden rule of 'prosting' – the boisterous clunking together of weighty beer mugs – is that you have to make meaningful eye contact with everyone around the table. Flashing each other mischievous grins, the students tell me that failing to both clink glasses and stare each other in the eyes can lead to seven years of 'bad sex'. Unsure whether they're just pulling my leg – and, I confess, intrigued as to what 'bad sex' might actually entail for rank-and-file Germans – I pull out my smartphone and pop into the gents' toilet to fact-check their claim.

It turns out they're dead right. Crouched over the loo

lid, I scroll through an article on *metro.co.uk* which blames the French for this superstition.

Time, surely, for another *Radler*.

Tour de Munich

Perched on one leg, arms arched overhead, I'm executing an impromptu 360° pirouette. Performing similarly eloquent motions alongside are 20 other individuals from Britain, Canada, America and Australia. Considering we're such a motley, unhomogenised crowd, we execute the whole thing in surprisingly good synchrony.

It would be comforting to think this was all part of a studious dance workout at some trendy converted-loft studio. The sort of dance academy where the instructor's name is Nigel and everybody calls each other *babe*. Sadly, that's not the case. We're actually on a guided cycling tour. And I've just leapt around ballerina style on the steps of the Neue Rathaus, Munich's neo-gothic town hall. 'Oh my gaahd!' chuckles our guide, as we complete this clumsy spectacle, 'I can't believe you just did that!'

The surrounding bystanders probably can't believe it either. Several of them, Americans most likely, are touting zoom-lenses, letting loose deep belly laughs as they play back our clumsy capers on their camcorders.

I laugh too. But more out of hysteria than amusement.

It's just 24 hours before the start of the Oktoberfest.

My parents have flown over and we've checked into Hotel Uhland, one of Munich's finest old-timey guesthouses. It's right opposite the entrance to the Wies'n, scene of all the action. It's been fun watching the comings and goings, especially the beer maids queueing up for selfies under the Fest banner, linking arms with butch-looking security guards. And sharing a *Mass* or more with each other. Curiously, at the very first Oktoberfest in 1810 not a single drop of alcohol was served. 30,000 guests invited to celebrate the wedding of Prince Ludwig to Princess Theresia of Hildeburghausen had to make do with just a horse race. Beer didn't become a staple commodity of the *Fest* until seven years later. These days, some six million thirsty visitors typically pour through the gates, each splurging an average of 63 euros per visit.

We'll go too. But today we have a different plan, and before sundown I'll have plunged through a crowd of naked sunbathers and dived into freezing cold fast-running water, letting myself be carried downstream to the best *Biergarten* in town.

Boy, I must be desperate for drink.

Wind back the clock an hour or so. The day begins with me joining Mike's Bike Tours for *The Classic Tour*. It seems a smart way of showing my parents more of Munich than they might normally experience by foot. Besides, despite living near Munich for over 16 years I'm still not really all that well versed on the city's facts, figures and history. As for what's what and what's hot, I always feel local guides are much better at explaining these things to visitors. Unfortunately, my parents pull out at the last minute – they're concerned we might be warming up for the next Olympics. 'We haven't ridden a bike in ages,' explains mum. 'Look Tim,' she says, pocketing the local transport day pass I've just handed her, 'why don't we just meet up in the beer garden when you take a break?'

I end up going along on my own.

Mum and dad needn't have worried. 'This isn't the Tour de France,' announces our guide called Abs, 'it's the Tour de Munich – way easier.' Which is just as well, because the steel-framed Dutch bikes we've just mounted evidently weren't built for racing.

We're assembled under the shadow of the Neues Rathaus on the Marienplatz, at the heart of Munich. Abs begins by describing the ritual of the daily Glockenspiel, acted out in the clock tower just above us. Referring to the spectacle that accompanies the chiming of Town Hall bells at 11 and 12 o' clock sharp, he warns 'Just don't expect anything exciting to happen, it's the most over-rated thing in Munich'.

Abs then enacts the *Schäfflertanz*. This is the dance performed twice daily by life-size figurines.

'C'mmon on everybody, let's do a twirl!' he encourages.

Which is how, in broad daylight, I come to be hovering on one leg in central Munich doing something like a pirouette.

Luckily, that's all the dancing I do today. From now on it's just plain biking. But, before we climb onto our vintage saddles, our guide wants to know if everybody can actually ride a bike. 'Hands up anyone who can't!'

he says. For a moment I feel like a six-year-old being quizzed by teacher on first day of school. 'Cool,' says Abs, as we all demonstratively dig our hands deep into our pockets. Poker-faced, he relates how the other day they had a woman from Texas on the tour. Putting on an accent he mimics: 'Oh yeah, I can ride a bike, I just can't turn left.' Abs tells the anecdote off the cuff, as if the lady's holed up somewhere in town, still recuperating from the ordeal. It's probably all part of a well-rehearsed script. Either way he's already won us over. Each time one of us says something smart – usually in answer to his dead-easy quiz questions – he zooms in for a high-five. Something most of our school teachers certainly never did.

We're soon off, weaving our way through crowds clogging the streets around the Hofbräuhaus. 'Any one need a bathroom?' asks Abs, pointing to the back entrance of Munich's most famous beer house, adding 'The very last free loo in town.' There's a useful tip. Munich is a pitiful place to get caught short in – you pay to pee almost everywhere.

First stop: Munich's most beautiful baroque church, the Theatiner Kirche. 'I can't pronounce that,' says Abs, 'so I just call it Tina Turner Church.' Abs explains how the church houses the Four Evangelists, lovingly sculptured by Balthasar Ableitner. 'So then, what's love got to do with it?' he quizzes. 'Everything!' calls out an American lady, sprightly clad in Lycra. 'High five!' retorts Abs, heading in for a hearty hand-slap.

We all cheer.

So far, so very good. On we go.

But you can't really do a tour of Munich's past without touching on a much grimmer chapter of German history. Just a few feet further, Abs has a sombre announcement to make. 'Sorry to dampen the cheery mood, guys,' he warns, 'but it's dark history time.' We're standing in the shadow of the Feldherrhalle, scene of the notorious Beer Hall Putsch. This, he explains, is where Hitler unsuccessfully attempted to storm the Bavarian Defence Ministry in 1923. Just before, I'd been humming that Tina Turner tune to myself, and everything had looked so peaceful in the sunshine. But suddenly a chill runs down my spine.

Originally from the USA, Abs has been in Munich for just a year but can already quote chapter and verse on the city's history. I'm impressed by his 'insider' knowledge of the Englischer Garten, larger than both London's Hyde Park and New York's Central Park. I also like how the Germans prefer to talk about green space as 'garden'. It sounds a lot more gentile than 'park', which often conjures up images of a place where yobbos fool around on broken kids' swings, amidst discarded syringes and overflowing litter bins. And the English Garden really is every bit as lovely as it sounds. Abs explains it's so called because it's laid out in the style of an English country park. No surprise there. What's new to me is that it was actually designed by an American. Working as an adviser to the Bavarian government, Massachusetts-born Benjamin Thompson was commissioned in 1789 to design a military garden where the soldiers could grow their own food in peaceful times. If it hadn't been for the French Revolution only a couple months later that's probably what it might still be – just an enormous vegetable plot. But Thompson smartly talked the government into redesigning the land into a public park, open to all citizens.

Cycling into the sprawling 37 sq.-km parkland, Abs tells us to look out for one or two 'local celebs.' I'm wondering which TV stars he's referring to, racking my brain to think of even just one local star. But it turns out Abs has something else in mind. There are six nudist 'zones' in Munich. Most of which are in the Englischer Garten. Abs informs us that nudists are actually protected by law, jokingly adding that you're allowed to photograph but not feed them. From the way he's talking, it feels more like Munich Zoo. Soon we're smack bang in the middle of the biggest nudist zone of all.

'You can't miss the Human Tripod,' says Abs, explaining that this nudist enjoys waving to cyclists. Pausing for effect, he adds 'but not necessarily with his hands.'

It's not every day you get to cycle amongst a mass of nude sunbathers and assorted exhibitionists. Some of the group prefer to take their time at this juncture, dismounting and wheeling their way through the clothes-free crowds. Quite content to forgo this – folks who strip off in public places are seldom the sort you actually *want* to see naked – I keep going. After riding along the Eisbach, a side channel of the River Isar, we finally all reassemble at the *Chinesischer Turm*. Gathering us round in a circle under the gargantuan five-story pagoda, Abs explains that the Chinese Tower is a monument to Europeans' craze in the late 18th century for all things oriental. The historic folly is surrounded by an enormous beer garden, the oldest and second largest in Munich, with seating for up to 7,500 drinkers. We join crowds queuing at the self-service counters, where we pile our plates high with piping hot *Currywurst* and chips. Traditional beer garden fodder has seldom tasted so succulent.

Refuelled, we pedal on towards our final stop – the Eisbach. The 'ice brook' is barely a ten-minute *Bummel* from the city centre. In summer crowds of spectators congregate on what's known as 'Surfers' Bridge', admiring athletic-looking Münchners as they queue to ride an artificial four-foot wave below. This practice, which was outlawed until 2010, remains highly dangerous. 'Surfers often used to be chased away by the police,' recalls Abs. 'And when they weren't being shooed away themselves, they were shooing away over-curious tourists. No one wanted to draw attention to themselves.'

Ironically, now that surfing the ferocious wave is perfectly legal, the riders seem to be competing with each other to see who can attract the most onlookers.

The four-hour tour is over far too quickly, and after cycling along the River Isar – passing some of the city's other five nudist zones on route – we rejoin the main thoroughfare, winding up right where we started. Just as I'm handing my bike back to Abs, mum and dad pop up. Since we're all hot and sticky, I suggest heading straight back to the Englischer Garten, possibly for a late afternoon dip in the Eisbach. Pedalling alongside the stream earlier, Abs had described how some locals like to dive in and let the current tug them downstream to the Chinese Tower. Some would then climb out of the water, sidestep the beer garden and jump straight onto the tram back into town. Wearing nothing but soggy g-straps, they'd often get into trouble. Not for indecent exposure but because they failed to purchase a ticket.

Soon we're back at the brook. Squeezing ourselves in between a mob of students stretched out on an enormous picnic rug, and a cluster of nudists squatting on nothing but their butts, we settle down and enjoy lazing in the sun too. All the while I'm contemplating a quick dip in the stream in spite of signs everywhere shouting 'Badeverbot!' No wonder bathing's banned – the icy water with its strong undercurrent can be life-threatening. In the past 10 years almost as many people have drowned in the Eisbach. But, amazingly, no one around us seems to be taking much heed of the warnings. Kids as young as four or five are paddling in the shallows. On a whim, I arrange to meet mum and dad at the beer garden under the Chinese Tower. Then, stripping down to just my pants, I take a running dive and let myself be pulled by the current in the same direction. I get there a good ten minutes before my parents who do the sensible thing and walk.

Although it might be better not trying to copy my foolish antics in Munich's treacherous Eisbach, I do recommend the push bike tour. For just €23 you manage to see far more than you would by foot in a whole day. Let alone in just one hour from an open-top bus. And, although the guide cracks jokes more likely heard in a male locker room, *The Classic Tour* definitely offers something for every age group. Mum and dad would have loved it.

On facebook that night I write 'September 13 and 24°C. Golden autumn! Just a couple more weeks like this please and then, for all I care, we can do winter...'

Bavarian Dwarves and Heimat Sex

I wake up with a jerk. Someone or something is massaging my belly. And whoever or whatever's doing it is soft and furry.

Very soft and furry.

A most pleasurable feeling. Particularly as I'd just dreamt of being packed off for a week's pampering in the Bavarian Forest. My application for a two-week *Kur*, or spa therapy, had finally been granted and my local *Krankenkasse*, all part of Germany's excellent health insurance system, was kindly footing the bill.

Ha. Only in your dreams.

Split seconds later, I'm both surprised and disappointed to discover a cuddly toy elephant doing the splits on my stomach.

'Ta-daaa!' the animal exclaims.

The voice is not dissimilar to that of my five-year old daughter.

'Ask Elli a question!'

'Uuu-gh,' I respond, rubbing my eyelids, still half stuck together with a layer of sleep crust.

'Ask Elli a question!' comes back the command.

For a moment I lie there wondering why on earth kids insist on calling their furry toys such predictable, unoriginal names. Tildy has a toy hamster called

Hamsti, a bear called Bärli and a *Marienkäfer* – German for ladybird – called, you've guessed it, Käfi.

'OK, Elli,' I say, giving in, 'what did you do last night?'

So, this is where expat life in Germany gets you – chatting up soft toys in bed.

'I played with my trunk!' comes the reply.

Ha, ask a silly question.

Saturday morning, 7 a.m. I'd so much been looking forward to a bit of a lie-in. Not a particularly long one, naturally. Everything in Germany starts early. Even at the weekend. Such as appointments at the local *Gartenverein*, the amateur gardeners' association who run a juice-your-own-fruit service every autumn. Our little orchard has produced a bumper crop this year. But there's only so many apples you can eat – and give away. So just after 8 o'clock, in a car crammed with 80 kg of apples and pears bulging out of laundry baskets, I head off to my juicing date in nearby Abensberg.

The whole process lasts less than an hour. I'm surprised just how quickly and efficiently my apples are turned into juice, all nicely packed in vacuum-sealed bags. But this is Germany, of course. And it doesn't cost the world either. €50 seems a very fair price for 16 five-kilo cartons, which will hopefully keep us supplied well into next year.

It's barely 10 o'clock, so rather than head straight back home I park in the centre of Abensberg and set off to explore this medieval town, which is often overshadowed by bigger brothers Regensburg and Ingolstadt. Abensberg boasts a jewel of a town centre, with a car-free main square, criss-crossed by scores of sleepy little alleyways, crammed with turret-fronted houses. Ideal for strolling on a clear blue-sky autumn weekend.

I sit for a while at *La Piazza Café Bistro* on the main square, savouring a cappuccino and *cornetti con crema al limone,* tasty Italian croissants stuffed with vanilla and lemon cream. I watch a group of tourists pile out of a coach straight into a *Gasthof* opposite for their *Frühschoppen,* the morning pint which fifty and sixty-something Germans traditionally enjoy either straight after, as part of, or simply instead of breakfast. Beer is, after all, officially regarded as a foodstuff in Bavaria. I could happily sit there all day watching the comings and goings at this quaint old guesthouse pub. But there's another place I want to visit while I'm here: a tower built for just one purpose – to pay homage to Bavarian beer.

Abensberg's best-loved landmark is the Kuchlbauer Tower, designed by world-famous artist and architect Friedensreich Hundertwasser. Completed in 2010, it certainly clashes with the town's otherwise oldy-worldy architecture. Anyone seeing this structure for the first time will probably do a double take in disbelief. Clad with dancing windows and topped with gold-leaved onion domes, it's almost unreal. The statement-making construction is part of *Kuchlbauer's Bierwelt.* Founded back in the 14th century, Kuchlbauer is the oldest wheat beer, or *Weissbier* as it's called in Bavaria. To climb the tower, you need to take the self-guided tour for twelve euros. Pricey, but worthwhile. We see not only the bottling side of the brewery but also Engel Aloisius, the patron saint of beer drinkers in Bavaria, the so-called 'wheat beer dwarves' – apparently they also speak in English on the international tour – and, tucked away in a corner of the cellar, a sensational half-scale interpretation of Leonardo da Vinci's The Last Supper.

Of his work, Hundertwasser said 'I want to show how basically simple it is to have paradise on earth. And everything that the religions and dogmas and the various political creeds promise, is all nonsense.' It's perhaps no coincidence that the church tower of Kuchlbauer's *Kunsthaus*, just next door, is three times wobblier than the Leaning Tower of Pisa.

All told, this tour's more about art than beer. Anyone interested in learning about beer making could probably discover a lot more at somewhere like Löwenbrau or Hacker Pschorr in Munich. Still, it's a colourful insight into one of the world's oldest breweries. I'll definitely do the tour again when we have visitors from the UK. Even if it's only to get a thrill out of seeing a bunch of Bavarian beer dwarves chatting away in hilarious *Denglish*.

German tourist boards sure know how to milk their home-grown celebrities – dead and alive.

Eisleben in the east, for example, markets itself as *Lutherstadt*, while Frankfurt does a supreme job of selling itself as 'Home of Goethe', with its flagship the world-renowned Goethe Institute. Bonn, in turn, has Beethoven to thank for pulling in the punters. Every September the ex-*Hauptstadt* holds a month-long

Beethovenfest in honour of its most famous son. Twenty years ago, new kid in town and just settling into my first job with Telekom, I went along to this festival. Half the crowd came dressed as the great composer – shocks of wild and unruly hair, pantaloons and high boots were *de rigueur*. More party than performance, it was all very camp and comic.

My adopted home of Moaburg also boasts one or two celebrities. The town's most prominent son is probably Franz Xaver Gabelsberger. Born in 1789, Gabelsberger worked as a chancery clerk for the *Landtag*, the Bavarian state parliament. Sensing he could speed up his work by using a simple shorthand system, the man from Moaburg did a very German thing. He sat down one *Feierabend* and invented one. The result was a stenographic system. Known as 'Gabelsberger shorthand', the system was ultimately adopted throughout Germany. Moaburg pays lip service to this august achievement by naming the high street, the local grammar school and an award-winning bakery after its most famous citizen. Yet ask locals what all the fuss is about and you'll probably be met by shrugs of indifference.

Question them about Alois Brummer, on the other hand, and you're likely to evoke a far more enthusiastic response. Born in Moaburg in 1926, Brummer worked as film distributor and cinema owner. But he soon found he could make much more money by shooting films himself. Porn films, to be precise. His first offering *'Graf Porno und seine Mädchen'* – Porn Count and his Girls – is said to be the first ever blue movie made in Germany.

Brummer's speciality was what he called 'Heimat Sex'. Anyone curious about 'Heimat Sex' should surf the web for the film producer's 1973 classic *'Unterm Dirndl wird gejodelt'*. The English title is 'How Sweet is her Valley', which one reviewer describes as 'absolutely dreadful'. Maybe they should have just stuck with the literal translation – Yodeling under the Dirndl Dress. Either way, it's a sort of sexed-up Heidi; bawdy and unashamedly *Carry On*.

Brummer died in 1984. But that hasn't stopped Moaburg from celebrating his birthday ever since. Just recently the town threw a party to mark his 90th. The *Stadtmuseum* invited burghers to a special screening of 'Heimat Sex'. Demand to see the naughty films far outstripped seating capacity – the museum had to turn away whole clusters of curious citizens. I couldn't get in either but I know someone who did; my hairdresser Nicole. When it comes to discussing carnal knowledge in public, Germans know few inhibitions and, since she just happened to mention the films in passing, I was curious to hear more. Our German-English dialogue, in between shampooing and snipping, went something like this:

'So, how was it then?

'Och, so lala.'

'What do you mean *so lala*?'

'Naja, mia hom nit vui gsehn.'

They didn't see very much.

'Oh, why not? Fade-out at first sign of hanky panky?'

'Hee. Na. So prude warn de aa ned.'

No, they weren't that prude.

'Well then, why didn't you see much?'

'Ja mei. 's warn jo de Siebziga, gell.'

It was the seventies. Presumably everyone was so hairy.

There was an elderly lady, hair bunched up in highlight foil, and several other retired-looking customers having their nails manicured.

All were in earshot.

No one so much as batted an eyelid.

Risiko or Routine?

'How does this sound?' I quiz Bea, in between mouthfuls of muesli diced with fried banana and lightly roasted crushed hazelnuts. Leaning into my laptop perched on the edge of the breakfast table, I start to read:

'Looking out into the back garden this morning, I'm thrilled to catch sunrise, and struck by the splendour of the sky. For a few moments, as the sun gently creeps up onto the horizon, the clouds resemble an enormous silk duvet, patched with streaky-bacon-like golden-orange pockets. It's Saturday and, filled with the hope of a day yet to unfold, I'm up early and enjoying...'

'*Ja, ja, bassd scho,*' Bea cuts in, reaching over for the last slice of honey-dew watermelon. By now she's quite fluent in local dialect. '*Bassd scho*' is perhaps the most Bavarian expression of all, and with the most nuances too. It can signal anything from total perfection to total fiasco – and a lot of apathy in between. Just like right now. Bea utters it with all the enthusiasm of an inmate waiting to go to the thumb screws. I sense she's only really been half listening.

Pity really, because I've just been describing a view which we'd travelled over 18,000 km to marvel at. It's that spectacular sunrise over Whangamata on the glorious Coromandel Peninsula of North Island, New

Zealand. Something which has been constantly on my mind since returning home six months ago. Right now, I'm just polishing off a blog I'd started writing, but hadn't quite finished during the long flight home. I'd no doubt been distracted by the delightful Meryl Streep peering at 'Mr. Perfect' over the rims of her tortoise-shell spectacles on the in-flight entertainment system.

Bea had adored New Zealand every bit as much as me, throwing herself with heart and soul into each and every one of our intrepid adventures. Several of which had stopped rather abruptly at the end of a rutted farm track. Indeed, some of the action was not without a certain element of risk. Such as following an invitation to doll up in drag together for a charity performance of *Fifty Shades of Grey* at the local theatre house. She'd had to rescue me from the advances of several muscle-bound young men who'd crowded around us, wolf-whistling as I tumbled out of the car in a Priscilla Queen get-up – sequin-studded frock and ostrich feather headdress. Incredulously, I seemed to turn them on more than Bea. Sporting stilettos and strapless polka dot dress with ruffles, she bore an uncanny resemblance to Marilyn Monroe.

Sadly though, Bea had made it clear right from the get-go that she had no intention of ever relocating to the southern hemisphere. Given her resistance, I should probably have just let it go. But no. Although we'd not discussed the subject together in any further detail since returning to Germany, I'd stubbornly clung to this 'oh-if-only…' idea. I'd even shot off some applications for teaching posts. One of the responders was headmistress of a high school in Timaru, South Island. Like most schools keen to lure new teachers, this one also described itself as 'thriving and oversubscribed'. Unfortunately, the advertised position had already been filled by a candidate who matched their requirements 'more closely'.

Not that I'm too pained by this rejection. Just the day before I'd heard from an experienced travel blogger that when it came to having a good time, Timaru was generally regarded as the ultimate no-thrills destination Down Under. Zealanders say things like 'Oh, it's about as much fun as a night out in Timaru.' Just as well, maybe, that I wasn't exactly a 100% match for the town's oversubscribed and thriving all-girls school. Although it did look rather swish; state-of-the-art campus set on landscaped parklands, and a mere stone's throw from Caroline Bay Beach.

While poring over scores of other job offers, many at locations probably not too unlike Timaru, something bugs me. For any school to seriously consider my application, they first require me to register with the authorities and have all my qualifications officially vetted by a designated office in Wellington. Fees for this small procedure are just shy of 1,000 euros.

Regardless, I'd gone ahead and filled in the online EC15 registration forms, laboriously detailing every single job I'd ever done, warts and all. This included the nightmare school I was posted to during teacher training. I probably couldn't expect to get too many job offers on the back of a reference from that place.

But I'm about to discover that paradise isn't all

picnics and pancakes. Browsing through the *New Zealand Herald,* I'm disturbed to read about a disruptive pupil in a high school in Auckland threatening his French teacher at knife point. Apparently, all Marie-Christine had done was turn her back on him for a split second to write some Key Stage 7 vocabulary on the whiteboard.

Not exactly best visiting card for any school seeking to recruit new teachers. And now this very school is advertised on the daily job alert which pings into my mail box late that night. Logging in next morning, I google the place. First hit is not their website but the knife crime report. Did I really want to apply there? To forsake all I'd built up in Germany just to end up held at knife point by a couldn't-give-a-toss schoolboy in the City of Sails?

The alert for this job's still in my box. I press 'delete'.

Sitting there right now at my laptop, finger hovering over PAY NOW, I've finally hit an impasse. What if I part with all that money and don't even receive one single job offer? And if I do secure a job, what if the grass isn't actually greener Down Under?

I'm reminded of the words of David, our b & b host in Takaka, just as we're about to head off to Auckland for our flight back home: 'If you have any doubts coming here for good you should forget it.'

PAY NOW, the icon is saying.

PAY NOW. It flashes again.

Do I pay or stay?

Proceed or cancel?

Risiko oder Routine?

Horror scenarios from 'Goodbye Deutschland', coupled with images of risk-adverse young Germans swarming back to Europe flicker through my mind.

I hit 'Cancel'.

'Spukschlösser' and Shit Storms

So that's it. Dice rolled, votes cast. We're leaving Europe.

Do half the folks back home actually realize what they've just gone and done? Not a single German I meet can work it out either. They each blink at me astonished when I pass at their question 'Why?'

Inevitably, they also ask: 'Where are you going to go now?

Again, I'm stumped for an answer.

'Ahmm. Uuugh.'

It's the best response I can manage. But probably not unlike the sort of reply you'd get from any of the 300,000 Germans living in Britain.

German newspapers and magazines are immediately fuelling the debate with song-title-inspired headlines such as 'Bye Bye Baby (Britain)' and 'Please don't go'. It's as if editors have plundered their CD collections for a suitable soundtrack to the whole grand débâcle. The tearful 'Bye Bye Baby (Britain)' evokes fading memories of a 1970s Scottish boy band, dolled up to the teeth in tartan. While the latter title recalls a ghastly cover version of KC and the Sunshine Band. Hardly *Zeitgeist* stuff. But my attention is attracted to a list of things that Germans say they love most about Britain.

Headlined 'God Save the Beans', the 18 July 2018

edition of *'Welt Kompakt'* devotes three full pages to Brexit, honing in on three British 'institutions' which Germans seem so fond of – baked beans, forming orderly queues and haunted castles.

Yes, haunted houses. The journal attributes Germans' fixation with what they call *Spukschlösser* to the fact that they have very few ghosts of their own. Save perhaps for political ones such as the ghost of communism. Personally, I put it down to pupils being force-fed a diet of stories invariably set in some or other spooky old building. German school textbooks for eleven-year olds, for example, typically feature sepia-toned pictures of mist-shrouded clifftop castles, accompanying short stories with such titles as The Ghost of Pucklebury Priory. Others, dealing the Horrible History card, devote page-long descriptions to how the ghost of Catherine Howard, fifth wife of Henry the Eighth, still haunts the corridors of Hampton Court Castle. No wonder Germans are far more knowledgeable about British haunted homes than Brits themselves. Find an Englander, for instance, who can name you the nation's most haunted house. Thanks to *'Welt Kompakt'* and school English, Germans can answer off pat. It's the Victorian Villa Borley Rectory in Essex.

The rest of the 'Best of British' list offers further insight into our European neighbours' beloved image of *'Inselaffen'*, or island apes as they affectionately call us. In almost idolizing tones, the newspaper article waxes lyrical about the British fondness for boiling hot and freezing cold taps (as opposed to the *'Mischbatterie'*, the mixer tap favoured in continental Europe).

'Do you want to be warmer or colder?' asks the 'Welt Kompakt'. I think they're implying that it's not so much about tap temperature but rather the British social class system. Warm water, claims the newspaper, is for Brits who attended boarding school, played cricket and race around in Aston Martins. Cold water, conversely, is for football-playing Brits who quit school at the very first opportunity, wear outlandish clothes and enjoy 'interesting' sex.

Ho. Could it be that the Germans are just a tad envious of us?

Actually, this very German practice of shoehorning us into one or the other box rather puzzles me. Yes, class still has a pervasive influence over British people's sense of identity, but Germans seem to have overlooked just one small thing – most Brits are actually quite normal.

And then, just when we think nothing can top Brexit, along comes the ultimate election disaster.

Straddling cheery Octoberfest and magical Advent, dull and dank November begins innocently enough. But on the ninth day of the month, I awake exhausted and bathed in a pool of sweat. My dormant mind is spewing out images of a man and woman belting each other around the head with a truncheon. Fireworks are exploding all around and the Star Spangled Banner is playing. It's a cross between seaside Punch and Judy show and The Fourth of July. Except that my two characters are baying for each other's blood and there's little cause for celebration.

It's almost like I'm getting a sneak preview of a far greater nightmare about to play out across the Land of

Endless Opportunity. On the day after the bombshell drops, Chuck, my colleague from the Midwest, appears. He's sporting an expression as glum as the grit-grey clouds etched ominously over the Bavarian skyline. 'Oh my gaahd!' he groans, shuffling into the staff room. For a moment it sounds like he's suffering from *Muskelkater*, those awful aching bones and limbs, about which you'll normally hear only Germans complaining.

My colleague's tired comment almost makes me choke on the *Brezel* I'm chewing. What comes out is half gag, half grunt, as I suddenly realize my mouth is full. 'Oh my God!' is of course the very expression splashed across most of today's headlines. And, underneath, as if an afterthought, following lengthy editorial debates whether readers would understand the perplexities of this foreign language lexical item – *'Geht's noch'?* Yes, that lovely expression which Germans mutter while slowly waving back of hand in front of face – Teutonic body language for 'Are you nuts?'. All this clearly points to one thing – German media is gearing up for the ultimate *Shit Storm*.

'Oh gosh, isn't it awful' I retort.

Chuck had been worried about how to broach the issue with his students. Even though I'd been at pains to reassure him that the unfortunate election result was not *entirely* his fault. But now he'd really gone and added fuel to the flames: 'I played them HIS Acceptance Speech, and one girl started crying. I've come to get some tissues for her.'

'Oh gosh' I repeat.

It's certainly not a brilliant start to any lesson. Deep

down inside I know I'm not going to have an easy ride today either. After all, we Brits ran the show in the USA for a while too. And we weren't the most popular landlords either. No wonder they threw our tea into the sea and sent us scuttling back to Blighty.

Suddenly however, I have a *Geistesblitz* – a flash of inspiration. I'll make the lesson topical yet totally avoid having to talk about HIM. I go in and show the students the video 'Why Americans love their flag'. The clip takes us back to the very first U.S. president, George Washington, and how the *Stars and Stripes* was born.

We all learn something new about American history. And – relief all round – there are no more tears.

Bavarian Olympics

While Britain's side-tracked by Brexit, and the US beats its brow over Trump, Bavaria's in an unequivocally festive mood. *'Man soll die Feste feiern wie sie fallen'* – celebrate special events as and when they occur – as the saying goes.

Hearing locals talk about Bavaria, with all its customs, folklore and die-hard traditions, you'd think the Free State had been around for ever. True, it began as a grand duchy in the sixth century, expanding into the Kingdom of Bavaria in 1805. But the present-day *Freistaat* has only just turned 100 years old. Following a peace rally in Munich between 7 and 8 November 1918, a journalist called Kurt Eisner proclaimed the creation of the state in face of almost no resistance. He was assassinated just one year later. But – typical German pragmatism at play – before shooting him they made sure he put his signature to the new constitution. Germany's largest state by land area, was born.

Here in Moaburg, festivities are already under way to mark Bavaria's grand centenary. Donning my beer-smeared lederhose, I go along to our local *Stadtfest*, and arrive just in time to join in the *Bayrische Olympiade*. While the organisers clearly mean well, it's difficult to see how they're actually going to stage these 'Bavarian

Olympics'. The 'sports field' is little more than a tiny rostrum. Squeezed in, almost as an afterthought, at the far corner of the market place.

I soon find myself chatting to Jörg, who's photographing the event for *Franns*, the local lifestyle magazine.

'So, any idea what this is all about?'

I'm pointing to the part of the programme where it says *Blindverkostung*.

'*Tja,*' Jörg replies pokerfaced, 'that's when you're led up onto the stage, blindfolded and have to swig and spit.'

'Huh?'

I'm genuinely confused.

Flexing the muscles in his right hand, Jörg starts to demonstrate the next competition, *Masskrugstemmen*: 'You've got to keep your arm straight and hold on like h......'

Jörg's demo is suddenly curtailed by the loudspeaker blaring out directly above us:

'*Wo ist der Engländer?*'

One of the participants has dropped out. Seems like I've been roped into taking their place.

It's a tough job, but someone has to do it – don a blindfold and identify half a dozen different beer sorts on sale at the nearby *Bierstrasse*, a whole street lined with beer-selling booths. Particularly tough when your tastebuds are already blighted by a variety of brands which all taste very much alike anyway. Even the most sober of punters must be hard pushed to tell the difference between *Ziegler Helles* and *Premium Bräu*.

Chances are you could almost win the *Spiel* without taking a single swig. Handing us taster after taster, Matthias offers just two options: *'dies oder das?* This or that?' But pure guess work would mean pouring damn good Zieglerbräu down the drain. The *Quiz Meister* is plying me with mini-litre samples quicker than I can knock them down the hatch.

I end up correctly guessing only two out of ten.

Matthias is already announcing the next challenge, and – since they seem to have run out of volunteers – I'm roped into this one too. Suddenly I become aware of another pressing matter. Having already drunk several litres on the *Bierstrasse* I'd meant to slip off to a nearby portacabin. But there'd been no time before the blind tasting competition. Following the free samples (all of which I naturally swallowed – far too good just to swig and spit out) my bladder feels like it's swollen to the size of a jackfruit. But there's no time to pop off for a pee now either. Pressing my knees together, I soldier on.

All this is hardly the best of prerequisites for the ensuing *Masskrugstemmen*.

Hoisting my *Mass* almost up to a right angle feels like child's play at first. Locked into a goofy *'Prost!'* pose, I probably look more like a living statue, beseeching passersby to throw money into a hat. Very soon, however, ease turns to discomfort, and discomfort turns to pain. My arm starts shaking. And, bit by bit, the rest of my body starts to follow suit. Within sixty seconds I've capitulated, sinking to the knees in defeat. Miraculously, I splatter the full contents of my *Mass* over no one but myself. Totally drenched, I collapse in a corner of the stage. I lie there in a drunken stupor until the final results are announced.

The winner apparently managed to keep holding his beer at chest height for a full minute and a half. A herculean feat, by local standards. But nothing compared to the world record. 28-year-old Matthias Völkl not only held 29 full litre beer mugs, he also carried them a full 40 metres from one end of the tent to the other. The mugs had a combined weight of almost 70 kilos. According to 'The Local', Germany's go-to news in English portal, the 'beefy Bavarian' trained for the challenge by carrying his female colleagues through the Munich Hofbräuhaus where he works.

As for my own 'heroic' efforts today, I come last in each competition. Apparently, I qualify for the booby prize, which they're calling me to collect as the winners, one by one, line up on centre stage.

That'll have to wait though – my bladder's full to bursting.

Nature's not just calling, it's screaming.

Spurring the award ceremony, I heave myself up and leg it to the loo.

'See that spot over there?' says Sue, pointing to a stretch of beach fronting a line of navy blue and green-striped beach cabins. 'That's where we did handstands together. Hand in hand in the sand! Me with a *Mars* in my mouth, you with a *Snickers*, remember?'

'Nah, nah, you got it wrong,' I tease, 'I had the *Mars*;

you had the *Snickers*!'

The playful incident happened a good forty years ago, yet it feels just yesterday. We did indeed perform handstands in the sand together, possibly on that very spot. With chocolate-smeared mouths, I dare say.

Back in Britain for the summer holidays, I've travelled to Mudeford (pronounced Mud-a-fudd) to see Sue. We two go back a long time. Our parents were closest friends. Wherever they went we either followed or were pushed ahead in our prams. Side by side in pushchair, we were best buddies and have remained so ever since. Sue now lives nearby in the New Forest. Less than an hour away from where we both grew up, this small seaside resort is one of my most favourite spots in Britain.

Mudeford Sandbank is most unique – an isolated area of sand on the South England coast, wedged between harbour and deep blue sea. When I tell friends in Germany that you can get there only by ferry or an hour's walk up and down a hill, they think I'm describing a remote hide-away in some far-flung corner of the world.

The picture-postcard sandspit is lined with brightly-painted beach cabins of all shapes, sizes and colours. My family once owned one of these cute little cabins too. Mind you, in those days we just called them 'huts'. That's all they were, very simple wooden shacks. Nowadays these 20-square-metre huts have been sexed up almost out of recognition. Some even have solar panels. And yet the coveted chalet-style lodgings still have neither mains electricity nor plumbing. Toilets and showers are all housed in communal blocks. And still they sell for around £ 300,000 a pop (roughly €350,000). That makes Munich property prices feel like a giveaway. It would easily buy you a neat little *'heisl'* in the Hoiertau. Obviously, a textbook case of Location, Location, Location.

I've come to the UK to take Tildy to a 'Summer Camp'. It's run by a nationwide organisation which have rented rooms at my old school in Bath. She's in good hands all week, so I take the opportunity to slip off to the seaside for a couple days. Which is how Sue and I come to be taking a trip down memory lane. And why, as we reminisce, Sue suggests we call round at old friends who still have a cabin just around the corner:

'Let's see if Sarah's there.'

She is.

I recognise Sarah immediately even though our paths haven't crossed for a good 30 years. Suddenly, it's just like old times again, chuntering away as if we'd never been apart. Except that last time I saw Sarah she was just starting at university. Now she has three grown-up boys who are at uni themselves. Sarah's telling us how the adolescents moved out of the family home, and had places of their own for a little while. But now, both back in their old childhood bedrooms, neither seem to be in any great hurry to leave. 'They've found it's cheaper than renting their own place,' she chuckles. Her twelve-year old daughter Eliza hovers around in the background and then disappears into the cabin kitchen. She returns carrying a tray of fresh-brewed fruit tea for everyone.

It's funny. Just like Sarah's boys, I've also found that sometimes you have to leave a place in order to learn how to love it. I feel I've grown much closer to and fond of my home land since leaving it almost exactly 20 years ago.

Many things that I used to take so much for granted – living so close to the sea, great beaches, bracing family hikes in wind and rain; swimming in the English Channel – I've come to appreciate much more. Probably because we're so far from the sea in Bavaria. I'm now seeing things in my home land from a totally different perspective.

It works both ways of course. Every time I return to Germany after holidays in England, I always appreciate life here much more. Even if it's just little things you can't get so readily in Britain, like fresh pretzels and organic coffee.

The following day I race back to Bath, just in case my child's missing me. But when I collect her from the school playground she looks quite distressed that I'm back so soon – she's made some girlfriends and they're in the middle of pelting each other with water bombs.

Some say schooldays are the happiest days of your life. I'm not sure mine were. But Tildy's lucky. She's thoroughly enjoyed her week at my old school. On the flight back to Munich, just as we're biting into our FlyBe sandwiches, she leans over and whispers 'Papa, England is cool.'

Step Five:

Join a Verein
– and drink like Weltmeister

*"Whenever three Germans get together,
they form a Verein."*

(German maxim)

Don't forget your Lederhose

Climb into your lederhose, drop in at any festival in Bavaria and you'll immediately spot them – the tightly knit groups of *'Stammgäste'*, or regular patrons, crammed around tables usually closest to the beer-serving hatch. Heads huddled down in conspiracy-like circles; their ranks remain firmly closed.

Unlike British pubs, often some of the easiest places in the world to mingle and mix, German beer gardens and festivals are some of the toughest places to meet new people. That might seem weird, given how willing Germans are to share tables with strangers (foreigners quickly learn the standard query *'Tschuldigung, ist hier noch frei?'* – is this seat free?). But, as I once discovered when turning up at a beer garden on my own, being offered a free seat at a stranger's table seldom means they want to talk to you.

How then, with odds heavily stacked against them, can outsiders still manage to infiltrate the closed ranks of Bavarians?

The answer, it turns out, is dead simple.

Join a *Verein*.

The biggest single club in Germany is the ADAC automobile club, boasting over 20 million members.

Some 1,750 regional divisions stage regular *Stammtisch* meetings where 'old timers' and 'young timers' dedicate whole weekends in a quest to out-trump each other with greatest engine displacement, torque, power and other remarkable statistics. Yet, luckily, when it comes to off-road distractions, everyone's a winner. In 2018, 36 million – almost every second burgher – belonged to one or more of the country's some 300,000 officially recognised associations. There's a *Verein* for almost everything. From putting out fires with the *freiwillger Feuerverein* to exchanging *Schnufftobak* with like-minded snuff fans. Many associations, such as the *Schützenverein*, or shooting sports club, seem to have an almost all-age appeal, from pre-pubescents to pensioners. Members are trained in 'everyday' skills, such as the art of muzzleloading weapons and shooting a bow and arrow.

For newbies interested in joining a *Verein*, but concerned they might not measure up to requirements, there's good news. Whether the association involves fighting fires, shooting clay pigeons or playing skittles – you don't actually have to *do* any of these activities. Rumour has it that some voluntary fire-fighting associations aren't even able to extinguish a disposable tin-foil barbecue. As for the multitude of musical associations, no one will so much as bat an eye if you can't play the relevant instrument. Germans even have a joke for this:

'How does a clarinet sound best? Quietly crackling in the fire, ha!'

Whatever the *Verein*, members normally need satisfy only two requirements: pay their annual subscription via direct debit and possess a bladder the size of jackfruit.

Here in deepest Lower Bavaria, burghers can either join a football club or sign up with a marching band. But that's just the problem. It's either or.

The closest British equivalent to *Blaskapelle* is a brass band. For many Brits this probably conjures up foggy-eyed images of musical ensembles in military uniform striking up outside a disused slag heap somewhere between Barnsley and Berwick-on-Tweed. Either that or the Brighouse and Rastrick Brass Band's classic appearance on Christmas Top of the Pops, ca. 1977.

In Bavaria, however, a brass band can be anything, from amateur hunting-horn quartet to full-blown symphony orchestra. Almost every single town, and many a remote *Kaff*, has its very own *Blaskapelle* – or 'blowing band'.

While tempted to give the 'blow' a go, I'm still haunted by the ghost of music lessons I endured at school more than forty years earlier. Being forced to play the flute in a windowless room no bigger than a broom cupboard put me off woodwind instruments for life. I found it impossible both to blow and keep my fingers over the holes at the same time. Miss Norris, my long-suffering music teacher, must have been at her wits end when she wrote on my school report 'Tim is totally devoid of all motor skills.'

This leaves only football.

Bavarians take their *Fuaßboi* extremely seriously. When they talk about 'The Kaiser', for example, they don't mean Wilhelm II, but Franz Beckenbauer.

Honorary President of FC Bayern, Beckenbauer is God of German football. And God is boundlessly good. Such is the logic that makes Bavarians baulk at reminders that he was accused of fraud and money laundering as part of the 2006 World Cup.

Football in Bavaria is a byword for *Vereinsleben* – life in the association. And whole lives in Bavaria literally revolve around these sports clubs. When the village *Fußballverein* plays, for example, women slave away at the stove all weekend, cooking up a storm to serve their menfolk after the game.

No doubt camaraderie in these *Fuaßboi* clubs is second to none. Sadly, I've never seen much sense in two teams chasing a leather ball around a field and I'm probably more hindrance than help to the housewives.

When it comes to joining a *Verein*, my options seem even more restricted than those of the average Lower Bavarian.

Like it or lump it, I'm going to have to go with the 'blowing band'.

Still, rather than rush into it, I decide first to seek a second opinion on my musical talent – if you can call it that. I contact music maker Stephan Ebn. Ex-drummer with pop diva Gianna Nannini, Stephan regularly tours with Scottish band Middle of the Road, best known for million seller 'Chirpy Chirpy, Cheep Cheep'. Hardly a day goes by without them playing this tune on Bayern Eins.

Foreigners often have this rose-tinted image of Bavarians dressed in lederhosen, all merrily marching to brass band music. Almost as if this were a dictionary definition of the music genre. Yet Stephan brusquely busts the myth that Bavarians play the best *Blasmusik.*

'*Mia san de schlimms*' – we're the world's worst – he announces.

Seeing my eyebrows shoot up in surprise, he smiles, explaining that Bavarians join a *Verein* not to play music but to get plastered. Stephan's revelation comes completely out of the blue. But it certainly explains why brass bands take such long breaks between sets whenever they appear in beer halls and gardens. Sometimes the impromptu interludes last longer than the actual performance.

I enjoy rummaging around the array of instruments in Stephan's underground studio, musing which to try out first. But, just as I'm lunging for the maracas, the accomplished musician gives me the throat-slash signal. I suspect he's already heard more than he can bear.

Fortunately, he just wants to share a secret:

'*Wa schlecht schbuit kriegt oafach moi de Dromme.*'

Anyone who can't play well in a Bavarian band lands up on drums.

For some that might be a bane, but for me it's a blessing. Ever since childhood, when I pinched mum's old pots, pans and cooking sticks for my own pop group called 'Image', I always wanted to play drums properly.

Standing astride a ginormous bass drum – 20 times the size of a regular pizza – Stephan demonstrates the basic marching beat, and then hands me the sticks. It's easier than I expect and, feet pounding up and down to the boom-boom, I soon get the hang of it.

Next up, Stephan squeezes behind the full drum kit

and demonstrates the 'roll' used to herald the start of a march. This is much harder, and he patiently watches as I try and retry to multi-task on cymbals and drums, whilst pumping the foot pedal. I give it my best, but a lot of my banging, for want of a better word, is literally hit and miss. *Mehr schlecht ois recht*, as Bavarians say.

The lesson is over far too quickly. Still, I've actually managed to play a musical instrument without murdering it. Stephan acknowledges my triumph with a fiery fist bump. Then, all of a sudden, the musician clicks his fingers.

'*Jawoiii!*' he whoops.

Next month, Stephan tells me, is the Gallimarkt, a four-day beer bonanza, second only – in Bavaria at least – to the Oktoberfest. The marching band will be guests of honour at the Fest, which hosts one of the liveliest fun fairs and booze-ups nationwide. It's a veritable magnet for rollercoaster riders, beer drinkers, and budding drummers.

Stephan seems to be suggesting that I audition for the role of drummer. The way he's talking, I'm an absolute shoo-in.

Coming in for a high five, Stephan suddenly retracts his hand. Stepping back, he glares at me sternly.

It's as if whatever plan we were hatching has just been scuppered. Perhaps I'm not the shoo-in Stephan had in mind after all. But then, pointing to my Bermuda shorts, he grins:

'*Vagiß ned ledahosn zua drogn, ned?*'

Don't forget your lederhose.

Squeezing the Queen

It's not every day you meet a queen. Well, not a crowned one, at least. Yet the one I've just met wears a very eye-catching coronet; it's decorated with an umbel of hops. This sovereign's sole role, apparently, is to consume copious amounts of beer and encourage others to do likewise.

As job descriptions go, this would normally be the stuff of dreams and fairytales. But here in deepest Lower Bavaria it's par for the course. 18-year-old Anna Baum was recently crowned very first Hallertau Beer Queen. Competition for the coveted title had been fierce. In three rounds, six finalists – all from local hop-growing families – vied with each other in a bid to lift the greatest number of litre mugs and correctly answer the most quiz questions on brewing techniques and ingredients. And – just like me at the *Stadtfest* – they'd also been blindfolded and challenged to taste the difference between yeasty lager and sweet wheat ales.

First and foremost, these savvy young ladies needed to woo the judges with their knowledge of a good brew. But from the moment Anna stepped onto stage, I suspect the all-male jury were more roused by something else. She's dressed in full regalia – traditional Bavarian *dirndl*, lovingly adorned with a frilly laced apron and pink and white bow. The strapless satin bodice hugs her chest like a dream. What does it for me is the sexy sash slung over her shoulder and hip. The golden lettering on a green and red background confirms her royal rank.

Standing there gawping at her – head lolling loosely, inane grin on face – I must have painted a pretty pathetic picture. As if drugged to the teeth with tranquilisers. Like someone about to be bundled into a little red van and carted off back to a building surrounded by a very high wall.

But there's another reason why I've gone so gooey-eyed.

Nothing's prepared me for this chance encounter with royalty. How to appropriately address people who go around carrying things like crowns, sashes and sceptres as part of their everyday attire? Should one bow and say '*Ihre Majestät, Ihre Exzellenze*?' And what's the German for 'Your Royal Highness?' Even more difficult – a typical German conundrum – should I say *Du* or *Sie*? In a land where it's customary to wait for the more senior person to 'offer' the *Du*, some Germans can get quite shirty if you address them as such without their prior consent. And with German nobility (that's anyone with *Graf, Gräfin* or *von* in their name) you're skating on even thinner ice if you accidentally breach aristocratic etiquette. Forgetting to address them as *Herr Graf* or *Frau Gräfin*, for example, can land you in yet deeper trouble.

I'm debating how to best behave without contravening pomp and ceremony in Lower Bavaria when Anna, sensing my dilemma, races to the rescue.

Abandoning royal protocol, with all its airs and graces, she says '*Mia könna uns gern dutzn.*'

All sorted. We're to say '*Du*' to each other.

It's the annual *Hopfazupfafest* and we've come together to demonstratively pick the last buds of this year's crop. Topping the bill of entertainment are alpine choirs, cowbell players and hearty young lads dancing the traditional folk dance of the *Schuhplattler*. They're all members of the local *Trachetenverein* or folklore society, an association you'll find in almost every single town in Bavaria. What would normally count as niche in Britain, and probably most other countries of the world, is mainstream in Germany. And – equally surprising, when compared with ageing British equivalents (think bell-jingling Morris Men) these ones are spring chicks. Most of the assembled folk dancers look like they're still living at home with mum and dad.

Having sat through multiple BBC travel shows on Bavaria, in which celebrity presenters act the goat while 'having a go', it's refreshing to see this difficult dance done properly. The twelve-strong all-male group leap, stomp and slap in time with the music. I'm out of breath just watching them. The *Schuhplattler* actually originated as a flirting dance. Whenever they felt a bit frisky and wanted to impress single young maidens, men (often, but not always single) would jump into their lederhose, don a feathered hat, and prance around in circles, slapping the soles of their shoes. The girls were apparently swept off their feet. The rest, presumably, was simply a case of 'Your *Platz* or mine?'

Chances of that happening tonight are pretty slim.

A pity really, as there are quite a few attractive young *Mädls* dotted around the audience. Each dressed in a beautifully laced dirndl, they all have that oldy-worldly period-drama look about them. As if they've just stepped off the pages of a Jane Austen novel. And with so much cleavage on show, it seems there's stiff competition to see who can exhibit the biggest eyeful. They must have spent hours on end in the bathroom, trussing themselves up like turkeys for the grand event. Yet very few appear particularly impressed by the flirt ceremony enacted for their benefit. In fact, most aren't even bothering to watch at all. They look more interested in taking selfies and scrunching their noses at the results.

Glancing over at the stage, I notice that the *Schuhplattler* are now onto the next instalment of their courtship ritual. Still whooping and stomping, they're prancing around a lump of wood, taking turns to hammer nails into it. By now the only spectators are a handful of pre-teens in the front row.

The eventful day had begun with me rising at the crack of dawn to help pick hop buds, known as umbels, from a small plantation at our local market square. Alas, my meagre pickings are no match for the lorry loads harvested by fellow volunteers – a five-strong, all-female workforce. These nimble-fingered *Omas*, with a combined age of at least 400, typically manage to fill a dozen baskets a day. Manual picking has long been mechanised, but the pensioners' performance is a nostalgic reminder that fields were once packed full of labourers during autumn harvest. Whole families would pitch in together. And if you wanted your kids to work the full fortnight, running around collecting in the baskets, a short note to teacher would get the child excused without any further ado. Nowadays you hardly see any locals at work in the fields. It's mostly East European labour.

The scene here at Moaburg's *Marktplatz* is very much a sign of the times. The neighbouring carpark is jam-packed with autos, yet only half a dozen drivers have volunteered to pick the buds. Similarly, while some parents still pull their kids out of school during term time, it's unlikely that they're being sent to labour in the fields.

I'm enjoying lending a hand in the hopfields when one of the volunteer grannies sidles up to me.

'Na los,' she says.

Oma is animating me to take something from her hand. It has a musty, stuffy sort of smell, and isn't exactly fragrance of the month. It's almost as if she's attempting to lead me astray when she whispers in my ear:

'Es wird Ihna den Kopf reining.'

I think she's saying it will clear my head. Feeling like a mischievous schoolboy lurking behind the bike shed, I furtively inhale the grains she dabs on my wrist.

Sadly, the stimulant sparks something rather less desirable. Firmly wedged halfway up my nostrils, it makes me sneeze. Big time. A whole umbel wreath flies off the table, stopping just short of *Oma's* over-flowing basket. But neither my spasmodic reflex act of breath expiration nor the flying decorative arrangement seems to have any impact on *Oma*. She's completely cool with the chaos. As I wipe the tears from my eyes and gradually regain my composure, I see she's busy dabbing her own wrist, ready to inhale too.

Snuff, or *'Schmoizla'*, is one the most popular natural stimulants in Bavaria. Looking as fit as a fiddle, it's obviously working for *Oma*.

Moments later, barely recovered from my sneezing fit, I'm introduced to the *Hallertauer Bierkönigin*. Clinking bier mugs, we're just getting nicely acquainted, when the local youth brass band, the *Jugendkapelle*, burst into a deafening *Radetzky* march. Suddenly I'm struggling to follow even half of what Anna's saying. I find myself listening and nodding rather dopily, desperately hoping I don't miss anything too important.

My ears suddenly prick up when I hear her 21-year-old sibling is 'Pussy Queen of Bavaria.' She utters these words in the same tone as neighbours might chatter over the garden fence about the weather. But maybe I misheard her. Perhaps she said *'Bussi* Queen'. *Bussi* is local lingo for a hug and kiss. Queen of Hugs, nice one. But then, as the band blasts out another thunderous number in relentless 2-0-1 tempo, Anna shapes her hands like a megaphone and bellows: *'Mu-siiik!'*

Ach so! The penny finally drops. Her elder sister is Music Queen.

Winning royal titles runs in the family. Anna's other sibling was a Beer Queen too. Anna Baum has a tough year ahead though, as she races from one *Bierfest* to the next. I can't help feeling just a tad envious of her contractual 'obligations'. Imagine being plied with free beer every step you take, and not even having to queue for a refill.

I enquire whether all the free refills aren't too much of a good thing. Anna laughs:

'i probier a bissal vo oiem!'

She likes to try a bit of everything.

But isn't she ever tempted to go for just a half litre – a *Mini-Mass?*

'Na, da voie Mass mua sei oiwei,' she insists, *'in Bayern is des noamal.'*

The mere thought of half measures seems to strike fear of God into Anna. The *Mass*, or full litre, is clearly a must, the only acceptable measure in Bavaria. Munich folk take their full litre of beer so seriously, in fact, that municipal authorities regularly send out plain-clothed 'beer inspectors' whose unannounced checks strive to hunt down, name and shame dishonest barmen. One story on the official Oktoberfest website reports how some secret-shopper officials at last year's festival were served as little as 0.73 litres a mug. 'Robbed of 2.43 euros!' declares the shock-horror headline.

Just before Anna heads off to her next appointment – blowing out the candles at a property developer's 50th birthday celebration in Sixthaselbach – we hurry over to a photo call in the hop garden. Only by now it no longer resembles much of hop garden. Stripped bare of all buds and leaves by the uber-industrious *Omas*, it feels more like some urban backyard. All that remains of the picturesque plantation is a row of poles cobbled together by metal wirework. Drape some underwear over the trellis and it could easily pass for a washing line. Yet we somehow manage to find the last remaining cluster of greenery and tug it over our hair and around our waists. Part comical, part theatrical, we stand there posing for a cameraman from *www.hallertau.info*. The reporter mouths *'danke schön'* – more for the benefit of Anna, no doubt. Upon which, snapping the cap back onto his zoom lens, he races off to his next shoot somewhere in deepest Lower Bavaria.

And then, just as nobody's looking, I do something that breaks with all royal protocol. Leaning in slightly closer, and taking full advantage of the leafy hops for camouflage, I give the Beer Queen a tight squeeze.

As the deafening military march plays on inside the beer hall, I'm reminded of my own mission. Something that started out as a practical joke has since snowballed into a serious challenge. Assuming the audition's a success, very soon I too will be marching in a brass band, making just as much of a racket as these guys.

That night I pen my latest feature for 'Expat':

'Cavorting with Beer Queen in hop garden and sniffing strange substances with great granny. LOL! So much for living the life. Expat existence doesn't get much better, surely?'

Maybe I've gone slightly overboard on the swagger. But I'm quite chuffed with the headline:

'Beauty and the Brit'.

Grinning at the wordplay, I mail the article – plus picture of Queen and I draped in hops – to the news desk in London.

The column's caption crew have dismissed every single playful headline I've suggested so far. But I'm buoyant they'll ride with this one. When the article goes online two weeks later I both sigh and smile. The Editor has decided there's more mileage in my drug 'discovery'. Headline: 'Time for a trip'.

Time for a trip? Right now, I just need to rest my head. No more sniffing strange snuff for me, thanks.

'How many m² has your home?'

It's 3 October, Day of German Unification, a national holiday commemorating the anniversary of East and West Germany reuniting in 1990. We've invited a few friends over for a leisurely brunch. There's Claudia and Martin, Rebecca and Tina. And there's Melanie, who's clearly not visited us before. She underscores that by asking directly:

'How many square meters has your home?'

It's the leading question whenever Germans step into one another's abode for the first time.

'95.5' I reply, quicker than a wink.

Melanie looks genuinely pleased with my answer.

Whenever Germans enquire how many square metres your home spans, and how much you pay per square metre, the trick is to follow their gaze and catch where it falls. Are they surveying just the living space or peering further afield into the garden, and hence the whole *Grundstück*?

It turns out Melanie is interested merely in our indoor surface area.

The solemn way Germans talk about their square meterage, you'd think they were discussing the complexity of geometrical submultiples rather than the place they raise their family. Square meterage is such a hot topic that the media regularly holds contests, awarding prizes to the town or region which affords greatest amount of personal living space to its burghers. In 2018 the happiest citizens were said to live in the Bavarian Forest town of Freyung. They enjoy 53.8 sq. m of housing space per capita. That's a grand six metres more than the Bavarian average and well over an extra 9 meters compared to the rest of Germany.

By contrast, you'll seldom hear Brits discuss the square meterage of a building. Well, not unless they're actually standing there, brick and mortar in hand, gainfully charged with building the place as you pass by.

Anyway. Everyone's brought along some finger food for the buffet. Martin, bless him, has brought his own home-brewed beer. 'Here in Bavaria it's a *Grundnahrungsmittel*,' he beams. Bavarians typically regard *Bier* as a staple food, or 'liquid bread' as they call it. Martin handles the bottles as if they were precious gold bars. One by one he pulls them out of a crumpled freezer bag from Aldi.

It's typical of Germans, however, that while they raise the subject of the host home's square meterage even before they're halfway through the front door, a good two hours elapse before anyone dares broach the thorny topic of politics. The *Bundeswahl* was only last week and yet nobody wants to be the first to mention it.

It feels like we're playing a game.

Don't Mention The Election!

Maybe we simply don't want to dampen each other's good mood on a public holiday. It certainly hadn't been a brilliant year for the ballot box. First the Americans with Trump, then the Brits with Brexit. Whole families in the UK suddenly seemed to have been torn asunder. Some of these IN youngsters were no longer on speaking terms with their OUT elders. Brexit had become a dirty word. It was everybody's worst nightmare.

And now it's the *Bundesbürgers'* turn to be devastated by a disastrous election result. One which had seen Germany's veteran leader suffer substantial losses. She was now hanging on to power by the skin of her teeth. All of a sudden, everything seemed to be fitting into a lovely logical but utterly calamitous pattern. It was like the last remaining pieces of a picture puzzle had finally been botched together in one single sweep of the hand.

Claudia at last takes the plunge. 'Right up to the last minute, I *really* didn't know where to put my two crosses,' she confides, glancing around the buffet table nervously, as if addressing members of a subversive underground movement, planning some sort of coup d'état. Voice scaled down to a whisper, she adds, 'I stood there, recited *Hail Mary* three times and planted a cross-shape sign on my forehead, stomach and both shoulders.'

The way she describes the unnerving experience, it sounds more like Sunday confessional booth than election ballot box.

'Don't tell me about it,' says Melanie, dismissing the remark with a casual waft of the hand, as if flicking away a pesky fly.

'I couldn't stand the sight of Merkel any longer so I voted for The Greens.'

And then, in a bid to justify her political affinity, she adds 'Everyone in Puchheim did.'

'*Aach!*'

It's Bea's turn to wade into the debate.

'I wish I'd voted Green too now,' she sighs. 'I *did* vote for her, I'm afraid.'

'No, you *didn't* vote for her, *she* wasn't on the list,' I say, rebuking my partner. 'You voted for the local CSU candidate. I had to show you where to put the cross, remember?'

In some way it's a shame that Merkel, now hanging to power by just a thread, didn't perform better in the polls. *Mutti*, or mummy, as Germans affectionately call her, had won quite a few plus points just weeks earlier by sharing her favourite recipe with glossy magazine *Bunte*. As an aficionado of *Grundnahrungsmittel*, she'd chosen one of the nation's best-loved dishes: *Kartoffelsuppe*. And to further boost her ratings in the polls, she'd been snapped digging up spuds from her very own garden in the Uckermark. If electoral victory simply meant furbishing the nation with basics, then she'd ticked all the right boxes. Down-to-earth politicians dig down-to-earth potato soup, don't they? Honestly, if I was eligible to vote in these federal elections, I'd have backed *Mutti* too.

Well, maybe not. But I do like *Kartoffelsuppe*.

At this moment, Martin, who up to now has been keeping his political persuasions quietly to himself, suddenly fixes me with an expression as black as thunder:

'*Waaas*? You are seriously saying you went *zusamma*? Both of you in one single *Wahlkabine*?'

Martin utters the German word for polling booth as if it's a den of iniquity.

'That's *strengstens verboten*!' he continues, nostrils flared in frenzy.

'No one is allowed to spy on others at the *Wahlkabine*! This can get you into *serious* trouble here in Germany!'

Our friend Martin is literally foaming at the mouth, his eyes lit up like billiard balls tossed around in a storm.

'You can land in prison for that, you know, *ja*?'

You could not meet a more peaceful, even-tempered man than Martin. I've not heard him so much as raise his voice to a flea. Right now, however, he's completely delirious. All at once, he motions as if to pull out his smartphone and, at a touch a few keys, deliver me up to the local *Ordnungshüter*. I'm almost expecting a vanload of police officers to pull up outside, and, gun barrel pressed tightly against my neck, be marched away in handcuffs. Flinching back in fear, I duck as if to avoid an imaginary blow.

But then the contrite expression on Martin's face slowly starts to fade.

All at once he breaks into a wide smile, pulling down on his lower left-hand eyelid. It's that typical Germanic gesture that means 'Sucker!'

Then, triumphantly, he raises his beer mug to me and cries '*P-R-O-S-T*!'

I've heard Bavarians say that *Prost!* is euphemistic for something like 'Screw the rest of the world and its problems!' A bit like *America First*, perhaps, only much more subtle. I've also heard it said that Germans in general have no sense of humour. But when it comes to uttering one single word that delivers the ultimate, twist-in-the-tale punchline, no one can hold a candle to the Bavarians.

Yes, why not?

Prost!

Whirls and Swirls

The question on the poster taped to a swing door at college is an instant attention grabber:

~ *Who fancies trying out Bavarian Dancing?* ~

Bavarian dancing. The words leap out at me, almost as if triggering a lightbulb moment. I was finally being offered the chance to boogy like a typical Bavarian.

Germans have a saying that goes '*Nichts hält jünger, als ein alter Tanz*' – nothing keeps you younger than an old dance. Maybe that's exactly what I need right now – an injection of youth. Very recently I'd celebrated another round birthday, landmarked by an embarrassing exhibition of daddy dancing. All captured on smartphone, of course. Good job the clip never made it onto facebook.

I sign up immediately.

'Bavarian Dancing', bizarrely, is not really Bavarian at all. It originated as an Austrian peasant whirl and twirl. It wasn't long, however, until the nobility got in on the act, popularizing it across the ballrooms of 19th-century Vienna. For the first time in history, dancing couples came really close and embraced each other. No wonder the waltz was considered by some as nothing short of scandalous. As for the 'Bavarian' polka, that's actually a Bohemian peasant dance which became fashionable around the same time.

But there's something else I discover.

Something rather saucy.

Conscious that Bavarian dancing is all about slapping both yourself and your partner on the hands and thighs, I naively believed that's as far as it goes. Alarm bells start clanging, however, when a search on YouTube unveils a clip in which the male dancer lays his partner on the ground and proceeds to slap her buttocks. I surf a bit further, just to check I haven't stumbled across an off-the-wall *Verein* that's taking the whole idea of whacking your partner's bum one naughty step too far. Incredibly, I discover scores of similar clips posted by traditional folk groups at dances all over Bavaria. Kids, youths, parents, aunties and uncles, even *Opas* and *Omas* – everyone, it seems, is grabbing, whacking and smacking.

Best to go with an open mind, maybe.

The big night begins with a disappointment. It turns out we're to dance in the very classroom I've been teaching in earlier that day. Embarrassingly, I hadn't even wiped the board clean. And that's not the only let-down. Clad in lederhose, I suddenly become acutely aware that my outfit feels a bit big. Even bigger than when I first wore it. Have I shrunk since the *Hoagarten*? My size 'M' was obviously tailored more towards the physique of the classic Bavarian *Bursche* – sturdy yet stumpy. I'm probably not getting enough *Heislmannskost* – good solid homemade meals such as pork knuckles and *Knödel* dumplings. Rather than cling to me, the whole outfit seems to hang off my backside. Just like those jeans that adolescents wear, with bum piece sagging significantly below the waist.

Apart from a colleague from the Student Advisory Service who's organising the event, I can't see anyone else dressed in full *Tracht*, the traditional yet once again trendy Bavarian costume. Merely one other male is wearing lederhose, and that's 'matched', for want of a better word, with a flashy *'Bondi Bitch'* t-shirt. What also strikes me is that females outnumber men approximately five to one. Bavarians call this *Damaübaschuß*.

Surplus women? No problem.

But then another let-down. Not one of them has donned a *dirndl*.

About two dozen of us, a mixture of students and teachers, are about to be serenaded by a five-strong band, Schreinergeiger, who have set up shop right in front of the blackboard. Our trainer for the evening is Magnus. It's funny how images we might have of the typical male dance teacher are so often hackneyed. Before tonight I would have probably pictured him prancing rather than dancing. Dressed in leopard-skin leotard, bracelets and bangles dangling from the wrists. A silver pendant swinging nonchalantly around the neck maybe. I imagine him fluffing his hair and saying things like 'Ding Dong, darling!' and 'Ooh lovey, just look at you!'

How wrong I am. Magnus is as straight as a tooth pick. Sporting suede leather jacket, tight polo shirt and skinny-fit jeans, he's very much a ladies' man. The man, no less, who grooms Munich's youth for the legendary *Kocherlball*, or 'Cooks' Ball'. That's the early morning dance-fest staged every June underneath the Chinese Tower in the Englischer Garten. After the briefest of introductions (*'i bin da Mognus'*) and minimum small talk (*'guad gell, laßt uns dann scho moi loslegn'*) – this is Germany, remember – it's straight down to business. Magnus explains that in Bavarian dancing it's always customary for women to request men to dance. And for women to take the lead in every ensuing step too. No problem for me; I'm more than willing to be led by ladies. My problem is of a different nature – I can't find a partner who's also willing. Everyone automatically pairs up with the person they arrived with and I'm left standing all on my own.

The whole thing feels like a cruel throwback to Year Nine all-boys school, when the sports teacher made us pair up to do exercises around the gym hall. Whenever we were an odd number of pupils, I was always the one left without a partner. Eventually the track-suited teacher would force two other boys to let me join them in a threesome. The pair would grudgingly accept me, at best, and heavily protest at worst. Several decades later, these memories return to haunt me. I fear I'll be left out again. Mercifully, Magnus races to my rescue.

'Hey, schau moi da.'

Our instructor is gesturing towards an attractive-looking girl in a zebra-striped singlet and snug-fit leggings. Standing over in the corner, she's also alone. Heaving an enormous sigh of relief, I take her hand and we gracefully slide in amongst the other couples to form one long polonaise, snaking around the room. I never pictured myself parading around my own classroom quite like this. It feels like we're warming up for a child's birthday party. That any minute someone will call out 'Food's on the table!' and we'll all race into the dining room and murder the cake. All that's missing here are party horns, paper hats and someone quietly throwing up in the corner.

All of a sudden, Magnus bids us to stretch our arms out and link together to form an archway. Standing right at the end of the arch, my partner and I are first to go under. Holding hands, we merrily canter through. It's a bit like we've just taken our vows up at the altar. Did I just sign something too? Maybe I'm taking this whole thing a bit too seriously, but something feels wrong when we emerge at the other end and no one showers us with confetti.

With everyone finally through the 'wedding tunnel', Magnus launches into the next routine: quintessential Bavarian-type hand-and-thigh slapping interspersed with slightly more elegant whirls and twirls, with the odd bit of tango and foxtrot thrown in for effect. Bavarian dancing has to be a hotchpotch of just about every single dance style under the sun. Some pairs manage the quick-step transitions quite effortlessly. The way Magnus is encouraging us to place a foot between our partner's legs makes me feel like we're more in Buenos Aires than Bavaria. I've never tried tango before and am trying exceedingly hard not to misplace my left foot when I suddenly squeal 'Ouch!' My right-hand toe is writhing with pain. My partner has just accidentally stepped on it. Still, I'm glad it's she who's committed the *faux pas* and not me. I'm generally the *Tolpatsch*, the one who always puts his foot in it outside the classroom.

During a short interlude, it's my turn to put the proverbial foot in it.

Thinking we're supposed to change partners, I turn to a colleague and ask if she'd like to be mine. '*Na, sorry,*' she replies, pointing to a diminutive lady with her back to us, presumably her partner for the evening. '*Pech kabd,*' bad luck, she adds. I know she doesn't mean it unsympathetically at all, but once again it feels like I'm back at school, seeking an elusive partner. Sheepishly, I return to my own partner, hoping to goodness she hasn't overheard this embarrassing exchange. Frankly, I'm quite glad no one has to change partners. We got off to a rather clumsy start, but I have the feeling we're moving nicely in time together now. I'm actually quite enjoying this.

Everything's going a treat until we have to pair up with another couple. We've got to slap-clap our partner's hands, whirl them around and then perform this very same 'act' on the two others. I don't know whether it's just because I wasn't following Magnus' demonstration carefully enough or I'm just plain uncoordinated, but this is where I suddenly start to lose it. I feel like those poor contestants in *The Generation Game*. That's the BBC 'have-a-go' show we used to howl at as kids. An expert would come on and demonstrate how to do something – such as modelling a vase on a potter's wheel or dressing up a shop window mannequin. They always made it look so dead simple. The competitors, typically mum or dad with either son or daughter-in-law, then had to copy the *Meister*, but usually in much less time. It's similar here. Before each new number Magnus demonstrates the moves. Beckoning to a different girl each time, he draws her close to his chest and swirls her around the floor. Nothing could look simpler.

Until we attempt it.

As soon as we break for slightly longer my partner slips off. I expect she's just grabbing a drink from the trestle table in the corridor and visiting the ladies' room. But I really wouldn't blame her if she seizes the opportunity to seek out a more competent partner. All went well until I screwed up on the step when you have to take your partner's left hand in yours and then your right hand behind her back to take her right hand in turn. I'm confused just thinking about it. Standing there, knotted together in this almost bear-hug-like embrace, our arms clumsily twisted around each other, I hadn't dared peer up to see the expression on her face. A look of horror, most likely.

Suddenly she reappears, sliding in alongside me as if she'd never been gone. For the second moment this evening I breathe a huge sigh of relief. Despite cavorting around the classroom almost nonstop for the last hour she's still looking as fresh as a buttercup. And – unlike me – still totally calm and composed. I'm just about to ask 'What's your...?' when the band suddenly starts blasting out the next tune. My last word is drowned in an ear-shattering wiener-schnitzel polka.

Falling into a hypnosis-like routine of twirls and swirls – briefly interspersed every now and again with a gentle mutual hand-slap – I remain on a high for the rest of the evening. I'm willing the whole thing to last just a tiny bit longer, but, spot on 9 o'clock – *deutsche Pünktlichkeit* at play once again – the band blow their final note. Sadly, next moment they're squeezing instruments back into cases and pulling on coats and scarves. It's almost as if they're racing to catch the last bus home. Beckoning everyone to form a tight circle, Magnus lavishes praise upon us, saying '*Ihr hobt olle note oins vedeant*' – you've all earned yourselves top grade.

Surprisingly, we've not paid a single cent for this evening's superb live music and expert dance tuition. It's all come courtesy of the Bavarian Ministry of Culture. My colleague explains afterwards that this government body paid the performers half a grand to come and amuse us for two hours. You hear so much about local government squandering public funds on this or that *Fehlinvestition*, or white-elephant idea. This, in contrast, seems a marvellous payback of tax payers' money.

Magnus dishes out flyers for another free dance session he's offering next month. This time it's at the world-famous Hofbräuhaus. I consider asking my partner if she'd care to go along too. Looking around, however, I notice she's vanished. The magical evening has ended all too abruptly. It's unfair. Why can't this finish like a fairytale ball? Lucky Prince Charming. At least he got the girl's glass slipper for keep's sake. Not only has my partner already bunked off, she's taken all her footgear too.

Leaving the classroom, I instinctively reach for the braces on my leather pants. During the dancing I'd had a job keeping them hitched up – they're definitely too loose. But I couldn't make them any tighter at all. There's obviously one hole too few on each suspender strap. Small wonder the whole outfit's hanging off me like a pair of saggy 'gangsta' pants. If I ever go Bavarian dancing again, I'm going in different lederhose. And they'd better be size 'S'.

That night, collapsing into bed, exhausted but exuberant, I post:

'First post-Brexit vote challenge on road to becoming Bavarian successfully completed!'

I soon drift off into deep comatose sleep. In no time, I dream I'm back in that classroom whirling and swirling my dance partner around the floor.

Stalking Prince Charles

'Measse vuimois.'

The blue-blooded Brit is speaking faultless Bavarian. Switching to English, he adds: 'I had one of these as a boy.'

Der ewige Thronfolger – the eternal heir, as he's called in Germany – has just been presented with a lederhose by Markus Söder, Minister President of Bavaria. Just one teeny-weeny problem – it's about 30 sizes too small.

Suddenly, coverage of Charles and Camilla in Munich jumps from Residenz to Hofbräuhaus. The commentator reveals that the lederhose is for the Prince's three-day old grandchild. What with proud parents Harry and Meghan parading the *Wunderkind* around Buckingham Palace and the announcement that Number Seven in line to throne's called Archie, it's been a right royal day.

Determined to catch up with Charles on his state visit to Munich, I'd stuffed a Union Jack into my bag and alerted students that our afternoon class would finish a few minutes earlier – just in case anybody wished to come along too. Sadly, I'm not too sure they do. 'You're *really* going?' one undergrad asks disbelievingly.

If I leave class at 3:15, I can just about make it to the Hofbräuhaus in time to wave my flag at the royal couple.

Perhaps they'll even autograph it.

What a blow then to arrive at the beer house to see large numbers of *Polizisten* in bullet-proof vests already packing away security cordon and climbing back into their vans. I've missed the Royals by just seven minutes.

It turns out that the Windsors are already on their way to the headquarters of Siemens. It's fast approaching 4 p.m., rush hour time in Munich. Surely, I can beat their convoy of limousines by jumping onto public transport?

It helps if you can read a *U-Bahn* plan the right way up. I end up taking the correct line but in the wrong direction. By the time I reach Siemens it's just turning 5 p.m. But it's the wrong branch of Siemens. Giving me side-eye, staff at the Welcome Desk have an unwelcome message: *'Sie san do foisch.'*

No wonder I'm in the wrong place – everyone milling around me is dressed in suits. I'm just in shorts and sandals. For a split second it looks like the reception girl's about to reach below her desk. Presumably to hit a panic button and summon security guards to guide me off the premises. Any moment I'm expecting swarms of officials in dayglo jackets to surround me, picking up commands on their ear-pieces and shouting feverishly into their mobiles. Instead, the receptionist calmly walks me out into the foyer and directs me down the street to Siemens Forum.

This time I think twice about entering. Quizzing the first group of dirndl-dressed employees leaving the building, I learn that Charles and Camilla took off a good 45 minutes ago. In the short time it's taken me to ride several stops on the subway, the royal party has made it across town through the *Berufsverkehr*, toured Siemens Forum and checked into their penthouse suite at the Bayrischer Hof.

As I turn to go, one of the Siemens secretaries says *'Herzlichen Beileid.'*

Doesn't that mean 'deepest condolences'? Something you'd normally say in hushed tones to the bereaved? Perhaps I really should be mourning. After chasing the Royals around Munich all afternoon I've twice missed them almost within a hair's breadth.

Heading back into the town centre, I stop off at the Residenz. That's where the royal couple walked the red carpet just a few hours earlier. Asking around, I discover that Charles passed right under the statue of König Maximilian Joseph. Squinting through the sunshine, I spot two pigeons doing a jig on Max's ears, before snapping their beaks and flying off, leaving a trail of bird paint dripping down His Royal Highness' majestic forehead.

Ah well, let's face it. That's probably about as close as I'm going to get to royalty today.

Luckily the day's not completely over. Today, it turns out, is Europe Day. The Bavarian Staatskanzlei, or Department of State, is staging a series of shows at the Marienplatz. Peppered all around the main *Platz* are little huts, plastered with posters encouraging Münchners to exercise their franchise at the forthcoming *Europawahl.*

Till now these elections had hardly bothered me. All that really interested me was whether Britain could pull out of Europe before being stitched into a straitjacket and forced to go along with the whole masquerade. But spotting a photo booth offering free selfies with an EU star-studded backdrop immediately converts me to the cause. Next moment I'm being photographed in front of a banner proclaiming *'Diesmal wähle ich!'* – this time I'm voting.

Meanwhile Ecco DiLorenzo Smart & Soul are playing a soulful mix of seventies, Chic-style disco. Just the right thing. Earlier, during harmonies from the *Deutsch-Französischer Chor*, I'd been lying back, luxuriating in one of the free deckchairs. But, as soon as I hear the opening chords to 'Le Freak', I leap up and join a handful of other revellers bopping up and down near the stage. Waving arms and legs around almost hypnotically, more Kate Bush than Beyoncé, we must appear quite comical to the rest of the audience, all superglued to their deckchairs.

The sun's still shining when just before 8 p.m. the band strikes up its final offering, the soul classic 'At the Carwash'.

At the Carwash?

I know this is an 'auto nation' and Germans love their cars, but it seems a funny choice of song title. Aren't they supposed to be encouraging everyone to abandon polishing their dreams on wheels on 26 May and get along to the polling booths instead?

But maybe that's not the point. What strikes me, boogying and bumping to Rose Royce is that I'm surrounded by a mass of merrymakers of all ages and mixed European backgrounds – grooving together as one. Staunch supporters of a United Europe. And all loving the moment.

Heaven knows what the *Herren* from The Bavarian Staatskanzlei make of our trance-like motions. But I hope they approve of our symbolic show of solidarity on the dance floor.

Prince Charles sure would.

Blow Brexit, I wanna be Bavarian!

'I solemnly declare that I will respect and observe the Basic Law and the laws of the Federal Republic of Germany, and that I will refrain from any activity which might cause it harm.'

In less than the ninety seconds it's taken to render all three verses of *Deutschland über alles,* and swear the oath of citizenship, I've suddenly become German. A photographer from the *Mittelbayerische Zeitung* has just snapped me receiving my *Einbürgerungszertifikat* from County Commissioner Martin Neumayer. There are a dozen or more other nationalities represented in the room. Hearing each one called up almost feels like casting votes at the Eurovision Song Contest – Croatia, Turkey, Poland, Lithuania, Bosnia-Herzegovina...

No jury points for anybody today though. In fact, the local press seems interested in only one single nationality. Clicking his camera from all angles, and zooming in on the Union Jack t-shirt I'd slipped on for a bit of fun, the reporter asks for my take on Brexit. I hesitate, wondering whether it's wise to reply at all. How much time has he got? Stepping down from the podium, I pass two other Brits next up to take the oath.

'Na, Glück gehabt. Hey, that was lucky,' quips the Commissioner a little later, as we mingle and mix over

Kaffee and Gebäck. Was he referring to the 'B' word? The dreaded date was just days away, but little did we know that only hours later it would be postponed. And postponed again. The way things were looking, it possibly wasn't going to happen at all.

Standing for the all-pervading Catholic state party of Bavaria, our local member of parliament appears to personify the quintessential German politician: stern, solemn and straightlaced to a tea.

Yet, face-to-face, only an arm's length away from the *Freistaat* flag, I can't help noticing a tiny twinkle in his eye.

Are you sure you want to be doing this?

There it goes again, that little voice inside my head. The one that waved the red flag as I was tossed and torn between Germany and New Zealand. And now it's questioning my sanity.

Sure, in a flight of fancy I'd toyed with the idea of joining my local brass band and beating the drum at the region's largest *Bierfest*. All in the notion, no doubt, that such a feat would somehow make me a fully-fledged Bavarian. Suddenly, however, the plan feels like a *Schnapsidee*, some crazy idea dreamt up while drunk. Why not simply call this whole Make-me-a-Bavarian thing a day while I was on a high? After all, I'd hobknobbed amongst the hops with a Beer Queen. Top that.

And I probably would have called it a day. Had it not been for a local lifestyle journal called *Franns*. This pocket-size magazine deserves an accolade for cramming a record number of photos into the minimum possible space. You almost need a laboratory magnifying lamp to pick up the detail in some of the images. Most of which portray adolescents dressed in dirndls and lederhosen. Captured in various states of sobriety, they all appear surgically attached to the litre jug of beer clutched tightly between their fists.

The brains behind *Franns* is a man called Jörg. We'd last met at the *Stadtfest* where I was roped into a blind beer-tasting competition. Jörg had also helped me out enormously when I desperately needed pictures to get my personal website off the ground.

It was our first weekend in the Hallertau, and I'd been on what felt like a wild goose chase, trawling town in search of a photographic studio. But there was just one small problem. When clocks chime midday on Saturday, almost everywhere in provincial Bavaria closes. Locals have a lovely expression for describing this closing down ceremony – *do wern de Biagasteige houchgeklappt*. Well, in Moaburg they don't even wait till nightfall to roll up the sidewalk. It's already packed away by lunchtime.

But it's not just in Moaburg. Anybody waylaid from clocking off at two o'clock on a Friday afternoon does their damnedest to ensure they get away by Saturday midday. I was just about to give up the search and head for home when I spotted a store that stood out from all the rest. Probably because of a purple banner festooned over the shop front, balloons floating from either end. The whole thing screamed 'New Kid on the Block'.

Local folk might say *'Na und?'* – what the heck. After all, stores and eateries are opening up and closing down here all the time. No big deal. But what struck me about this *Neue Eröffnung* was the Very English banner: 'The Sour Cherry'. Curious to discover whether a fellow expat had set up locally, I'd pulled up alongside to take a closer squint.

The man at the door is wearing bright orange trousers. I'm expecting him to tell me, politely but firmly, to go away, since he's probably just about to head off on his well-earned *Feierabend*. Instead, however, he smiles almost apologetically, introduces himself and invites me in:

'Hallöchen! Ich bin der Jörg!'

Anyone who talks like this has to be a *Zugeroasta*. An outsider. Bavarians don't go around saying *'Hallöchen!'* They say *'Servus'*, *'Griaß di'* and *'Naaa'*. Or – some Bavarians can be exceptionally gruff – just lower the head a fraction. Hearing *'Hallöchen!'* here in Bavaria is a bit like having some camp type sidle up in Stoke-on-Trent and say 'Well he-llo there!'

Jörg, it turns out, hails from Saxony in former East Germany. *'Komm rein,'* he says, beckoning me in. When I explain I need shots for my website he leads me into a brightly lit studio and starts flashing away before I've even had time to straighten my jacket or comb my unruly hair into place.

I'm thrilled with the results. Jörg throws in one or two extra pictures for free and adds a neat little caption.

It says 'Tim Howe, saving the world and just *lurrving* it.' I chuckle. One shot shows me posturing in a smart Sacco jacket, copy of *The Daily Telegraph* rolled up in hand. The East German seems to be casting me as Her Majesty's secret service agent. The pose I'm striking bears an uncanny resemblance to a James Bond cardboard cut-out. One in which 007 is seen saving the universe from the clutches of some monstrous villain. Lovely stuff.

We soon become friends and I often pop into Jörg's studio whenever I need professional photos taken. On one occasion I run my 'Make me a Bavarian' idea past him. He must like the idea because he immediately pulls out his smartphone and starts scrolling through his personal planner. In a flash, he's pencilled me in for a full-page feature in the next issue of *Franns*.

It's not long before news of my exploits becomes a staple feature of the local 'what's-hot-what's-not' magazine. Clicking onto the publication's website, I grin at the headline: 'What's it like living as a *Zugeroasta* in the Hallertau? And just what do we locals make of this Brit?'

There was a high risk that locals might say 'Not a lot.' In my first serialized instalment, I'd poked fun at *Wunschkennzeichenfahrer*. That's what they call motorists who willingly fork out twenty euros or more for personal licence plates. In this case, the vanity plates all carry the letters 'MAI'. Short for Mainburg, MAI is pronounced exactly the same as the English 'my'. It's the cherry on the cake for local burghers, who get a kick out of making wordplays with their initials. As opposed to

'KEH' for Kelheim – the regional administration town, some 40 km up the road. Many natives turn their noses up at vehicle registration plates from Kelheim. Not because KEH bonds less beautifully with their initials but simply because Kelheim's so far away. Yes, 40 km is a mighty long distance in the eyes and minds of *Moaburger*.

Interestingly, most other Germans tend to treat personalised plates more as visiting cards, typically displaying both their initials and birth year. The registration M JS5 68, for example, reveals that the driver is from Munich, their first name is likely to be either Johannes or Johanna and their surname probably Schönegge or Sedlmeier. It also signals this is their car number five and they were born in the heady year of 1968. All this feels worlds apart from the British penchant of treating 'wish' plates purely as a joke. Think HIP DJ.

Germans happily dig deep into their pockets for anything and everything to do with their beloved *Autos*. According to *Welt.de* they fork out an average of 335 euros a month on car-related expenses. Yet when it comes to most other pleasures, it's more a question of *Geiz is geil* – tight is right – to quote the slogan of Saturn, the electronics retailer giant. Germans can be alarmingly tight-fisted. Local burghers, for instance, feverishly take to the barricades every time Guiseppe at *Eiscafé Venezzia* jacks up the price of a single scoop by ten cents.

But right now something totally different is creating a stir amongst my fellow citizens. It's the hoops I'm leaping through in a bid to become one of them myself.

Growing numbers on social media are firing off questions faster than I can reply. It seems they're egging me on to 'up the ante' or *oins ostàndig draud machn*, as they say around here. 'Hey, Mister British Man', posts Lisa-Marie on FRANNS' facebook page. Reverting to dialect, she enquires:

'Wirst Du boar voa weihhnochd?

Will I be Bavarian by Christmas? Typical Germans, constantly pressing for deadlines.

Other followers, mostly males actually, have seen my picture posing with the Beer Queen among the hop buds. They're inviting me to drink *Bruadaschoft*. How flattering that so many Bavarians should want to join me, an Englander of all people, in this very Germanic ritual of male bonding. Although I rather suspect it's the *Bierkönigin* who's been fuelling their fantasies more than a loony Brit larking around in oversized lederhosen. Whatever, there's no getting away from this time-honoured act of locking arms and drinking the pledge of eternal friendship. Bavarians don't normally do *Bruadaschoft* until they've known each other for a good twenty years. And, even then, only on very specific occasions, such as marriage/divorce or successfully surviving a mid-life crisis together. Yet here I am being fast-tracked to the fore, catapulted to the cusp of discovering what it means to call yourself a *Boar*, a true Bavarian. And teetering on the brink of becoming one myself. By Christmas, possibly.

Given this volume of public interest, it would be downright disingenuous to back down.

I call Christian, the *Kappellenmeister*.

It turns out Stephan has already spoken to his colleague about an Englander aspiring to join their ranks. Better still, he's persuaded him to give me an audition. The band leader seems delighted to have me on board:

'*Super, kimm mang zu Probevoastäiung!*'

Rehearsals begin tomorrow.

The Accidental Cymbalist

'*Du schbuist doch aa Beckn, naaa?*'

Basti is speaking in thickly accented *Niederbayrisch*. So thick, in fact, that it's any outsider's guess what he's saying. And this time no one's leaping to my rescue with a translation.

Registering the blank expression on my face, Basti repeats the question painfully slowly – in something more resembling *Hochdeitsch*. When Bavarians speak High German, they often labour each word, as if it were some intrinsically difficult foreign language:

'*Du-uu spie-elst doch auuuch Be-cken, naaa?*

You *do* play *Becken, don't* you?

Pointing his little finger at me as if an admonishment, Basti is clearly not making some polite enquiry. More likely, he's issuing a firm command. As for '*Naaa?*' it's one of those multi-functional Bavarian words that can mean either 'yes', 'no', 'how are you?' or simply 'let's get a beer together'.

But it's unlikely that Basti is enquiring about my health. And he's certainly not inviting me for a drink. Right now, I think he's simply signalling end of discussion.

Shame. I'd turned up hoping for a score-card analysis

of my musical potential. Or, at very least, some sort of action plan regarding my potential role in the band. But Basti doesn't do pep talk, and he definitely isn't about to conduct a performance appraisal. Like most Bavarians, he's hardwired for cutting straight to the chase. My fate, it seems, has already been decided.

A fortnight has passed since I made the call to the *Kappellenmoasda*. Basti has been my mentor – and a very patient one too – while I've worked out on drums. I was so looking forward to banging the instrument in public. But suddenly he's relegated me to *Becken*.

'*Ahhm, jaaaa?*' I respond, half answer, half question.

It turns out that my name came up in an *Ausschusssitzung*, the sort of committee meeting which Germans willingly endure long into the night. They've decided my drum skills aren't quite up to scratch. But what exactly are *Becken*? When Germans talk about *Becken* they can mean either basin, bowl or pelvis. Bastian is obviously talking about none of these at all. He goes on to explain that their cymbals player has quit just two days before our public appearance. They've searched the Hoiertau high and low for a replacement, yet failed to find one. He doesn't say so directly, but the message is clear.

I'm their very last resort.

It's cymbals or sod all.

And when it comes to cymbals, I really do know sod all. The only member of the percussion family I've ever played is the triangle, and not since junior school in 1977. Cymbals typically weigh in at around 3.5 kg. Holding them up to my chest, it feels like I'm auditioning for Iron

Man at the local branch of INJOY.

Sliding into the back row, I join the rest of the band for their final rehearsal that evening. We haven't even finished practising the Bavarian theme tune *Weiß Blauer* and my hands already feel like they're about to disconnect from my limbs and slide off. How on earth will I survive this ordeal when we perform in public?

Basti ends the shortest induction in German history as tersely as it began:

'*Na, dann bis Feidog um fünf, bassd?*'

Sure, Basti. See you Friday at five.

But, driving home after final rehearsal, I begin to have second thoughts. Under my breath I go through the motions of making a farewell speech. I thank the band for the enlightening experience and vow to pull out gracefully, before making a complete muppet of myself.

Just one small problem. Pulling out right now would mean not giving the statutory 12 hours' notice. And Bavarians don't do short notice. They probably require me to announce my standing down at least one month in advance – countersigned by local bank manager, rubber-stamped and dispatched recorded delivery.

On the big day, however, I find myself walking out of the house with a spring in my step. Overnight I had some crazy dream about riding up the steps to our local *Rathaus* on a red carpet, cymbals clanging all around me, clattering together like tin cans trailing behind a newlyweds' honeymoon vehicle. It's funny what you can end up fantasising about after living in Germany for almost two decades.

This is it then. It's do or die.

The Gallimarkt is the Hallertau region's biggest and brashest *Bierfest*, and one of Bavaria's most ancient, dating back to 1397. On the opening night we're scheduled to play in front of the Town Hall and then head the procession of clubs and associations towards the beer tents. Marching time: approx. one hour. Having squeezed myself into my increasingly stinky lederhose, I arrive at the meeting place at five o'clock on the dot – exactly as instructed. But the street corner is completely deserted, devoid of band and spectators.

So much for *deutsche Pünktlichkeit*.

I panic. Maybe I've got the wrong place, wrong day, wrong time even. Could *fünf Uhr* possibly mean five in the *morning*? Knowing the Germans' penchant for getting up and going to work half way through the night, that wouldn't surprise me at all. Clutching my mobile as if were my last lifeline, I step into a shop doorway. Glancing nervously from side to side, I feel like a flustered school kid, gutted at the prospect of being stood up on a first date.

I pretend to look busy by scrutinising my WhatsApp account.

No calls, no messages, *nix*.

That's it. I'm going. But then, from round the corner, I suddenly hear a buzz of voices. It's the band. Next thing, curvy-shaped cases are being cranked open all around me and dozens of shiny brass instruments start appearing. One of these is my pair of cymbals. 'Ta-daaaa!' announces Basti, handing me the tyre-size clashers with exaggerated ceremony. The irony of Basti making such a fuss over me doesn't escape some of my fellow musicians. They've been busy rehearsing for this grand event for months on end. I started practising just a few days ago.

As I hoist my weighty cymbals into a 45-degree position – they feel more like 5-kg dumbbells than a musical instrument – band leader Christian beckons me over for a final briefing: 'When we march off, start on your left foot and just count *oins-zwoa*, one-two. *Alles klar?*'

Just about.

Our short performance in front of the *Rathaus* goes surprisingly smoothly, actually. Well at least I don't drop the cymbals. But it's questionable whether the noise I'm making can actually be classified as music. Spectators soon start to clasp hands to ears and scuttle off to the sidelines. Some band members do so too.

Warm-up show over, the procession slowly starts to move off. Although I'm making a point of keeping an eye glued to my marching steps, this doesn't feel much like a coordinated march at all. At the pace most of us are going, it's more like a shuffle. Somehow, no one around me seems all that bothered.

We're flanked by some 60 associations, including voluntary firefighters, boy scouts, homing pigeon breeders and choral societies. Padding alongside, dressed in bonnets and delightful check-print pinafores, are the ladies from the local *Gesangsverein*. Wedged in right behind us, meanwhile, is the *Burschenverein*. This is the association whose sole *raison d'être* appears to be erecting tents in the middle of woods and staging *Titty Twister* parties. It feels great, parading down the streets lined with onlookers clapping and cheering us on like minor celebrities. It's almost like we're being swept along on a red carpet. Ah, last night's daft dream! Unfortunately, I remember very little else of the march. Apart from the deafening din of my cymbals.

Our destination is *Dausinger* – an enormous beer tent, festooned with giant bauble-like balloons and garish paper chains. The long trestle tables are all lovingly decorated with white and blue crepe tissue-paper cloths and matching serviettes. It looks like they've been laid for some gigantic tea party. Instead of Alice and The Mad Hatter, however, I'm surrounded by hundreds upon hundreds of beer-thirsty Bavarians. Just as we take our seats, the *Bürgermeister* slips on a neatly-ironed apron, preparing to perform the *Anstich*, the ceremonial tapping of the keg. Before I've even unfolded my napkin, the rest of the band are ordering mountain-size servings of *Schweinshax'n*, roasted pork knuckles, and *Hoibs Hendl*, half a chicken. I'm always amazed how Germans can gobble down XXL portions with every litre *Bier*. Having marched for an hour with the equivalent of my weight in gold bullion bars, I'm far too tired to eat anything at all.

Soon we're all sloshing steins and swapping stories. Everyone's drinking away merrily but no one's overdrinking. That's another feather in the Germans' felt cap, their *Trinkfestigkeit* – literally their 'steadfastiness' when it comes to drinking – and knowing when to call it quits.

I strike up conversation with trumpeter Maria:

'Are you still fit after blowing two hours nonstop?'

'Bäh, des is jo nix.'

That's nothing, apparently. Tomorrow they'll play six hours.

These Bavarians sure have stamina. I say how much I've enjoyed being their guest cymbalist and, laughing, she suggests I come to more rehearsals. Nice to hear they want to see me again. But Maria clearly isn't pussyfooting with me:

'Du soist a bisserl mehr übn.'

I ought to practise a bit more.

Impressive though it is, the 600-year-old Gallimarkt is bush league compared to the *Volksfest* we visited just a fortnight earlier. Attracting six million visitors who knock back 7.5 million litres of beer between them, Munich's Oktoberfest is the world's largest *Bierfest*. But unlike the Gallimarkt, you can't just walk into just any tent you wish. For each tent you need a colour-coded band. These are like gold dust and there are only two ways to get one. Either you arrive first thing in the day or – months in advance – you reserve a table in one of the raised 'boxes' spanning the side of the tent. Which we were lucky to secure in the *Ochsenbraterei* pavilion this year, thanks to our dear friend Daniela who works at the *Bayrischer Bauernverband* (Bavarian Farmers' Union). As the dirndl-clad *Kellnerin* hovered around our luxury loge taking orders, it felt a bit like airline First Class. The waitress-cum-hostess just stopped short of offering to plump up our cushions. But, glancing down at the mass of merrymakers squashed together like sardines, we clearly had the best deal on legroom.

Back to the Gallimarkt. The whole atmosphere is

strikingly similar to *Fasching*. Masses of merrymakers dressed up in clothes they wouldn't normally dare wear, revelling with people they wouldn't normally party with. And all of them performing jigs and gestures far too embarrassing to talk about.

Such as wiggling index fingers up and down to the tune of 'Mamma Mia'.

Weaving my way through a crowd of Abba aficionados, I suddenly spot the Hallertau Beer Queen bouncing towards me. After the lengthy official proceedings, the evening is only just starting for young Anna. It's lovely to see her again. But up against the deafening sound of the brass band blowing away for all its worth right behind us, once again I can barely make out what she's shouting about. The gist seems to be that they're all going to the after-show at *Almhüttn*, an alpine-style log hut just behind the big tent. Will she be dancing on the tables too?

'*Ha,*' Anna laughs, '*so wos machn grod de jüngrn*' – that's just the young ones.

By now I'm a little hoarse from trying to make myself heard over the ear-splitting sound of *Froschhaxn Express* giving all they've got up on stage. After marching with two 3.5 kilo weights, I can no longer feel my arms. I have the feeling that at any moment they'll quietly detach themselves from the rest of my torso and drop to the ground.

Anna is right, we're best leaving table dancing to the youngsters.

Aside from one or two senior moments such as this, my mission to become a Bavarian – a Hoiertau Bavarian

– is practically accomplished. I'm one of the gang. For one night, at least. Admittedly, I'm not the most accomplished cymbals player to ever swell their ranks. But at least I've given it Best of British.

Calling it a day, I hand my clangers back to Basti and make for the exit.

If this were theatre, we'd now be into curtain call. We'd have the whole cast assembled in one long line front of stage, hands linked and held high, ready to take their final bow amidst a storm of applause.

End of show, curtains down, lights on.

But there's one final act, as yet unscripted. After sobering up from the brass band challenge, I suspect the greatest challenge is still to come. The cymbal bashing has been a great rehearsal. But I'll need to exert myself to an even greater physical degree if I'm serious about becoming a true *Boar*.

Of course, it's not enough just to catch up with the Bavarians. Physically, you need to keep up with them too. And it's crystal-clear where this struggle is either won or lost.

On the running track.

Step Six:

Finish race
(with or without cheating)

– and order *Bier* properly

*The average German guzzles 110 litres a year
(that's a giant jugful every two to three days).
Yet they stay as sober as a judge.*

The Full Litre

It's late evening on Friday the Thirteenth. Just like four in five Brits and two thirds of Germans, I don't believe in superstition. But supposing bad luck were to strike today? It's sure taking its time. Second thoughts, this could well be my lucky day, because I've just made a new friend. We've hit it off awfully well.

But then he goes and asks me a rather odd question: 'Did you know that two out of three traffic cops these days are women?'

I've no idea what makes Martin suddenly ask this. Germans don't normally go around dressing up fun facts as questions. At least not when you've only just been introduced to each other. Besides, we've just been making small talk about the soaring price of pumpkins.

The other thing is, only half of me is listening to him. The other is more preoccupied with the bizarre-tasting *Bier-Wein-Mix-Getränk* in my hand. Drinking beer mixes has always struck me as an unsmart way of getting sloshed. I mean, beer is a perfectly refreshing good drink on its own. You don't need to go squirting other stuff into it – like raspberry syrup, as customary in Berlin. And you certainly don't go stretching it with other perfectly good drinks. Least not of all wine. Beer mixes ought to be banned in Germany.

And yet that's exactly what I'm offered just before I

meet Martin. I'm at the Sour Cherry Photo Studio, which tonight is celebrating its *Verflixte Siebtes Jahr*, or Seven Year Itch. À propos classic film titles, no sign of any Marilyn Monroe look-alikes here, sadly. We've all been asked to bring a little lucky charm with us. Mine's creating a bit of a bulge in my trouser pocket, actually. It's a *Muschel*, a little conch I picked up on the beach in Poland.

Martin's expecting an answer. So, feigning interest, I reply 'Really?'

'Well,' he explains, 'the other day I parked for just two minutes outside Witmanns to get cigarettes. When I came back a traffic cop was writing me a ticket. A woman of course. And guess what?'

'What?' I respond. If this is a guessing game, I'm not sure where it's leading us.

'I know her,' replies Martin, 'she's one of my customers. I do her accounts!'

He speaks the last sentence like a punchline, as if it were some enormous joke. I'm uncertain whether to laugh or just feel sorry for him. Gazing sceptically, I ask 'You weren't rude to her, were you?'

When it comes to disputes with German police and traffic wardens, impertinence can cost you dearly. Just the other day I read in the ADAC *Motormagazin* that German civil law lays down exactly how much you pay for every specific insult. Calling cops a *Hurensohn* or 'son of a bitch' can set you back €1,600. Say *Arschloch*, or a*** hole, to a law enforcer and you're fined *only* €1,000. Unless you happen to be ex-footballer Stefan Effenberg, who several years ago had to cough up €10,000 for saying this to a *Polizist*. Germans are typically penalised according to how much they earn. Curiously, however, when it comes to exercising *Redefreiheit* (freedom of speech – a basic right anchored in German constitutional law) there's no fine for such insults as *'Sie können mich mal!'* or 'sod you.'

Fortunately for Martin, he hadn't called this traffic cop any nasty names. He'd insulted no one whatsoever. All he'd done wrong was forget to display the obligatory parking disc behind his windscreen.

'So,' I query, 'you work for this cop and she *still* gave you a ticket?'

'Ja,' nods Martin. He'd pleaded for common sense to prevail, of course, in the interest of their business relationship. But she simply handed him the ticket and said *'des wern mia scho moi sengs.'* End of discussion.

'Well,' I brood, 'you could have just refused to pay.'

'Na, na, naaah,' he responds, 'here in Germany you can get sent to the slammer for that.'

Martin's command of idiomatic English is impressive. He even says *na* instead of 'no'. But he pronounces 'Germany' like a typical German: *'Tschoermeny.'*

Jörg, who's been standing on the sidelines, quietly taking this all in, suddenly speaks up: 'Ooh, I wouldn't mind being handcuffed by a woman in uniform!' To underline this wishful thinking, he takes three short steps forward, raises his hands in mock surrender and says 'Please, take me – wherever you like!'

I'm bemused. Only in deepest Lower Bavaria, it appears, can you be talking one moment about the price of pumpkins and then move on, so effortlessly, to share manhood fantasies about being led away in chains by female traffic wardens.

Still, it's been an enjoyable evening and I end up arranging to meet Martin the following day. We've dared each other to compete in *Crosslauf*, the annual six-kilometre run organised by Moaburg's *Sportverein*.

Just hearing the word *Sportverein* puts the wind up me. Don't its members meet for running practice three times a week? Expressing my reservations about this to Martin, he pats me on the back and grins: 'Don't worry, I'm totally out of practice too.'

The following morning, I rise at the crack of dawn and do something I've shied away from since my run-in with the hunter.

I go for a jog.

Leaves streaked with autumnal yellowy-brown hues flitter from the trees as I enter the dense woodland. The sky is truly Bavarian blue, not a single cloud to be seen, and it's unusually warm for mid-October, a pleasurable 17 °C. I arrive back home slightly sweating but beaming with joy. And all geared up for the 'real thing' – half a dozen laps up and down the hills of Moaburg.

After lunch, however, it's so warm that I flop onto a sun lounger under the shade of our apple trees. I immediately fall asleep, and proceed to dream about cruising over the *Crosslauf* finishing post to tumultuous cheers and applause from the crowds. Waking up at ten past two, I panic. I have just twenty minutes to get to the starting point and register for the run. Tyres screeching, I pull up outside the club, and race over to the starting banner. The only person still officiating the start of the race is a young girl squeezed behind a trestle table. She's counting ticket tabs as she puts them back into a Tupperware box. I immediately bombard her with questions:

'I'm late, yes? 'They've left, right? I can still run, OK?'

The girl, sitting there with her tabs and Tupperware, looks me up and down suspiciously. It's as if I've just proposed running the race with nothing on except white sneaker socks and my competitor's number tag. I fear she's about to turn me away, because she says *'Sorry, online Omeldeschluss war heit fria.'* I've missed online registration, alas. But then suddenly her eyes light up, she smiles and says *'I vastehe, is 's just for fun, gell?'*

'Sorry' and *'just for fun'* are some of those Anglicisms which Germans bandy around so liberally, as if they're blissfully unaware these words are *not* actually German.

'Ja,' I reply, palpably relieved, *'just for fun.'*

Reaching into another Tupperware box, the assistant pulls out a quarter banana. *'Do a boh vitamin,'* she says, pressing it into my sweaty hand.

All of a sudden, just as I'm bending down to tighten my laces, a grey-haired contestant pops up. He looks about seventy. Taking a bite of banana from Tupperware Girl, he's off again. And, before I'm even back on my legs again, he's disappeared into the distance.

I've hardly ran 100 metres when I hear the sound of feet padding the ground behind me. It can't be runners who started the race even later than me, surely?

No. These competitors are already on their second

lap. Glancing behind, I see they're signalling to me to move over to one side so they can overtake. It's a bit like those big black Audis that tear down the autobahn almost faster than physics allows. I notice that a number of runners who promptly proceed to pass me are a fair bit older – and a whole lot fitter too.

How weird. Chatting last night to Martin – he's nowhere to be seen, incidentally – about doing the race, we both had in mind that everyone would be running at a much more leisurely pace, casually chatting to each other about what else they were doing this weekend, and maybe also commenting on the glorious weather we're having for this time of year.

Fat chance of that happening right now.

These runners are clearly in it to win. Judging by the determined expressions etched on their faces as they speed by, they have no time for idle banter. When it comes to sport, it seems that Germans apply exactly the same principle here as they do at the workplace. You do your job of work first and then you take a break to talk. In Britain, of course, it's the other way around. Small wonder no one shooting past me has bothered to utter anything at all. As the next person proceeds to race past, I call out *'Den wievuidn?'* – how many laps have you already done? Instead of slowing down to give me a verbal reply, he simply speeds up. With a hands-up-in-air-surrender gesture, he surges past, leaving me behind almost instantly.

Next to overtake is a svelte-limbed blond in black leggings and garishly yellow Lycra shirt, dripping with sweat. I ask her the same question: *'Den wievuidn?'* This runner is slightly more communicative – she holds up four fingers. Presumably to indicate she's now onto her fourth lap. At this stage of the race I've not even completed my second.

Straggling towards the finishing post among a small group of runners lagging some way behind the rest, I can't help feeling a bit of a bluff package or *Mogelpackung*. But to carry on running might draw attention to the fact that I'm at least two laps behind all my fellow competitors. Better to pretend I'm almost finished and just pray no one notices the discrepancy. Breaking into a sprint at the final leg, I speed past the finishing line to a round of cheers from either side of the track

Just as I'm reaching for a glass of water behind the banner marked *Ziel*, Tupperware Girl pops up. '*Sie hom's aa no gschofft!*' she calls. She's right, I have done it – of sorts, at least. Right at that moment, Martin also appears.

'I've been looking for you everywhere!' he pants.

Martin actually finishes the race *behind* me. But then he reminds me that he did at least manage *all* six laps.

Slowly regaining breath, we celebrate in style – with a plastic cup of fizzy water.

It's agreed that we both need to shape up if we're to stand any chance at all in next year's race. We muse the idea of seeing if the *Sportverein* Moaburg offers something a little more 'gentle' – ping-pong or badminton club night maybe. We also mull over doing a few gentle jogs through the woods together.

'We'll leave the serious stuff to the others,' Martin

calls over his shoulder as we part.

At the *Siegerehrung*, the presentation ceremony, instead of being awarded lovely shiny trophies or medals, the winners in each age group are presented with a five-litre barrel of beer. No one seems to mind. One lucky winner accepts the prize patting his stomach and joking *'des is mei eigana Six Pog!'* – here's my own six-pack. As everyone's leaving, I saunter out onto the *Sportverein* balcony. Looking down at some half a dozen tennis courts and running tracks, I'm struck by how fortunate the Germans are. Everywhere you go, from the largest city, right down to the smallest *Kaff* – villages just like ours – burghers of all ages reap the benefit of extensive state-of-the-art sports facilities. I enquire afterwards about the price of an annual family membership. It's just €100, which sounds remarkably good value. They also offer a *Schnupperdog*, a free trial day.

Perhaps tagging along with the other uber-fit joggers for regular workouts and practice runs is the key to cracking *Crosslauf*. As for my performance today, the upshot is that I start the race a good lap or two behind all other competitors and – despite blatantly cheating – still manage to come in comfortably last. I take a cursory glance at the list of individual participants' timings. My name's nowhere to be seen among the 209 sprinters. I don't even show up as an also-ran. Unofficially I was the 210th runner – the one who simply hadn't got their act together and registered in advance.

So yes, I had effectively fluffed my final challenge not only when it came to physical fitness, or rather lack thereof, but also basic organisation. No wonder Germans register online for everything. It's so much less hassle. Instead of going out with a big bang, I'd limped off with a woeful whimper.

For my fellow sprinters, on the other hand, the run had been more like a relaxed stroll through the woods. I wonder what sort of distances they're normally used to running. I'd noticed that while bucketloads of sweat were pouring off me, all the other competitors still looked remarkably composed. It was as if they'd just jumped up from the sofa and popped into the kitchen to put the kettle on.

As I chew this over on the sports club balcony, I suddenly begin to feel thirsty. Turning around, I notice the bar is still open. Earlier, during the prize ceremony, I'd ordered only a 0.25 measure of draught beer. This had caught the *Fräulein* somewhat by surprise. Fully unprepared for such a small order, she'd gone down on all fours and rummaged somewhere beneath the sink for an appropriately dainty-sized glass. Eventually she found one. Filling to overflow, she handed it to me like a trophy. I'd certainly earned it. But as every good Bavarian will tell you, a quarter litre is nothing – a mere *Klecks*, something just to moisten the palate or whet your whistle. Barely an apology for a drink. It's what they sip in needle-thin glasses up in the Rhineland.

Gazing over the running track, mini mug clasped close to chest, I realize there's one final thing I need to do in order to become Bavarian. *Modus operandi* for every typical Bavarian – regardless of whether or not they've just run fast enough to earn the equivalent of a six-pack.

It was something The Beer Queen had been quite adamant about at the hop-picking ceremony. Something about such and such a size being the only acceptable measure of beer in Bavaria.

Flashing the maid a toothy grin, I say in broadest Bavarian:

'Bitte a Mass.'

One litre, please.

And, this time, please make it the *full* litre.

Epilogue

Over twenty years have elapsed since I languished in that clippings' cubicle, frantically fishing around for stories to stick into Deutsche Telekom's scrapbook. That *Alleskleber* sure was effective. Sometimes I even managed to stick my fingers in there too. I must have been very attached to the job.

What ever became of my artwork on that first job?

I search the web. The language service is still going strong; its press releases are peppered with cutting-edge jargon announcing the arrival of 'Push Tolerance', 'Balanced Score Card Basics' and 'Reactive Data Mining'. And that's just the German texts. One report catches my eye. It's a vague promise that within five to ten years every single German household will enjoy fibre broadband 50 Mbit/s. It's a giant jump from just 2% right now. I draw a total blank with the Clippings Department though. Scrolling down the vernacular of the *Sprachendienst* page, nothing whatsoever suggests that my former work station ever even existed.

And the push to be as physically fit as a Bavarian? I've sort of succeeded. Having agreed with Martin to start off with something soft and gentle, we went along to a *Schnupperomd* at the local badminton club. I thought *Badminton* and *Federball* were both the same thing. But with members whacking balls to me at almost 200 km/h (the world record stands at 280) it was quite clear that these two sports have nothing in common whatsoever. The amazing thing is that Germans take their not-so-gentle badminton even *more* seriously than they do their jogging. We'd barely removed our tracksuits and they were already running laps around the gym hall, doing press-ups, stretch-outs and numerous other invigorating warmups. They somehow managed to contort their limbs and body parts into places you'd think were physically impossible. By the time we finally moved on to play a bit of badminton I was absolutely exhausted.

The end result? I survived this 2½-hour Bavarian endurance test too. I even managed to return a few backhand shots before the evening was over.

Mind you, like every good German, I woke up the following morning with a mighty *Muskelkater*.

Postscript

Germany celebrates its 150th birthday in 2021. Later in the year, when burghers head to the polls to elect a new government, I – and almost a quarter million other Brits granted German citizenship since 23 June 2016 – will be allowed to vote alongside for the first time.

Appendix

How to be normal in Germany

With so much pressure to be punctual, risk averse, uber-organised and disciplined in everything you do in Germany, it's often easy to feel like you're constantly breaking the rules, messing up and looking like a *Vollidiot*. But it doesn't have to be like that. Let's face it – not even the Germans are *total perfekt*.

So, whether you're here just short term or, like me, you've washed up in Germany for good, just relax. Here are the top twenty uber-*Deutsch* things which, in the land of sausages and fairy-tale castles, will guarantee you blend in beautifully with your fellow burghers:

… referring to your mobile phone as your 'handy'.

… bringing cake to work on your *Geburtstag* (when, by all rights, your colleagues should be bringing you one instead).

… expecting your weekend to begin on Friday, 2 p.m. sharp. And, if it doesn't, complaining you're doing too much overtime.

… getting pretzel withdrawal symptoms each time you leave Germany for longer than a week.

... picking up litter on the street, approaching the nearest stranger and saying 'Ha-llo! I think you've lost something?'

... pronouncing OK as 'O-kaaay' (half question, half statement).

... turning up to work in shorts, white socks and Birkenstock sandals.

... spotting a speed trap on the way to work, pulling in and phoning the local radio station to report it.

... saying 'ja' and 'ja, genau' in almost every other gulp of breath.

... climbing into a cow costume or dressing up as a jailbird every *Fasching*.

... automatically uttering '*Tja*' whenever shit hits the fan.

... calling in sick with ailments known only to Germans: *Kreislaufstörung, Muskelkater* ....

... taking your street shoes off before you go indoors (bonus points for bringing your own carpet slippers with you).

... smothering your pommes frites with both mayonnaise *and* ketchup.

... linking arms and swaying in tune to Seventies songs you used to loathe (and, yes, it really is fun to stay at the 'Y.M.C.A.').

... joining a roundabout without signalling (completely legal in Germany).

... flashing your lights at the car ahead of you, demanding they pull aside to let you overtake (commonplace yet illegal in Germany).

... taking time off work (having applied for the day off months in advance, of course) to sort your recycling waste.

... joining the local shooting sport club (*Schützenverein*) even though you jump out of your pants at the sound of a gun going off.

And, last not least,

... complaining.

About everything, of course.

Danke....

To all *Moaburger* and *Oabensbeger* who helped me out with my challenges: Maria, Stephan, Basti, Anna, Martin, Horst, Ingo, Editor 'Bob' and, last not least, all fifty Wolpis. It was often a case of *gute Miene zum bösen Spiel* – putting on a brave face to a bad game, literally – but I've mentioned you by name wherever I felt it safe enough to do so...

To Jörg & Co. at The Sour Cherry. You helped me appreciate that there's a lot more to Moaburg that initially meets the eye.

To all the *Direktors*, teachers and students, without whom this book just wouldn't be complete. You provided me, albeit unwittingly, with some of my best material. Names have been changed for all the usual reasons.

To our good friends Claudi and Martin, and of course to the rest of our 'Freising Clan'. *Danke Ihr Lieben!*

Special thanks to graphic guru Christoph, for knocking the layout into shape and the amazing cover.

Last not least, to Bill Howe, without whom this self-published book would probably still be languishing on the shelf. Thanks for supporting me, dad.

And to everybody else I may have missed here who also helped me in the course of my 'challenges' to become a Bavarian.

Germans, we love you. Especially your *Bier*.
Measse vuimoi!

Dear Reader,

I hope you enjoyed reading this book as much as I enjoyed writing it. If you think others might like it too, I'd be thrilled if you could leave a nice little comment under Amazon's 'Customer Reviews'.

Big thank you

Tim Howe

Printed in Poland
by Amazon Fulfillment
Poland Sp. z o.o., Wrocław

85754366R00190